Subsistence Strategies and Craft Production at the Ancient Egyptian Ramesside Fort of Zawiyet Umm el-Rakham

Bloomsbury Egyptology

Ancient Egyptians at Play, Walter Crist, Anne-Elizabeth Dunn-Vaturi and Alex de Voogt

Ancient Egyptian Technology and Innovation, Ian Shaw

Archaeologists, Tourists, Interpreters, Rachel Mairs and Maya Muratov

Asiatics in Middle Kingdom Egypt, Phyllis Saretta

Burial Customs in Ancient Egypt, Wolfram Grajetzki

Court Officials of the Egyptian Middle Kingdom, Wolfram Grajetzki

The Egyptian Oracle Project, edited by Robyn Gillam and Jeffrey Jacobson

Foreigners in Ancient Egypt, Flora Brooke Anthony

Five Egyptian Goddesses: Their Possible Beginnings, Actions, and Relationships in the Third Millennium BCE, Susan Tower Hollis

Hidden Hands, Stephen Quirke

The Middle Kingdom of Ancient Egypt, Wolfram Grajetzki

The Unknown Tutankhamun, Marianne Eaton-Krauss

Performance and Drama in Ancient Egypt, Robyn Gillam

Subsistence Strategies and Craft Production at the Ancient Egyptian Ramesside Fort of Zawiyet Umm el-Rakham

Nicky Nielsen

BLOOMSBURY ACADEMIC
LONDON • NEW YORK • OXFORD • NEW DELHI • SYDNEY

BLOOMSBURY ACADEMIC
Bloomsbury Publishing Plc, 50 Bedford Square, London, WC1B 3DP, UK
Bloomsbury Publishing Inc, 1385 Broadway, New York, NY 10018, USA
Bloomsbury Publishing Ireland, 29 Earlsfort Terrace, Dublin 2, D02 AY28, Ireland

BLOOMSBURY, BLOOMSBURY ACADEMIC and the Diana logo are
trademarks of Bloomsbury Publishing Plc

First published in Great Britain 2024
This paperback edition published 2025

Copyright © Nicky Nielsen, 2024

Nicky Nielsen has asserted his right under the Copyright,
Designs and Patents Act, 1988, to be identified as Author of this work.

For legal purposes the Acknowledgements on p. ix constitute
an extension of this copyright page.

Cover design: Terry Woodley
Cover image: A Ramesside globular jar found in Area K at Zawiyet Umm
el-Rakham (© S. Snape)

All rights reserved. No part of this publication may be: i) reproduced or transmitted in
any form, electronic or mechanical, including photocopying, recording or by means
of any information storage or retrieval system without prior permission in writing from
the publishers; or ii) used or reproduced in any way for the training, development or
operation of artificial intelligence (AI) technologies, including generative AI technologies.
The rights holders expressly reserve this publication from the text and data mining
exception as per Article 4(3) of the Digital Single Market Directive (EU) 2019/790.

Bloomsbury Publishing Inc does not have any control over, or responsibility for,
any third-party websites referred to or in this book. All internet addresses given
in this book were correct at the time of going to press. The author and publisher
regret any inconvenience caused if addresses have changed or sites have
ceased to exist, but can accept no responsibility for any such changes.

A catalogue record for this book is available from the British Library.

Library of Congress Cataloging-in-Publication Data
Names: Nielsen, Nicky, author.
Title: Subsistence strategies and craft production at the ancient Egyptian Ramesside fort
of Zawiyet Umm El-Rakham / Nicky Nielsen.Other titles: Bloomsbury Egyptology ; 10.
Description: London ; New York : Bloomsbury Academic, 2024. |
Series: Bloomsbury Egyptology; 10 | Includes bibliographical references and index.
Identifiers: LCCN 2023029667 (print) | LCCN 2023029668 (ebook) |
ISBN 9781350327368 (hb) | ISBN 9781350327375 (paperback) |
ISBN 9781350327382 (epdf) | ISBN 9781350327399 (ebook)
Subjects: LCSH: Excavations (Archaeology)—Egypt—Zāwiyat Umm ar Rakham. |
Zāwiyat Umm ar Rakham (Egypt)—Antiquities.
Classification: LCC DT73.Z36 N54 2024 (print) | LCC DT73.Z36 (ebook) |
DDC 932—dc23/eng/20230729
LC record available at https://lccn.loc.gov/2023029667
LC ebook record available at https://lccn.loc.gov/2023029668

ISBN: HB: 978-1-3503-2736-8
PB: 978-1-3503-2737-5
ePDF: 978-1-3503-2738-2
eBook: 978-1-3503-2739-9

Series: Bloomsbury Egyptology

Typeset by RefineCatch Limited, Bungay, Suffolk

For product safety related questions contact productsafety@bloomsbury.com.

To find out more about our authors and books visit www.bloomsbury.com
and sign up for our newsletters.

Contents

List of Figures, Colour Plates and Tables		vi
Acknowledgements		ix
Abbreviations		x
Preface		xi
1	The Fortress at the End of the World	1
2	Subsistence	25
3	Manufacture and Decoration of Pottery from Area K	61
4	Craft Production	83
5	The West Delta and Marmarican Fortresses	107
6	Subsistence and Production Strategies at Early- to Mid-Ramesside Forts	119
Conclusion: Living and Working at Zawiyet Umm el-Rakham		131
Appendix: Catalogue of Area K Ceramic Vessels		135
Bibliography		191
Index		213

Figures, Colour Plates and Tables

Figures

1.1	The plan of Zawiyet Umm el-Rakham produced by Alan Rowe	2
1.2	Plan of the fortified enclosure at Zawiyet Umm el-Rakham highlighting the main areas excavated by the University of Liverpool mission	10
1.3	Plan of Area K at Zawiyet Umm el-Rakham	12
1.4	Plan of Area K highlighting the main buildings in the Area, Buildings 1–5	15
1.5	The main types of houses found at Zawiyet Umm el-Rakham based on the typology developed by Tietze (1985)	18
2.1	Photograph showing the granaries found in Area H	28
2.2	Space KG (right) and KS (left) looking north, showing an embedded mortar in KS in the forefront of the picture and ZUR/KD/57 in the background	30
2.3	Spatial overview of tools related to grain processing (circle: mortar; rectangle: hand stone; triangle: quern; rhomboid: basin)	33
2.4	The Area K faunal assemblage in comparison with contemporary material from sites in the Nile Valley	52
3.1	The main types of local ceramic produced at Zawiyet Umm el-Rakham, being (from top to bottom) ZUR A, ZUR B and ZUR C	63
3.2	Berlin 20363	70
3.3	Bologna 1888	71
3.4	The royal camp at Qadesh	72
3.5	The different types of decorative scheme utilised on the polychrome pottery from Area K, Zawiyet Umm el-Rakham	76
3.6	ZUR/KM/13, a blue-painted plate depicting a duck or other waterbird taking flight over a pond with waterlilies	78

3.7 Illustrations of the three pot marks found in Area K at Zawiyet Umm el-Rakham on ZUR/K2A/21, ZUR/K2H/19 and ZUR/KK1/11   80
4.1 Spatial overview of tools related to textile production (triangle: spinning bowls; circle: spindle whorl; square: loom weight)   87
4.2 Possible loom support found in Area G, scale bar in picture is 15.0 cm   88
4.3 Overview of Area K showing the main structures, architectural type as well as some of the uncovered door jambs and lintels   91
4.4 Polishing stone ZUR/N34/8   102
4.5 Spatial arrangement of locally produced bone pins   103
5.1 Map showing the location of the Marmarican and West Delta fortresses   108
6.1 Ramesside fortified settlements discussed in Chapter 6   120

Colour plates

1 Material related to the processing of grain excavated from Area K
2 Material related to (a) fishing and hunting and (b) textile production excavated from Area K
3 Material related to stone working and imported stone artefacts excavated from Area K
4 Bone pins excavated from Area K

Tables

2.1 Amount of arable land required to sustain 230 occupants at Zawiyet Umm el-Rakham   38
2.2 Amount of arable land required to sustain 500 occupants at Zawiyet Umm el-Rakham   40
2.3 Labour requirements for agricultural production at Zawiyet Umm el-Rakham.   42

2.4 Count of unidentified mammalian, avian and mollusc elements; the two former classified by size, the latter unidentifiable due to poor preservation 46
2.5 Taxonomical classification for the Area K faunal assemblage 46
2.6 The Area K faunal assemblage in comparison with contemporary material from sites in the Nile Valley 52
3.1 Samples selected for pXRF analysis 64
3.2 Chemical composition of ZUR A–C 65
3.3 Chemical composition of ZUR A–C and measured samples of Nile silt 67
3.4 Egyptian Nile silt and Marl fabrics from Area K 69
4.1 Area K assemblage divided by material type 94
4.2 Types of lithic material found in Magazine Six 95

Acknowledgements

A great many individuals have been instrumental in the completion of the research that lies at the foundation of this monograph. In particular, I would like to thank all of my colleagues and friends at the Department of Archaeology, Classics and Egyptology at the University of Liverpool where I undertook both my undergraduate and postgraduate study. I owe a particular debt of gratitude to my PhD supervisor Professor Steven Snape who not only encouraged and guided my research into the site of Zawiyet Umm el-Rakham, but also – as the site director – gave me access to the materials excavated from Area K. Without him, neither the project, nor this publication would be possible. I would also like to thank Professor Ian Shaw and Dr Glenn Godenho who also supervised parts of the research which forms the basis of this publication. I am also grateful to Dr Matthew Ponting, Dr Susanna Thomas and Dr Sue Stalibras.

I would also like to thank Dr Valentina Gasperini for her help, advise and support both in Egypt and the United Kingdom, as well as Dr Huw Twiston Davies and Dr Cecelie Lelek-Tvetmarken, Dr Edgar Pusch, Dr Henning Franzmeier, Mandy Mamedow and other members of the Qantir-Piramesses team for the many stimulating discussions about life in the Ramesside period in general and Ramesside ceramics in particular. I should also like to thank the Arts and Humanities Research Council who provided funding for the project through a PhD block grant. I would like to extend my gratitude to Professor Christopher Eyre and Professor Paul Nicholson for examining the thesis upon which this publication is based and providing valuable insights on the research.

The greatest thanks of all, however, are reserved for my wonderful wife and partner in crime Dr Diana T. Nikolova for all her support and love through the years, as well as my parents Gitte and Leif without whose unceasing belief this project could never have been completed. It is to these three, and to my grandmother Ingrid, that I dedicate this study.

Abbreviations

Ä&L	Ägypten und Levante
ASAE	Annales du Service des Antiquités de l'Egypte
BACE	Bulletin of the Australian Centre for Egyptology
BASOR	Bulletin of the American Schools of Oriental Research
BIFAO	Bulletin de l'Institut Français d'Archéologie Orientale
CAJ	Cambridge Archaeological Journal
CCE	Cahier de la céramique égyptienne
CRIPEL	Cahier de Recherches de l'Institut de Papyrologie et d'Égyptologie de Lille
GM	Göttinger Miszellen
JAEI	Journal of Ancient Egyptian Interconnections
JAOS	Journal of the American Oriental Society
JARCE	Journal of the American Research Center in Egypt
JAS	Journal of Archaeological Science
JEA	Journal of Egyptian Archaeology
JFA	Journal of Field Archaeology
JNES	Journal of Near Eastern Studies
JSSEA	Journal of the Society of the Study of Egyptian Antiquities
JWH	Journal of World History
LibStud	Libyan Studies
MDAIK	Mitteilungen des Deutschen Archäologischen Instituts, Abteilung Kairo
RdE	Revue d'Égyptologie
REE	Revista de Estudios de Egiptologia
SAK	Studien zur Altägyptischen Kultur
ZÄS	Zeitschrift für ägyptische Sprache und Altertumskunde 000

Preface

The research upon which this monograph is based was conducted at the University of Liverpool as part of an AHRC-funded PhD project from 2012 to 2016. The project was based on a methodical re-examination of an assemblage of materials (small finds and ceramics) excavated within Area K of the Ramesside fortress at Zawiyet Umm el-Rakham. The site itself was identified in April of 1946 by Sheikh Fayez Awad, a farmer from the village of Zawiyet Umm el-Rakham from which the site derives its name. The site was then excavated briefly by Alan Rowe in the summer of that same year, and subsequently by Labib Habachi in 1949 and from 1953 to 1955. A short excavation by the Egyptian Antiquities Organisation was conducted in 1991 before the site was excavated from 1994 to the present day by a team from the University of Liverpool led by Steven Snape.

In 2014 the present author re-examined the archaeological materials excavation from Area K in 1998–2002. The bulk of these materials remain to this day in the Mersa Matrouh MSA magazine with a small amount on display in the Mersa Matrouh Museum and a few other materials in storage in the Grand Egyptian Museum in Cairo. This re-examination provided the bulk of the research data which underpin this study, although, as will be noted where relevant, not all the excavated material could be located and in some cases the analysis is built not on a comprehensive sample of certain material types, but rather a representative one. This is particularly the case for the quern stones of which only a few remain in the magazine. Instead, the analysis of this material is based on the smaller amount still in storage as well as the original descriptions, photographs and drawings made by the excavators.

The aim of this monograph is to provide an overview of the subsistence and craft production strategies undertaken by the Ramesside inhabitants of Zawiyet Umm el-Rakham and contextualise these findings within the broader framework of the daily life of the Egyptian inhabitants of liminal military sites during the Late Bronze Age. Chapter 1 provides an introduction to the site of

Zawiyet Umm el-Rakham itself, its excavation history and the different areas explored by the University of Liverpool mission from 1994 to 2010. This section also includes a detailed exploration of the spatial layout of Area K, the domestic and industrial area of the site under investigation in this publication.

Chapter 2 explores the archaeological evidence for agricultural production at the site, in combination with investigations of contemporary textual data, as well as ethnographic observations to address the issue of how an Egyptian garrison used to an inundation-based agricultural system, adapted to the rainfall-based agricultural strategies necessary to successfully grow crops in the *wadis* south of the fortress. This chapter also contains an investigation of some of the faunal remains found in Area K as well as the archaeological evidence for fishing and hunting.

Chapter 3 focuses on the largest body of archaeological evidence from Area K, namely the ceramic material which comprises an assemblage typical early- to mid-Ramesside shapes. As part of this investigation, the chapter also provides the results of a pXRF analysis of a smaller samples of ceramics which suggests that nearly half of the pottery utilised by the Egyptian garrison was produced locally rather than imported from the Nile Valley.

Chapter 4 focuses on the three best-evidenced craft productions undertaken at the site, namely: the weaving industry, stone working (including lithic manufacture) and the manufacture of bone hairpins, of which more than forty have been found all across the site. Chapters 5 and 6 seek to contextualise the archaeological material from Area K, firstly by placing Zawiyet Umm el-Rakham within the broader framework of early Ramesside fortified structures built in the western Delta and along the Marmarican Coast and secondly by providing an in-depth discussion of subsistence and craft production strategies undertaken at contemporary and comparable structures in the western Delta, the Sinai Peninsula and Nubia.

The overall aim of this monograph is not merely the presentation of a corpus of archaeological data. The data simply provides a lens through which the issues of domestic life, industrial production and food security at liminal sites can be explored. The archaeological remains of Zawiyet Umm el-Rakham and the corpus of small finds left behind by its inhabitants represent a way to study the foreign policies of the early Ramesside rulers, in particular Ramesses II, divorced to a certain extent from the bombastic and often misleading proclamations found in royal monumental inscriptions. The significance of the assemblage cannot be overstated. As the site of Deir el-Medina and the materials excavated from it have provided invaluable information about daily life in a state-sponsored artisans village, so the material from Area K at Zawiyet Umm el-Rakham provides an insight into the daily life and priorities of an isolated population of, mostly, Egyptians living hundreds of miles from the Nile Valley on the very edge of what was considered the Ramesside sphere of influence.

1

The Fortress at the End of the World

1.1 Site history and terminological definition

The initial archaeological exploration of the site of Zawiyet Umm el-Rakham ('Rest house of the Mother of Vultures', 31.3985° N, 27.0419° E) was made by archaeologist Alan Rowe in the summer of 1946 after being alerted to the presence of inscribed limestone fragments at the site by Sheikh Fayez, a local farmer (Rowe, 1953, 1954 and Snape and Wilson, 2007: 1). The precise location of Rowe's excavations (Figure 1.1) within the site cannot be determined, as the plan which he produced cannot be reconciled with any excavated features discovered either by Labib Habachi in his explorations of the site from 1949 and 1953–5 or by the University of Liverpool team (Snape and Wilson, 2007: 1). The fort came to greater attention in the wider Egyptological community with the publication of Labib Habachi's seminal article chronicling the results of his personal survey in the Western Delta and along the Marmarican coast, visiting and exploring the sites of Kom Firin, Tell Aqa'in, el-Alamein and Zawiyet Umm el-Rakham (Habachi, 1980). Habachi also published a brief description of his work at the site at an earlier date (Habachi, 1955), as well as a series of summary reports by J. Leclant (1954, 1955 and 1956).

Habachi focused the majority of his 1980 article on his excavations at Zawiyet Umm el-Rakham as well as a detailed overview of Alan Rowe's previous work at the site. While Rowe's finds had primarily consisted of inscriptional evidence (most notably the first evidence of the fort's commander Nebre), Habachi also investigated the architectural remains of the fort, locating a small temple in the north-western corner of a large mudbrick enclosure wall and a series of private stelae from the same area (Snape and Wilson, 2007: 93–129). On the basis of this heavily fortified wall, Habachi suggested an

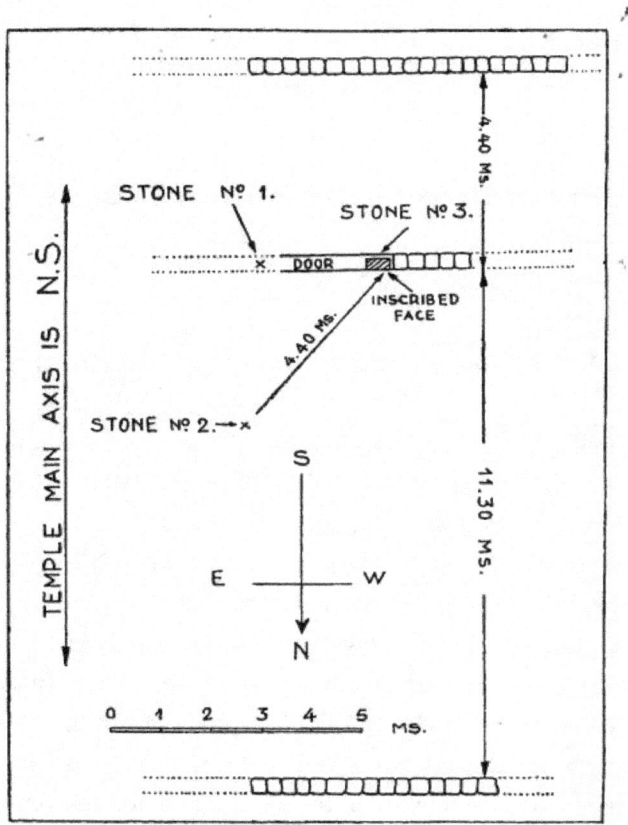

Figure 1.1 The plan of Zawiyet Umm el-Rakham produced by Alan Rowe (Rowe, 1948: Fig. 5).

exclusively military function for the installation and in conjunction with Egyptian documentary evidence from the reign of Ramesses II, he proposed that the fortress at Zawiyet Umm el-Rakham had been constructed in response to an encroaching threat from the Sea People (Habachi, 1980: 30).

Significant work was not continued until 1994 when the University of Liverpool resumed excavations at the site. In one of the first preliminary accounts, Snape (1998) argued that the fortress of Zawiyet Umm el-Rakham did not exclusively fulfil a military purpose, but more broadly a role as a port of call in a proposed anti-clockwise Mediterranean trade circuit. This claim is supported both by the excavations of Bate's Island, but also by large amounts of imported Mycenaean pottery at the Magazines at Zawiyet Umm el-Rakham. Additionally, Snape argued that the fortress guarded strategically important water-sources, thereby limiting large population movements (Snape, 1998: 1083–4). The presence of foreign pottery at the site in large quantities was discussed in greater detail by Susanna Thomas (2000) who highlighted the similarity between the Zawiyet Umm el-Rakham corpus of Mycenaean pottery from Magazine 1 and the ceramic corpus from Kommos in Southern Crete.

Three PhD theses were written on the basis of work conducted at the site in the late 1990s and early 2000s by Thomas (2000), Hounsell (2002) and Simpson (2002). Thomas elaborated on Snape's (1998) preliminary work and discussed the role of Zawiyet Umm el-Rakham in the Eastern Mediterranean trade network during the Late Bronze Age (Thomas, 2000: 318–48) and also the spread of certain technologies in the Eastern Mediterranean such as Egyptian blue pigment. Hounsell and Simpson discussed the issue of Egypto-Libyan relations in the area by employing respectively ground-surveys of Bedouin encampments in the area in an effort to identify Late Bronze Age material, although this method was largely unsuccessful (Hounsell, 2002) and a discussion of non-Egyptian material and architecture found at the site which was convincingly attributed to Libyan squatter activity following the site's abandonment (Simpson, 2002). Surveys in the *wadis* south of the site by the Liverpool team together with Hulin (2001) provided further evidence for cooperation between local Libyans and Egyptians in the form of mixed Libyan and Egyptian sherd scatters dating to the Late Bronze Age. The current author completed his own PhD thesis concerning material from Area K upon which this monograph is built in 2015 (Nielsen, 2015).

The strictly military aspects of Zawiyet Umm el-Rakham were further discussed by Snape (2003). Snape initially showed that the Libyans themselves were too technologically unsophisticated to have overwhelmed a garrison inside the walls of Zawiyet Umm el-Rakham, although he also noted that the subsistence strategies of the garrison appeared at least partially dependent on local production of foodstuff and, by extension, on the goodwill of the local Libyan population. Another article by Snape (2004) constitutes a general description of the work carried out since the commencement of excavations.

Two further publications by Snape (2010 and 2013) are respectively a preliminary discussion of the issues of self-sufficiency at the site with respect to food production and local industries (Snape, 2010) as well as the possible transit routes along which a supply chain could be maintained from the Nile Valley to Zawiyet Umm el-Rakham by sea and overland (Snape, 2013). The issue of local industries at the site has also been briefly discussed by Hulin (2009), who concluded that metal smelting crucibles associated with Late Bronze Age Libyan squatter activity at the site is a direct argument against the commonly held view of the contemporary Libyans as wholly a-metallic (Hulin, 2009: 19–20, contra conclusions reached by Simpson, 2002: 194 and 199). Excavations at the site were interrupted by the outbreak of the 'Arab Spring' and the subsequent unrest in Egypt. Further research into the provisioning of the fort, its ceramic corpus and the evidence for Egypto-Libyan cooperation at the site was explored by the current author (Nielsen, 2015, 2016 and 2017). Subsequent research into the wider area during the Late Bronze Age and its potential as a harbour has also been conducted by Hulin (2018).

The inscriptional evidence from Zawiyet Umm el-Rakham identifies the structure as one of a series of '[…] *mnnw*-forts upon the foreign land of Tjemeh […]' (Snape, 1995: 171) constructed by Ramesses II. Evidence from the biography of Nebre also labels the site as '[…]The Town (*dmiw*) of Ramesses II […]' (Snape and Godenho, in press). These terms are not necessarily conflicting and evidence from the reign of Ramesses III suggests that they were used with some degree of interchangeability (K*RI* V, 14:12–13 and 43:10–12). Zawiyet Umm el-Rakham is one of several fortified structures built, fortified or expanded during the reigns of Seti I and Ramesses II in Sinai, Libya and Nubia, and includes the *ḫtm*-forts of Tell el-Retaba and Tell Heboua I, a term defined by Morris (2005: 804–9) as larger forts guarding entry points to the Nile Valley, Tell el-Borg and the *mktr* of Haruba A-289 (Morris, 2005: 512) and Deir el-Balah (Dothan and Brandl, 2010: 255–6). The term *mktr* has been defined by Morris (2005: 817–20) as smaller fortified structures or migdols exclusively located in North Sinai. The final group of Ramesside settlements of this type are the the Nubian *mnnw*-forts of Aksha and Amara West and the probable *mnnw*-forts (Spencer, 2014: 33) of Kom Firin and Tell Abqa'in in the Western Delta (Morris, 2005: 809–14) which are architecturally similar to Zawiyet Umm el-Rakham. As discussed by Morris (2005: 627) and Snape (2013: 442) a *mnnw*-fort has been defined as a fortified population centre of some size, although precise size criteria are not clear.

The similarity between the Nubian and Libyan *mnnw*-forts constructed during the early nineteenth Dynasty are striking, primarily the presence of architecturally similar temples (Snape and Wilson, 2007: 69–92). Tell Abqa'in may also have housed a temple, dedicated to the goddess Anath (Thomas, 2011) but further excavation at the site is needed to confirm its existence. In her publication of New Kingdom fortifications Morris (2005: 809–14) makes an extensive architectural comparison between the Nubian and the Libyan *mnnw*-forts of the early Ramesside period. She postulates that the Libyan *mnnw*-forts were more militaristic in nature than their Nubian counterparts, that they were built to withstand a real threat and that they – like the contemporary fortified installations on the Sinai – were built along a high-way to blockade the advancement of a population group which the Egyptians wished to keep away from their borders (Morris, 2005: 812–13).

Inscriptional evidence from the site of Zawiyet Umm el-Rakham (Snape, 1995: 171) however, shows that the site was not located on a highway leading to potential enemies in a manner reminiscent to the Ways of Horus but was in fact in the middle of a foreign territory. Morris' evidence for the hypothesised increased level of militarism found at Zawiyet Umm el-Rakham and the Libiyan *mnnw*-forts over their Nubian counterparts is the two towers which fortified the gateway at Zawiyet Umm el-Rakham by comparison to the wider gates at sites such as Amara West and Aksha (Morris, 2005: 813), the blockage of stairways to the walls at Nubian forts (813), the presence of a glacis outside the walls of Zawiyet Umm el-Rakham and the lack of construction outside the walls of Zawiyet Umm el-Rakham, when construction was evident outside the protection of the enclosure at Amara West (813).

However, from a purely defensive standpoint, the heavily fortified gateway at Zawiyet Umm el-Rakham is merely a single feature. The enclosure wall of Zawiyet Umm el-Rakham for instance lacks the buttresses found at Amara West and Aksha in Nubia making it more vulnerable in the case of a siege. The argument that no structures were built outside the walls of Zawiyet Umm el-Rakham and that this is an indicator of a hostile environment is an oversimplification. No structures have so far been found because no one has looked for them. The magnetometric survey of Zawiyet Umm el-Rakham, for instance (Snape, 2010: 277), only included the fortress enclosure itself. It can be noted for instance that the digging of a ditch by local farmers to the west of the fort's enclosure wall revealed a great amount of Ramesside pottery immediately beneath the surface (Snape, pers. comm.), which may be indicative of structures outside the walls although further work will be needed to determine their type and extent. Finally, the proposed glacis is only partially found at the northern wall (Snape, 2010: 276), and whether its purpose is similar to the 'southern ditch' at the site (to collect flood water and as an area of rubbish deposition) is still unknown (Snape, 2010: 276) and as such considering these ditches as evidence for a raised threat-level is premature.

1.2 Egyptian relations with Libyan groupings through the Late Bronze Age

The study of Egypto-Libyan relations has been almost exclusively achieved through Egyptian source-material as the ancient inhabitants of the Western Desert have left no textual – and very little archaeological – material behind (cf. Carter, 1963). Initial studies by Bates (1917) and Holscher (1955) are tainted by contemporary colonial attitudes. Discussions of Egypto-Libyan relations during the Pharaonic period on the basis primarily of textual documentation have been published by Spalinger (1979b), Osing (1980), Kitchen (1990), O'Connor (1990), Snape (2003), Morris (2005: 611–21) and most recently by Garcia (2014).

1.2.1 Pre-Ramesside contact

While Egypt's relationship with its western neighbour was, as Snape (2003: 93–4) states, less developed than the relationship with other foreign territories, evidence for contact nonetheless appears already from the early Dynastic period and the 'Libyan Palette' found at Hierakonpolis, which contains an early hieroglyph associated with the word 'Tjehenu' ($thn(w)$) used in conjunction with the term 'Tjemeh' (tmh) throughout the Pharaonic period to denote a specific group of nomads or a specific area of land in the Western Desert (Snape, 2003: 97). Evidence from the Old Kingdom is predominately in the form of stylised monumental representations of Tjehenu-Libyans being dominated by the King (such as the relief of Ne-User-Re (Borchardt, 1907: 47 and pls. 9–10) and Sa-Hu-Re (Borchardt, 1913: 10–15 and Pl. 1) and cursory mentions in the biographies of Harkuf (*Urk.* I, 120–31) and Weni (*Urk.* I, 98–110).

A raid by Mentuhotep II recorded at his chapel in Denderra (Habachi, 1963: 21–3 and Pl. 5) and also on a fragmented inscription from Gebelein (39), constitutes the earliest evidence of Middle Kingdom relations with the Tjehenu-Libyans. Another raid by the Egyptians against the Tjehenu is alluded to in the Tale of Sinuhe (Sethe, 1929: 3–17) and also on a private stela from the reign of Senwosret I (Stela Berlin Museum 1199). The Tjehenu also appear in the Execration Texts (Posener, 1940: 25), but no information about names of chiefs or toponyms is listed. The inclusion of the Libyans instead appears entirely symbolic, rather than representative of an actual threat, perceived or real. The references to Tjehenu and Tjemeh in the pessimistic literature of the period, such as the Prophecies of Neferty (Helck, 1970: 55) and the Dialogue of Ipuwer and the Lord of All (Enmarch, 2008: 14.13) similarly provides no detail about Egypto-Libyan relations as such, but present the Libyans as stereotypical enemies of Egypt and harbingers of chaos and disorder.

Slightly more substantial evidence for Egypto-Libyan relations appear during the eighteenth Dynasty where the Tjehenu-Libyans appear occasionally as minor trading partners on for instance the Karnak Obelisk inscription of Hatshepsut (*Urk.* IV, 373). Considering the typical African goods which the Libyans trade (ivory tusks and panther-skins), Osing (1980: 1021) suggests that the Libyans of the Western Desert functioned occasionally as intermediaries handling typically Nubian goods. Some hostility during this period is also suggested by an inscription from Soleb dating to the reign of Amenhotep III wherein the king claims to have seized Tjehenu Libyans in a raid and used the captives as a labour force (Urk. IV, 1656). The Meshwesh (*mšwš*) and possibly the Rebu (*rbw*) constituting other Libyan groupings also appear in the Egyptian records during the later eighteenth Dynasty (Snape, 2003: 98–9). A papyrus from Tell el-Amarna now in the British Museum (BM EA 74100) furthermore seemingly depicts a group of Libyans, not identified by any accompanying texts, attacking and slaying an Egyptian soldier (Parkinson and Schofield, 1995).

1.2.2 The Libyan campaigns of Seti I

By the early nineteenth Dynasty, further evidence of hostile contact between Libya and Egypt is described in the battle reliefs of Seti I from the Karnak temple (Oriental Institute Epigraphic Survey, 1986; *KRI* I, 20:15–24:5), which may depict a battle against Meshwesh, rather than Tjehenu-Libyans (Kitchen, 1990: 17). These have been studied in detail primarily by Murnane (1985: 151–3) and Spalinger (1979a: 34) and also discussed by O'Connor (1990: 87) and Morris (2005: 613–15).

Murnane in particular argues that the generic style and lack of any detail in the account of Seti's Libyan campaign may indicate that the campaign – unlike his campaigns in the Near East – served little military purpose (1985: 151–3).

Morris (2005: 614) and O'Connor (1990: 87) however argue for an increasingly hostile situation between the Egyptian state and some Libyan groups during the nineteenth Dynasty, even to the extent of suggesting that the campaigns of Seti I were a response to actual Libyan invasion attempts (Morris, 2005: 813). Morris (2005: 614) cites three sources as support for this hypothesis: a private stela from Wadi es-Sebua recording the use of Tjehenu prisoners-of-war as labourers (KRI III, 95:12–14) and the two pieces of royal monumental inscription which detail the settling of Libyans within cities bearing the name of Ramesses II and their use as soldiers (2005: 614).

However, the passivity of the Libyans in their reaction to Seti's attack - hiding in the desert rather than facing the Egyptians (KRI I, 22:5-6) – could be perceived as an argument against any type of decisive pitched battle, which – as Morris (2005: 614) also notes – the Libyan semi-nomadic groupings would have no interest in fighting. As Kitchen (1990: 17) suggests, Seti's campaign may have pacified the region and allowed the construction of the line of forts along the Marmarican coast in the reign of Ramesses II, which also includes Zawiyet Umm el-Rakham. It is unclear however, whether this pacification was the intention of Seti's campaign. By Year 5 of the reign of Metenptah, groups of Libyans, including the Tjehenu, Meshwesh and Libu bolstered by groups associated with the 'Sea People' launched an invasion or migration against Egypt (Snape, 2003: 99 and Manassa, 2003) driven possibly by an environmental disaster in Libya (Kitchen, 1990: 20). This invasion attempt may also have prompted the abandonment of the settlement at Zawiyet Umm el-Rakham as no inscriptional material post-dating Ramesses II has so far been found.

1.3. The 1994–2010 Liverpool excavations at Zawiyet Umm el-Rakham

While the majority of the data utilised in this study was excavated from Area K in the southern portion of the fortified enclosure of Zawiyet Umm el-Rakham (Figure 1.2), it is only one area within a broader architectural context comprising both sacred and domestic structures explored elsewhere within the enclosure.

1.3.1 The temple and chapels

Labib Habachi initially excavated the temple in the north-western corner of the site in 1954–5 (Habachi, 1955; Leclant, 1956 and Snape and Wilson, 2007: 3). The temple was left partially exposed by Habachi, before being re-cleared by the Egyptian Antiquities Organisation (Snape and Wilson, 2007: 3) and re-excavated during the mid-to-late 1990s by the University of Liverpool team under the auspices of Dr Steven Snape. The temple itself is built on an east-west axis and abuts the external enclosure wall. It is similar in general appearance to other early Ramesside temples as Snape has argued such as temples found at Akhsa, Amara West and Gurob (2007: 69–92). The temple is constructed from slabs of the poor-quality local limestone, and includes an external courtyard with a barque shrine and the remains of ten columns, of which only the bases remain.

To the west of this courtyard are two transverse chambers (Outer and Inner Vestibule) and three sanctuaries (Northern, Central and Southern). The rear of the temple stands on a platform, raised in places to a level of 45 centimetres above the courtyard (Snape and Wilson, 2007: 9–12). No small finds or ceramics were noted in the temple area, most likely due to the repeated excavations and re-excavations in the area since the 1950s. Immediately south of the Temple, the University of Liverpool mission re-excavated three chapels (C1–C3) originally cleared hurriedly by Habachi's workmen in the 1950s (Snape and Wilson, 2007: 33). Clearing the three chapels revealed an assemblage of ceramics, which had been overlooked or ignored by Habachi's workmen, primarily consisting of Egyptian marl-ware vessels and imported materials such as Canaanite storage jars and coarse-ware stirrup jars (Snape and Wilson, 2007: 57–60). A collection of twenty-one private limestone stela were also recovered from this area by Habachi's excavators and published by Snape and Wilson (2007: 93–129).

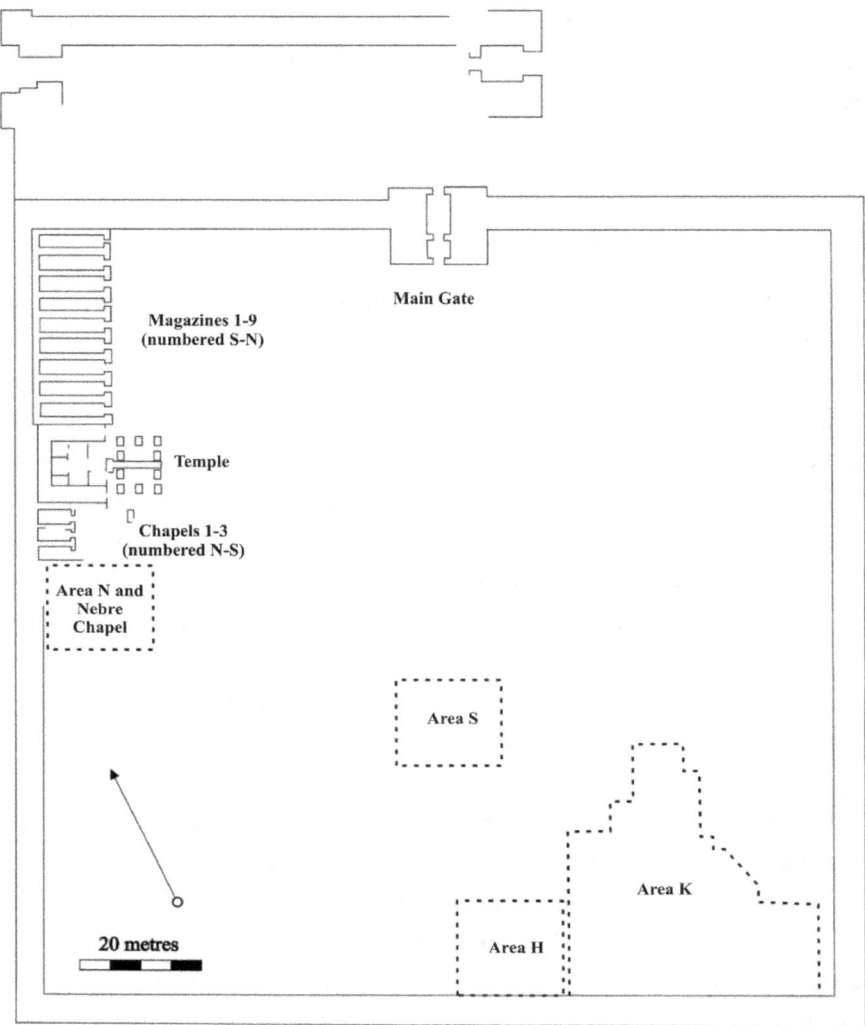

Figure 1.2 Plan of the fortified enclosure at Zawiyet Umm el-Rakham highlighting the main areas excavated by the University of Liverpool mission (S. Snape and author).

1.3.2 The Magazines and Nebre Chapel

North of the Temple, the Liverpool team located a series of nine rectangular magazines measuring 16.5 by 3.5 metres. Their original roofing had vanished, but in situ limestone door lintels carried the cartouches of Ramesses II as well as in one case, the fortress commander Nebre (Snape, 2004). Eight of the magazines were empty, but Magazine 1 contained a large assemblage of Canaanite storage jars and Mycenaean stirrup-jars. The discovery of this assemblage, studied by Thomas as part of her PhD research (Thomas, 2000), prompted extensive discussions about the role of Zawiyet Umm el-Rakham in the hypothesised counter-clockwise Eastern Mediterranean trade circuit during the Late Bronze Age (Snape, 1998, 2003, 2004 and 2010), especially considering the similarity between the Magazine 1 ceramic assemblage and material uncovered at the Cretan site of Kommos (Thomas, 2000: 528).

The Nebre Chapel is – together with Area N – one component of a hypothetical Governor's Residence, immediately south of the Temple and Chapels. The chapel, which measured 10 by 5 metres was discovered by the Liverpool expedition in 2000, and found to contain a limestone naos dedicated to Ptah and Sekhmet, as well as a ⅔rds life-size statue of Nebre made from fine non-local limestone. The entrance to the chapel is fronted by limestone doorjambs dedicated to Ptah and Sekhmet. The full publication of the Nebre chapel has yet to appear, but brief descriptions have appeared in works by Snape (2001 and 2004: 151). Excavation in this area is ongoing.

1.3.3 Area N

Area N is situated immediately south-east of the chapels and south of the Nebre Chapel. The area was excavated in a single season in 2008 by Glenn Godenho and Steven Snape and measures 10 by 10 metres. Only two small structures, both seemingly part of a larger complex, were discovered in the area and are architecturally similar to the structures in Area K. Area N may form a small part of a larger complex constituting the headquarters and mansion of the fort's commanders (Snape, pers. comm.).

1.3.4 Area S

The south building comprises three rooms, the walls of which are built from limestone cobbles held in a mud matrix (similar to the domestic architecture in Areas K and N). The cultic nature of the building has been hypothesised by Snape (2004: 150) on the basis of the presence of large uninscribed limestone monoliths in two of the three rooms (similar to Canaanite *massebah* shrines) and an assemblage of small offering bowls scattered on the floor of the rooms (Snape, 2004: 150).

1.3.5 Area H and Libyan squatter activity

During excavations between 1996 and 1999, eight circular stone structures were discovered immediately east of the main temple at Zawiyet Umm el-Rakham. These structures were investigated by Simpson (2002: 95–184) who convincingly suggested that they had been constructed by local Libyans as

Figure 1.3 Plan of Area K at Zawiyet Umm el-Rakham (S. Thomas and author).

shelters shortly after the abandonment of the fort by the Egyptian inhabitants (2002: 182–4).

1.4 Spatial layout of Area K

Area K is located in the south-western corner of the fortress enclosure and at the present comprises some 410 metres^2 of excavation (Figure 1.3). The nature of the area is wholly domestic, with low cobblestone walls as well as ovens, mortar emplacements and other evidence of food production activities (Snape, 2010). The walls are preserved to a height in places of a metre and more, and their relatively smoothed surfaces have caused speculation that they may have been topped by mud brick courses (Snape, 2010: 278) as is indeed evidenced in one instance where a substantial mud brick wall is still preserved on top of a foundation of cobblestones held in a silt matrix.

As argued by Snape (2010: 272) on the basis of inscriptional evidence, there seems to be only a single short occupation of the fortress during the early- to mid-nineteenth Dynasty, coinciding with the reign of Ramesses II. Nothing in the archaeological record in Area K suggests major later occupation of the site (Snape, 2010: 272). Some indicators however, suggest minor changes to the site during the Egyptian occupation. One structural element in particular shows evidence of repeated reconfigurations: the fifteen domed ovens excavated within the area. These domed bread ovens are identical in their construction to contemporary structures found for instance at Deir el-Medina (Bruyère, 1937–9: 72–4) and the Workman's Village at Tell el-Amarna (Samuel, 1999 and 2000: 566) in the Nile Valley and the archaeological record at Zawiyet Umm el-Rakham suggests that they were not used in synchronisation. Only six were found complete upon excavation, with the remainder showing signs of deliberate attempts at removal.

1.4.1 Buildings in Area K

The buildings in Area K are similar to other domestic structures from settlement sites excavated in Egypt in that they comprise a series of interconnected walls forming structures of ascribable and comparable types

(Shaw, 1992: 148; Tietze, 1985). The buildings differ however in their use of local limestone cobblestone held in a silt matrix rather than the far more common mud brick. This change is clearly an adaptation to the wetter conditions at Zawiyet Umm el-Rakham due to the autumn and winter rains causing some flooding of the *wadis* south of the fortress which in turn washes across the floodplain upon which the fort is built. As Snape (2010: 278) has concluded, the cobblestones either comprised the entire wall, or provided a sturdier foundation for mud brick walls, with the added benefit of raising the exposed mud brick above the level of some flooding to which the site was exposed. The utilisation of cobblestone and mortar architecture can therefore be seen as an adaptation to a geo-environmental condition. Seven structures in total have been identified within Area K (Figure 1.4).

Building 0a

Building 0a corresponds to the earliest construction phase at the site, and underlies rooms KM and KN in B.4. The longest surviving structural component of this building measures 5.10 metres. Two shorter walls originate from it measuring 2.20 and 1.90 metres respectively. A fourth cobblestonewall may originally have connected the two shorter N-S oriented walls. The four cobblestonewalls are all substantially thinner than the later Phase 3 walls related to B.1–5.

From this it is clear that the walls could not have supported a significant structure, and the building most likely represents a temporary shelter (perhaps in combination with lean-tos) similar to those found at the eighteenth-Dynasty fort at Tell el-Borg, where they may have functioned as temporary housing for the men who worked on the construction of the site (Hoffmeier, 2004: 90). The most likely conclusion is that B.0a originally served as one of multiple temporary shelters used during the construction of the settlement, which were later removed to make room for more substantial and permanent structures in Area K.

Building 0b

As with B.0a, B.0b comprises a series of thinner cobblestone walls than those used in later construction, and it appears contemporary with B.0a. The structure comprises four low walls which were deliberately removed almost to

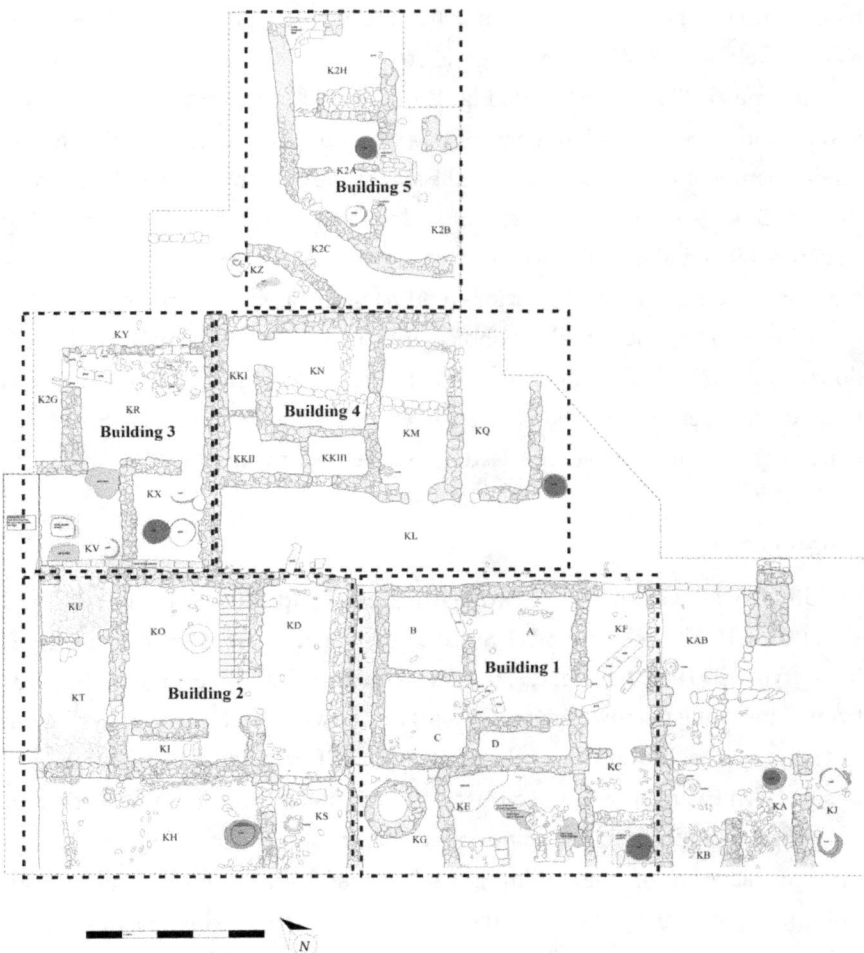

Figure 1.4 Plan of Area K highlighting the main buildings in the Area, Buildings 1–5 (S. Thomas and author).

ground level in order to facilitate passage from KF directly through to KJ and the eastern extent of Area K. Its function was most likely, as with Building 0a to house workers at the site during the construction of the settlement.

Building 1

Building 1 and its associated structural components were excavated over an extended period. In the 1999 season, Spaces A–D were uncovered as well as a blocked up passageway, Space E. In 2001, four further spaces, KC, KE, KF and KG were excavated. While the original structure resembles a typical Egyptian house Type 1b (Tietze, 1985: 65, Fig. 1.5), the adjoining areas E, KE, KC, KG and KF have been considered part of this structure, as their relationship to any other existing buildings are unclear. The size of the main nucleus of B.1 (Rooms A–D) is 5.0 x 6.0 metres (30 metres^2) and with the addition of the supporting structures listed above, the whole complex is roughly 8.8 x 8.0 metres (70.4 metres^2). The exterior and interior dividing walls are uniformly constructed from local limestone rubble (cobblestone) held in a silt matrix, and most doorways are flanked by limestone lintels and door jambs. The structure was floored with densely packed sandy soil except for a small area in Space KE where part of the floor is comprised of exposed bedrock.

Building 2

Building 2 was excavated over two seasons, 2001 and 2002 (2001: KH, KI and KJ; 2002: KD, KO, KT and KU). Structurally the building is similar to Tietze's house type 2c (1985: 66, Fig. 1.5) in that it constitutes a single large room (KO) fronted by a long narrow entry way (KD) as well as a small, narrow store-room (KI) and two to four ancillary chambers (KU, KT, KH and KS). The structure is square, measuring 8.8 x 8.8 metres (77.4 metres^2). The construction of Building 2 is linked to construction phases elsewhere in Area K. Phase 3.a saw the construction of the building itself, most likely contemporarily with Buildings 1–4. During Phase 3.c the east wall of KD was widened, most likely to facilitate the blocking of Space F, which lead to Space KG and the Well KW.

Building 3

Building 3 is the smallest structure in Area K, and is reminiscent of Tietze's Type 1a (1985: 64, Fig. X1.5) and also MS.XI from Tell Heboua (el-Maksoud, 1998: 143). The structure comprises a main space (KR) with two additional work and/or storage spaces (KV and KX) in the rear of the building, which measures 4.8 x 6.5 metres (31.2 metres^2) with the addition of the slightly larger shape of KV which breaks the rectangular outline of the structure and adds an additional 0.6 x 2.7 metres (1.6 metres^2) providing a total square area of the building as 32.8 metres^2.

A number of contexts within Building 3 suggests several structural alterations. A shared cobblestone wall related to Space KO in Building 2 suggests that the two structures were built simultaneously. However, following the collapse of the north-eastern cobblestone wall of KU, Building 2 and the addition of a new mudbrick wall, it seems that a dividing wall with a buttress was raised to divide rooms KV and KX, which had up till that point most likely constituted a single space. The later reconfigurations of the internal room structure are apparent, but their precise interrelationship is difficult to determine.

Building 4

Building 4 was excavated in 2001 and 2002. The main elements of the structure (Rooms KM, KN, KQ and KK1-3) is similar to Tietze's 1.C (1985: 66, Fig. 1.5), that is to say a main quarter (KN) surrounded by smaller auxiliary chambers (KK1-3) and an entrance room (KM). An additional wind-break was added which create an outside work area (KZ). The nucleus of the structure (KM, KN, KP and KK1-3) measures 5.0 x 6.6 metres (33 metres^2) and with the addition of areas KQ and KZ the total area of Building 5 and its environs is roughly 46.44 metres^2. The stratigraphy of the structure is unique, as the walls of an earlier dwelling, B.0a, are visible running through the main area of the structure.

Building 5

Building 5 comprises a larger domestic structure which is only partially excavated with three areas excavated in the 2002 season (K2A, K2B and K2H). Considering the largely unexcavated state of the building, a type is difficult to ascribe, although the room configuration is suggestive of a larger unit than Buildings 1-4, and on the basis of the three individual chambers on the southern side of the building, and the fact that these clearly continue further north-east, the most likely type is a larger structural hub such as Tietze's Type 2d (1985: 69, Fig. 1.5).

1.4.2 Courtyards and streets

A number of outdoor areas such as courtyards and streets which connect the main buildings are clearly identifiable within Area K. Some, such as Courtyard

Figure 1.5 The main types of houses found at Zawiyet Umm el-Rakham based on the typology developed by Tietze (1985).

KL were clearly planned early in the construction of the area, as several other structures are built to face it, while others such as Courtyards KA, KAB, KB and KJ are the result of a reconfiguration of an existing building into a far more open space which seems unlikely to have been roofed due to the removal of interior walls which could have acted as supports for a second storey or a roof.

Courtyards KA, KAB, KB and KJ

The communal zone or outdoor area comprising KA, KAB, KB and KJ is intrinsically linked to the demolished B.0b. This is primarily due to the shared nature of several walls that remain standing which were clearly part of the original structure of B.0b before its removal. There is a heavy concentration of grain processing implements in the area (three out of five mortar emplacements from Area K are located there), indicating a communal processing of grain prior to baking (similar to the communal zone found at E13.13 at Amara West [Spencer, 2015: 189]).

Courtyard KL

The courtyard KL is the primary unifying feature of B.1–2 and B.4 in Area K. All these structures have direct points of access to the area. No structural remains which might commonly be found in contemporary courtyards, such as shrines (found for instance in the courtyard of P.24 at Tell el-Amarna [Stevens, 2006: 222–3] or in larger dwellings at the same site [220–1]) have been located in KL. Significant portions of the faunal remains recovered from the site were found in four clusters located within the courtyard, along with tools. This could signify that the courtyard functioned as a butchering area and/or an area intended for waste disposal. The courtyard is roughly 17 metres^2.

Courtyard KY and K2G

KY and K2G may form a part of an open space courtyard, but their relationship and extent will need to be defined by further excavation. Very few finds were discovered in this area. Space KY also leads directly to both Space KZ and the 'street' K2C, and as such provided access from B.3 to B.5. The boundaries of the excavated portions of KY and K2G are too uncertain to provide meaningful measurements.

Street K2C

Knowledge of the extent of the elongated space or 'street' K2C, which divides B.4 and B.5, hinges upon further excavation to the east of these structures, but it seems plausible based on observed surface remains that K2C continued eastwards, providing a northern point of access to Space KQ before curving south to join with the Courtyard KL, effectively providing all the excavated structures (as well as further structures located to the west of Area K via Space KY) with access to the main courtyard KL and more easily facilitating movement within and between the somewhat confined architecture of the area. The excavated portion of K2C is roughly 14.5 metres^2.

1.4.3 Discussion

The utilisation of cobblestone and mortar architecture in Area K served a practical purpose of lessening the impact of a flooding of the site and therefore an adaptation to a geo-environmental condition. Furthermore, with the Hamada-type desert widespread on the nearby Marmarica Plateau, limestone cobbles would also be readily available, and the choice to go from the coastal plain up the escarpment to the plateau above and simply collect these stones may have been considered sensible procurement strategy as it in turn reduced the number of mud bricks which had to be created from local silt (such as was done for the enclosure wall).

Whether or not the seeking out of significant raw material on the nearby plateau (or alternatively a smaller number of suitable stones washed down from the plateau to the edge of the coastal plain) was a viable exchange for manufacturing fewer mud bricks, the availability of the choice itself is significant. If it is correctly assumed that the earliest structures in Area K (B.0a and B.0b) are roughly contemporary with the early construction phase of the fortress itself, the choice to construct from Hamada stones show that even at a relatively early point in the permanent Egyptian military presence, enough control was maintained in the area to make such excursions away from the primary hub of Egyptian activity safe enough to consider.

This in turn shows a significant control or pacification of the nearby area and the locals who periodically inhabited it from a relatively early stage in the Egyptian presence in the area of Zawiyet Umm el-Rakham. Even though it seems likely that a smaller fortified structure was erected to protect the builders of the larger fortification, who were housed in structures such as B.0a and B.0b, the choice to stray to the edge of the coastal plain and the plateau can still be interpreted as an expression of at least a basic measure of local security.

A noticeable feature which the structures from Zawiyet Umm el-Rakham generally share with most architecture from ancient Egypt is a degree of fluidity concerning especially the interior wall arrangements (see an extensive discussion of similar architectural re-configuration of domestic structures at Amara West [Spencer, 2015]). In respect to this restructuring of interior and exterior profiles and structures, it is curious to note that while some of these were conducted with a high degree of care and expertise, others suggest a somewhat more lethargic attitude to structural maintenance. This may be indicative of differing groups of occupants, soldiers or civilians, utilising different skill sets and setting alternating priorities during the occupation of the fortress. It may also evidence a degree of ownership over individual structures, that those occupants – whether a single-family unit or several groups – associated with specific structures had a personal choice in their lay-out and architectural modifications.

As for the function of Area K, the architectural lay-out of the structures suggest the housing of people, probably the soldiers of the garrison and possibly also their families, although evidence for the presence of partners and children remain speculative. The concentration of tools and the clear evidence of intense industries conducted in the area might be considered suggestive of a busy multi-craft workshop environment, however as discussed extensively by Spence (2015), craft production was an inherent element of the Egyptian household, although the precise location for such production within the house various (Spence, 2015: 94–6). As Spencer (2014: 46) also notes, there was little actual difference between the modern terms of 'house' and 'workshop' in Pharaonic Egypt and it is entirely likely that portions of the occupants slept, ate and worked within Area K. Further excavation north of the area however, may yet reveal a more ordered occupational zone, such as barracks, similar to those found at Askut (Smith, 2003: 100).

1.5 Population composition at Zawiyet Umm el-Rakham

The individuals and groups which constituted the 'elite' at early Ramesside forts are known from inscriptional evidence (stelae, door jambs and statues) found either at the settlements or in associated cemeteries at Tell Heboua I (el-Maksoud and Valbelle, 2005), Kom Firin (Spencer, 2014: 27) and Tell el-Borg (Hoffmeier and el-Maksoud, 2003). At Zawiyet Umm el-Rakham private stela set up in a series of chapels located south of the temple complex (Snape and Wilson, 2007) record several standard-bearers, some of whom are known from monuments elsewhere in Egypt (Snape and Wilson, 2007: 128), as well as two high-ranking officers; a general (*imy-rmš wr*), Panehesy (Snape and Wilson, 2007: 128) and the Troop-commander (*ḥry pḏt*) and Overseer of

Foreign Lands (*imy-r ḫ3s(w)t*) Nebre, who functioned as the fort's commander (Snape and Godenho, in press).

Considering the primarily military elite at the site, it is reasonable to assume that the majority of the common inhabitants at Zawiyet Umm el-Rakham were soldiers. Their ethnicity however, is a more complex issue. The majority of archaeological material from the site is convincingly Egyptian in nature, and parallels most aspects of contemporary Egyptian culture so precisely that it can be assumed that the majority of the occupants at the site were culturally Egyptian. However, other groups are also attested at the site (see Morris, 2005: 633 for further discussion). Textual evidence from the reign of Merenptah attest to the presence of at least two non-Egyptian ethnic groups associated with *mnnw*-forts in Libya (aside from the Medjay, a word which may not at this point in time refer exclusively to an ethnic group), the *ṯktn* and the *n3w* scouts: 'The forts [*mnnw*] are left to themselves, the wells (lie) open, accessible? to messengers. The (high)-walled battlements are undisturbed, it is the sunlight that (alone) awakens their guards. The Medjayu-militia [*md3yw*] lie fast asleep, the Niau [*n3w*] and Tjukten [*ṯktn*] scouts are out in the meadows as they wish' (*KRI* IV, 18:5–18:9 and Sagrillo, 2012: 441). Both groups are poorly represented in contemporary texts, although *ṯktn* most likely refers to Egyptian soldiers of Libyan blood (*Wb* 5, 411.3). A further reference to the cooperation between the *ṯktn* and the Egyptians is the Medinet Habu inscriptions of Ramesses III, which refer to a hostile Libyan chief seeking peace with the Egyptians according to similar terms as those enjoyed by the *ṯktn* (Sagrillo, 2012: 441). The role of these *ṯktn* within Egyptian society and the scholarly debate caused by the geographic origin is also extensively discussed by Sagrillo (2012: 440–5).

At Zawiyet Umm el-Rakham, the *ṯktn* are also directly referenced in the biography of Nebre, the forts commander:

> The Town of Ramesses II, the place known to the king, which he built for these Libyan people [*ṯk*], who had been living on the desert like jackals. He made them masters of the town, so that they would plant trees [*dg3 šn(wt)*]; so that they would work many orchards/vinyards [*k3mw*] in the countryside [...]
>
> Snape and Godenho, in press

This policy of settling Libyans in towns (*dmiw*) bearing the name of Ramesses II is also alluded to in an inscribed block from Suez: '[...] [Resettling the]

Libyans in settlements (*dmiw*) bearing his name, Lord of Crowns, Ramesses II [...]' (K*RI* II, 406:3, see also a discussion of the nature of the relationship between the sedentary Egyptians at Zawiyet Umm el-Rakham and the semi-nomadic Libyan pastoralists in Nielsen, 2017).

Archaeological evidence (primarily in the form of ceramics and ostrich egg-shell) also suggests the presence of Libyans at Zawiyet Umm el-Rakham both during and immediately following the Egyptian occupation of the site (discussed by Simpson, 2002: 443–54). Sherd scatters containing a mixture of Egyptian Late Bronze Age shapes and local Marmaric fabric shapes discovered in the *wadis* south of the settlement (Hulin, 2001) further support both the textual evidence and archaeological material from the site. The use of Libyan troops as part of the Egyptian army is also described in the Rhetorical Tanis Stela II: 'Libya (Tehenu) is cast down under his feet, his slaughtering has prevailed over them. He has captured the country of the West, transformed into soldiery, to serve him'. (K*RI* II, 289:18–21).

The possible *massebah* from Area S discussed above viewed in conjunction with locally produced Canaanite objects such as house shrines, and a Canaanite stone plate suggests that a portion of the occupants were Canaanites travelling with the Egyptian army (for a discussion of the use of mercenaries and the problematic nature of the term in the New Kingdom army, see Spalinger, 2005: 7–8). The presence of Canaanites at Zawiyet Umm el-Rakham in Libya can be explained by the practice, alluded to by Ramesses II, of re-settling prisoners-of-war far from their native regions: '[The King] carries off the land of Nubia to the Northland (or Delta), and the Asiatics to Nubia; he has placed the Shasu in the Westland, and he has settled the Libyans (Tjehenu) on the ridges'. (K*RI* II, 206:16–18). So while the majority of the occupants at Zawiyet Umm el-Rakham were from the Nile Valley, it is likely that groupings of both inhabitants from the local area as well as Canaanites constituted a portion of the occupants in the settlement although their precise role is far from clear.

Only limited information concerning the gender distribution of the occupants at Zawiyet Umm el-Rakham exists. Some evidence in the form of a stela belonging to Nebre and showing him in the company of his wife (Snape and Godenho, in press) may suggest that at least members of the elite within the fort were accompanied by their families. More information may however be inferred from contemporary forts containing nearby cemeteries or human remains, such as Amara West (Binder, Spencer and Millet, 2011) and Tell el-Retaba (Gorka and Rzepka, 2011). The preliminary research into the human and inscriptional remains at Amara West suggests a relatively diverse occupancy during the New Kingdom, with inscriptions testifying the presence of various officials such as messengers, priests and scribes (Binder et al., 2011: 48), along with the presence of burials of both females and children (52).

Amphora burials containing children, dated to the nineteenth Dynasty have also been found at Tell el-Retaba (Gorka and Rzepka, 2011) further supporting the notion that family groups were living at the fort contemporarily with the fortification of the site by Ramesses II (98–9). It is still unknown whether cemeteries existed in the vicinity of Zawiyet Umm el-Rakham although considering the estimated lifespan of the site of fifty years, it is plausible that some may be found during future surveys. The presence of some type of family groupings at contemporary fortress sites in Sinai and Nubia may indicate a similar situation at Zawiyet Umm el-Rakham, although it is problematic to unquestioningly assume similar social situations in the various geographical regions considering the differences in the political and historical context in which the structures existed. However, along with the presence of non-Egyptian groups at Zawiyet Umm el-Rakham, the possible presence of women and children serve to highlight the potential diversity of a population that cannot be considered as exclusively comprising male members affiliated with the Egyptian military.

2

Subsistence

2.1 Agricultural production

Bread and beer were staples of both Egyptian daily life and a primary component in the Egyptian offering cult throughout the Pharaonic Period (Helck, 1971; Verhoeven, 1984; Samuel, 2000; Peters-Desteract, 2005), and as a result cereal agriculture was a cornerstone of Egyptian society, expressed especially in the frequent use of grain as a principal trading commodity in an otherwise cashless economy, and the payment of grain as salaries and rations (Janssen, 1975, 2004; Spalinger, 1987; Murray, 2000: 508). It is therefore unsurprising that the most well documented subsistence industry conducted in Area K at Zawiyet Umm el-Rakham is related to cereal processing, baking and brewing. The significance of this topic has also resulted in a vast amount of scholarly literature on the issue, necessitating the following assessment on the state of current scholarship utilizing the most significant publications within the field. Following the seminal studies of respectively Murray (2000) and Samuel (2000), this assessment of scholarship has been divided into two components, grain processing and baking and brewing respectively.

2.1.1 Cereal production and processing

Cereal production and processing have been defined by Murray (2000: 506) as the processes spanning '[...] the initial land preparation prior to sowing, to the storage of the cereals in granaries'. It must however be noted that agriculture at Zawiyet Umm el-Rakham was by its basic nature highly different from cereal agriculture as conducted in the Nile Valley, due to the absence of the River Nile and its annual Inundation. Zawiyet Umm el-Rakham is located between the escarpment cliffs of the Marmarica formation and the Mediterranean Sea.

Overlaying the Marmarica Limestone Formation is the littoral zone or coastal belt, composed primarily of sedimentary loamy soil and clays, described in some detail by the traveller and scholar Oric Bates in the early nineteenth century (Bates, 1914: 2-8). The fortress of Zawiyet Umm el-Rakham is situated roughly half-way between the tide-line and the foot of the southern escarpment, meaning that all major land-use by the occupants was confined to the coastal belt, and therefore heavily influenced by two significant factors: (a) what vegetation could be supported by the area and (b) the availability of water.

Due to a relatively high annual rainfall, the wild flora of the littoral zone is both extensive and varied, more so than elsewhere in Egypt (Zahran and Willis, 1992: 21-2), and domestic plants such as emmer wheat and barley have historically been grown successfully in the area (Royal Geographical Society, 1916: 133). More recent studies, such as that conducted among Cyrenaica and Marmarican Bedouin by Roy Behnke (1980) found that while agriculture in these environments always exists on slim margins, several areas – the bottom of *wadis* even on the dry steppes, the crestline and plateau of the Jebel Akhdar and most notably the fertile strips of clayey soil along the coast – can provide a moderate yield of grain, usually utilized as supplements to the primary pastoral subsistence strategy employed by the Bedouin (Behnke, 1980: 9-25).

A 1966 UNESCO survey of the entire Qattata Littoral Zone found the area useful both for grazing of domestic animals, as well crop growth, made possible both by the winter rainfalls, and the use of wells and cisterns. The modern reintroduction of non-cereal crops such as grapes and olives has also been successful, as has the continuing exploitation of pre-Roman and Roman desert cisterns (Meigs, 1966: 85). As such, cereal agriculture was an available subsistence strategy to the inhabitants of Zawiyet Umm el-Rakham, although most effectively conducted in the relatively fertile *wadi* floors. No evidence of New Kingdom cisterns or similar attempts at water storage has been found at, or near, the site.

As discussed by Murray (2000: 507-8) earlier Egyptological studies related to agrarian practices tended towards a focus on tomb depictions within general introductions to Egyptian daily life (such as Erman, 1894), disregarding the inherent complications of relying on depictions governed to some extent by a stylistic repertoire. Textual sources have also been employed especially in the analysis of grain transport (Janssen, 2004) and the role of both grain and land within the Egyptian economy (cf. the Deir el-Medina ostraca [Černý, 1954] or the Heqanakhte Letters [Baer, 1963 and Allen, 2002]).

Ethnographic studies have further added to this scholarship through the study of the pre-mechanized Egyptian agricultural practices (Foaden and Fletcher, 1908; Murray, 2000: 508). The introduction of archaeobotanical research practices using flotation added a further dimension to this field of research with pioneering studies at settlement sites such as Kom el-Hisn (Moens and Wetterstrom, 1980) and Tell Ibrahim Awad (Roller, 1992) as opposed to the primary analysis of plant remains from tomb assemblages (Murray, 2000: 509). Archaeological finds have also aided the interpretation of grain storage, notably Middle Kingdom granaries discovered at Kahun and the Middle Kingdom forts in Nubia (Kemp, 1986). Other archaeological evidence such as hoes and sickle blades has also been found at Egyptian settlements (cf. Petrie, 1917: 46 and 54–5).

With regards to grain storage, depictions in the form of tomb paintings (Tylor and Griffith, 1894: Pl. III and Badawy, 1954: Fig. 81) and tomb models, such as those from the Middle Kingdom tomb of Meketre (Winlock, 1954), show that the grain – in the case of emmer wheat – was most likely stored in the form of emmer spikelets rather than clean grain (Murray, 2000: 527). Excavations at settlement sites such as Tell el-Amarna (Peet and Woolley, 1923: Pl. VII), Abydos (Wegner, 1998: 9, 15 and 21–2), Tell Edfu (Moeller, 2010: 89-100), Lahun and the Middle Kingdom Second Cataract Forts (Kemp, 1986) as well as Tell Heboua (el-Maksoud, 1998: 137) have identified circular or rectangular granary structures where this storage was conducted.

In 2001, a series of circular structures were identified immediately west of Area K at Zawiyet Umm el-Rakham (Area H, Figure 2.1). When excavated, it became clear that the structures constituted a series of three (H1, H2 and H3) granaries constructed from the same limestone cobbles and silt-mortar as the walls of the Area K buildings. These structures have been discussed in-depth by Simpson (2002: 401–16) who demonstrated both the primary use of the granaries, as well as the secondary use of one of them as an enclosed structure for baking (with the addition of ovens), and furthermore demonstrated their typical Egyptian appearance. The evidence of grain storage by no means evidences cereal production, but taken together with the evidence in the form of sickle blades found at the site – many with evidence of sickle sheen - some local production of grain can be suggested.

2.1.2 Baking and brewing

As with grain production and processing, investigations of ancient Egyptian baking and brewing initially had a strong focus on textual remains (such as Eisenlohr, 1897) which to some extent continues to modern times (cf. Spalinger, 1986). However, the discovery of installations such as ovens related to baking, notably from Tell el-Amarna and Deir el-Medina (Samuel, 2000: 542) have added archaeological evidence to the existing textual corpus.

Samuel herself has been perhaps the most prolific scholar studying the production of bread and beer in ancient Egypt (Samuel, 1989, 1992 and 2000) pioneering an interdisciplinary approach utilizing biological science and techniques, for instance residue analysis and correlative microscopy (Samuel, 1996) and experimental archaeology in order to learn the precise application of various tools from the archaeological record including hand stones and querns (Kemp, Samuel and Luff, 1994: 143–66 and Samuel, 2000: 561–3 and 2009) as well as using anthropological theories to investigate social relationships and their significance for food production in small communities such as the Deir

Figure 2.1 Photograph showing the granaries found in Area H (photograph by S. Snape).

el-Medina workmen's village (Samuel, 1999). As such, Samuel's collected bibliography remains one of the most far-reaching investigations into the techniques related to ancient Egyptian baking and brewing. Further experimental work focusing on breadmoulds and their function in the baking process has also been conducted by Bats (2019 and 2020) as well as Borojevic and Childs (2018). Further exploration of how workforces, including distantly deployed workforces, were provisioned has also been conducted by Malleson (2022)

2.1.3 Archaeological evidence for cereal processing from Area K (Plate 1)

As discussed by Samuel (2000: 559–60) with reference to ethnographic parallels for instance from Turkey (Hillman, 1984: 129–30), the first step in flour production was the pounding of the emmer spikelets in mortars using wooden pestles under a covering of water (Samuel, 2000: 560) to produce a mixture of bran and damp grain to be dried in the sun before a secondary winnowing process to remove the broken husks from the cleaned grain. The primary tools surviving in the archaeological record to evidence this process are limestone mortars and pestles (Samuel, 1999: 124), although no wooden pestles have been found at Zawiyet Umm el-Rakham, most likely due to the poor preservation of wood in the high-saline ground. Five mortars were found during the excavation of Area K, all of which were produced from local limestone (Figure 2.2) and of a shape similar to contemporary objects found at Memphis (Giddy, 1999: Pl. 61.28). The mortars were placed in depressions and surrounded by an emplacement of mud brick, stone cobbles and plaster, similar to arrangements found at the Tell el-Amarna Workmen's Village (Samuel, 2000: 561, fig. 22.11) and in the city itself (Kemp and Stevens, 2010b: 420).

The milling of the grain was primarily conducted in ancient Egypt with saddle-querns and hand stones/grinders (Samuel, 2000: 560) and unsurprisingly, a great number of querns (Pl. I) and quern fragments have been found in Area K, all made from local limestone. Eight hand stones or grinding stones (Pl. I) were found in the area, the majority of which are made from imported harder stones, of similar types to the contemporary assemblage from Tell el-Amarna (Kemp and Stevens, 2010b: 423–37). Four (ZUR/K/276, ZUR/KD/16, ZUR/K2A/15 and ZUR/KQ/13) are made from quartzite, quarried most likely in

Figure 2.2 Space KG (right) and KS (left) looking north, showing an embedded mortar in KS in the forefront of the picture and ZUR/KD/57 in the background (photograph by S. Snape).

Lower Egypt from Gebel Ahmar (Aston, Harrell and Shaw, 2000: 12) and brought to the site from the Valley and two (ZUR/KQ/11 and ZUR/KQ/16) are made from dark granite, either from the Eastern Desert or from Aswan (Aston et al., 2000: 35–6). The remaining two are made from local limestone (ZUR/K/297 and ZUR/KQ/11). The preference for hard-stone hand-stones may imply that the Egyptian occupants were aware at an early stage that there were no sources of hard rocks available in the local area, and that while workable querns could be made from local limestone, the local environment necessitated import of hard-stone hand stones from the Nile Valley. Baking scenes from the New Kingdom, such as one from the eighteenth-Dynasty tomb of Nebamun at Thebes (Samuel, 2000: Fig. 22.14) show figures mixing dough in large bowls with round or flattened bases. Several ceramic types from Area K were ideally suited to the large-scale mixing of dough, in particular two large vessels made from the ceramic fabric Nile C.

However, a large trough (ZUR/KD/57, Fig. 2.2), produced from local limestone and measuring 1.00 x 0.30 metres and found in Space KD could also have been effectively used. While no direct evidence was found in the form of residue within the trough, its proximity to both a mortar installation in the neighbouring Space KS, a quern stone in the neighbouring Space KG, a hand stone in Space KD itself, an oven in the neighbouring space Space KH and a water source in the form of the nearby well KW, it nonetheless was eminently suited for mixing large quantities of dough in a self-contained operation situated in these three rooms in Building 2.

As discussed by Samuel (2000: 554), one step in the brewing process was to filter or sieve a mixture of cooked grain and uncooked malt through a sieve using water. Only a single example of such an object has survived from Area K: ZUR/KAB/20 is a fragment of a slightly curved sieve (Pl. I), most likely curved to fit more securely over the neck of a larger vessel. The irregular holes in the sieve were pierced prior to firing. The large quantity of black particles within the ceramic matrix suggests that the sieve was locally produced from the ZUR B fabric. In itself ZUR/KAB/20 does not provide much evidence for the production of beer at the site, although it remains the only tangible proof for such procedure in the archaeological record.

The archaeological evidence suggests strongly that a significant grain processing industry was functioning in Area K. The majority of the tools used in the industry are also of local manufacture, in particular the mortars and quern stones. The only imported element of the production are the hard-stone hand stones, most likely brought to the site due to a known lack of suitable stones in the area. This suggests either a caution on the part of the initial garrisons, or perhaps a basic knowledge of the local geology. The role of the grain processing in Area K and the details of its function however can be most profitably studied through the dual investigation of its spatial arrangement within the site, and extrapolation of information regarding grain processing from contemporary texts.

2.1.4 Spatial arrangements and scale of agricultural production

Social interactions in the context of grain processing, baking and brewing has primarily been investigated by Samuel (1999). Samuel's conclusions regarding the self-sufficiency of individual households in the production of bread (1999: 139–40) are however potentially unhelpful for the site of Zawiyet Umm el-Rakham. While the Workmen's Village at Tell el-Amarna was a similarly state-sponsored settlement, it nonetheless contained individual households, whereas most of the available evidence from Zawiyet Umm el-Rakham suggests rather a predominately military settlement with less differentiation on the basis of households, although the presence of families or other groupings associated with individual structures within Area K cannot be excluded. It is for instance noticeable that each individual structure is associated with at least one oven, although the presence of only a single water source (KW) may reinforce the notion also suggested by Spencer (2015: 189) on the basis of evidence from Amara West, that baking and brewing was a largely communal affair, possibly regardless of the nature of occupants within a structural enclave.

The spatial arrangement of tools and installations related to grain processing, baking and brewing in Area K (Figure 2.3) does indeed show a preference for working in the outside/communal areas, such as Space KL and Spaces KA, KB and KAB. Aside from in Buildings 3 and 5, ovens were generally located in front rooms of buildings or in outside communal areas, possible to avoid smoky and cramped conditions inside the structures. The tools related to baking, querns, hand stones and mortars, are likewise generally grouped around these exterior ovens. This is particularly noticeable in Space KL and KQ where a majority of all discovered hand stones and querns were located in a close spatial arrangement around an outside oven. Another outside work area, Space KZ, also has two querns associated with an oven. A pile of ash found associated with the two quern stones may suggest the process of controlled burning of the quern surfaces for hygienic purposes described by Samuel (2000: 561, note also Miller, 1987: 14–16).

No individual saddle quern emplacements have been found in Area K (see Samuel, 2000: 551–654), although it is possible that the large mud brick platform in Space KO in Building 2 served as a large emplacement intended for several querns at once. The need for a structure to house multiple querns operated simultaneously, as opposed to the smaller individual one-quern emplacements found in Tell el-Amarna (Kemp et al., 1994: 160) might be explained by the requirement for much larger quantities of food to feed the entire garrison of 500 men, rather than merely a household.

The lack of any significant concentration of implements related to the processing of grain in the western portion of the area, in particular in Building 3 is problematic considering the large quantity of ovens located within this structure. However, most of these ovens had been effectively dismantled prior to the abandonment of the site, and were preserved only as lenses of ashy

Figure 2.3 Spatial overview of tools related to grain processing (circle: mortar; rectangle: hand stone; triangle: quern; rhomboid: basin) (S. Thomas and author).

deposit surrounded by the low base of their ceramic shell. The lack of tools in the area then further suggests that the focus of activity had shifted away from this portion of the area to the eastern side, although the reason for the modification remains unclear.

2.1.4.1 Population size

Discussions of the type and significance of grain cultivation to the economic life of the occupants at Zawiyet Umm el-Rakham requires quantification. In order to define the amount of grain required to sustain the site and by extension the amount of arable land needed for cultivation, the demography of the site must be discussed. Attempts to identify population size at ancient settlements have, as Mueller (2006: 94) argues, been fraught with uncertainty. Among the most common method has been the multiplication of the physical size of a settlement with a constant of inhabitants per hectare. As shown by Zorn (1994: 34) these constants have fluctuated from 100 inhabitants to 1000 inhabitants.

A more recent method championed by Mueller and Lee (2005 and Mueller, 2006: 95–104) has been the dual use of settlement size distribution (that is identifying the size of a settlement by investigation of the size of another known regional settlement and determining their respective size within a settlement hierarchy wherein all settlements are ranked by descending population size) and multi-linear regression (whereby population size is calculated on the basis of the presence or absence of specific facilities). Both methods have failings; determining population size by ranking regional settlements on the basis of the rank-size rule (Mueller, 2006: 94) requires both the presence of a group of regional settlements and also that the population size of at least one is known in order to determine the size of other settlements in the grouping. The multi-linear regression method requires either considerable archaeological data or – more commonly – textual data (Mueller, 2006: 101) in order to determine which facilities were present within a settlement. Neither method is applicable to Zawiyet Umm el-Rakham as a relatively isolated and also partially excavated settlement.

Attempts to determine the population size at Zawiyet Umm el-Rakham have been directed towards identifying military officials associated to the site and extrapolating amounts of troop under their command with reference to their titles (Snape and Wilson, 2007: 128). Stela 6 found by Habachi standing against the south wall of the temple at Zawiyet Umm el-Rakham (Snape and Wilson, 2007: 108) preserves two possibly different standard bearers. On the basis of research conducted by Schulman (1964: 69), that a standard bearer (t_3i $sryt$) commanded a company (s_3) of either 200 (Faulkner, 1953: 32–47) or 250 (Schulman, 1964: 26–32) men, Snape and Wilson (2007: 128) conclude that the standing garrison at Zawiyet Umm el-Rakham was between 400 and 500 men.

Similar calculations have also been done by Raedler (2003: 157) who asserts that between 800 and 1,000 men were stationed at Wadi es-Sebua during the reign of Ramesses II on the basis of four different standard bearers listed on stela from the temple at this site (see also Exell, 2009: 116). However, a further three stelae from Zawiyet Umm el-Rakham (Stela 4, 9 and 17, Snape and Wilson, 2007: 104–5, 112–13 and 119–21) also preserve images of standard bearers, which might, following this argumentation, increase the garrison estimates to between 1,000 and 1,250 men. Furthermore, the location of both stela 6 and 17 stacked in between a mud brick wall and the south-western corner of the temple might also suggest a secondary storage facility for stela taken from their original context by the Egyptian inhabitants (Snape and Wilson, 2007: 94), possibly because their dedicators were no longer associated with the fort, having either died or left.

A further issue with the use of military titles to estimate population size in this manner is the assumption that the occupants were exclusively male soldiery and therefore quantifiable as a 'company'. The lack of any evidence of centralised food production in Area K (as is seen for instance at the industrial bakeries at Kom el Nana [Kemp, 1995: 433–8]) taken together with the commonly gendered tasks of, for instance, grinding grain (see especially Samuel, 2009 and Robins, 1993: 102) suggests a domestic setting which would likely involve both women and children (also evidenced at other fortress sites from the nineteenth Dynasty in the form of female and child burials at Amara West, Binder, Spencer and Millet, 2011: 52, and infant burials at Tell el-Retaba, Gorka and Rzepka, 2011: 98–9). Due to this presence of an unspecified number of 'civilian' occupants at the site, the purely military estimation of population size by presence of commanding officers cannot be wholly reliable.

Another possible strategy for establishing the approximate size of the population at Zawiyet Umm el-Rakham is a dwellings-based estimate following Zorn (1994: 32). Using this method, the number of domestic structures or dwellings within the excavated portion of the site is scaled up to include the known extent of the site. Taken together, the temple, chapels, magazines as well as Areas N, G, S and K comprise roughly 2,360 metres^2 or 16.39 per cent of the fortress enclosure of 14,400 metres^2 (measuring 120 metres on a side). Within this area, five contemporary domestic units have been identified within Area K (see Chapter 1) with a further two to three smaller domestic units identified within Area N (Snape, pers. comm.). Following the advice of Zorn (1994: 33) and considering five occupants per dwelling, this provides a conservative estimate of between thirty-five and forty occupants within the excavated area. Scaling this number up to encompass the entire known area of the settlement by multiplying it with a factor of 6.101 suggests between 214 and 245 occupants (230 on average) at the site. This number is of course biased by the lack of investigation of possible structures outside the enclosure walls which could conceivably have provided shelter for more occupants. Similarly, it assumes an even distribution of domestic units across the unexcavated areas of the site.

2.1.4.2 Water management, agricultural yield and crop types in the eastern Marmarica region

Herodotus' claim that the 'eastern region of Libya, which the nomads inhabit, is low-lying and sandy as far as the Triton river' (Herodotus IV: 191) and that as a result the nomadic occupants of Eastern Libya were sustained exclusively by milk and the flesh of their animals (Herodotus IV: 186) has in recent years been challenged by surveys of the eastern Marmarica region between Mersa Matrouh and Zawiyet Umm el-Rakham (White, 1999: 932; Hulin, 2001: 74; Vetter, Reiger and Nicolay, 2009; Rieger, Vetter and Möller, 2012; Vetter, Reiger and Möller, 2013; Vetter, Riegre and Nicolay 2014), which has helped to create a more nuanced picture of the agricultural potential of the coastal zone in particular and the many *wadis* which bisect the area. Pap. Vatican II dating to the second century AD from the Marmarica region lists barley, but also some wheat and beans as well as vines, olives, figs and dates as the primary crops grown in the area in Classical antiquity (Johnson, 1959: 58–62). Complimenting this textual evidence are a series of Ptolemaic settlements identified in the area south of Zawiyet Umm el-Rakham at Wadi Umm el-Ashtan (Rieger et al., 2012: 166–8), Wadi Qasaba and Wadi Magid (Vetter et al., 2014: 50–3) as well as a widespread network of cisterns, embanked fields and other evidence of 'water harvesting' dating primarily to Classical antiquity spread throughout the surveyed area (Vetter et al., 2013: Fig. 13).

Of particular interest to the current study are a series of water harvesting structures discovered at Wadi Magid, located 8 kilometres south-east of Zawiyet Umm el-Rakham. The survey in the area identified lateral terraces constructed to exploit hilltop run-off before the water ran onto the *wadi* floor during the winter rains in the area (Vetter et al., 2014: 51–2). Analysis of soil samples associated with the terraces at Wadi Magid using optically stimulated luminescence (OSL) provided absolute dates for the construction of the two structures at respectively 1193 BC and 1153 BC and placing them within the

Egyptian New Kingdom (or, including potential error, dating between the early New Kingdom and the Third Intermediate Period) (Rieger et al., 2012: 167). Similar dating of embanked fields at Wadi Umm el-Ashtan (located 2 kilometres south of Zawiyet Umm el-Rakham) provided a range of dates from The First Intermediate Period through to the Ptolemaic Period (Rieger et al., 2012: 167).

Ceramic surveys by Linda Hulin revealed concentrations of Egyptian and Egyptian-style local pottery in the *wadis* south of Zawiyet Umm el-Rakham, close to the areas discussed above (Hulin, 2001: 68). Considering the presence of Egyptian material and chronologically contemporary water-harvesting structures south of the fortress, it is likely that the Egyptian occupants of Zawiyet Umm el-Rakham exploited these fertile areas for agricultural purposes. However, it is more questionable how Egyptians, raised in the Nile Valley with an inundation-based agriculture, had the technological expertise and local knowledge of the hydrological conditions to effectively irrigate the soil. However, on the basis of OSL dates provided by Rieger et al. (2012: 167–8) it is clear that farming in this area pre-dates the Egyptian occupation by several hundred years, at least from the Middle Kingdom onwards. Ethnographic evidence from the Cyrenaica region of Libya highlights the seasonal agriculture conducted by nomadic tribes (Behnke, 1980: 40–8). A similar situation is also described by travellers in the region in pre-industrial times (Lyon, 1821: 44).

It is likely then that a similar opportunistic agriculture was conducted by Libyan nomads in Pharaonic times as a means of supplementing a diet based around their animals. Such agricultural pursuits would have required a knowledge of the hydrological conditions in the eastern Marmarica region described above and it is therefore a likely hypothesis that the Egyptian occupants at Zawiyet Umm el-Rakham relied on information and help from local Libyans familiar with this type of agriculture in order to farm in the *wadis* south of the site. It is in this context that the following quote from the biography of the Zawiyet Umm el-Rakham's commander Nebre should be viewed:

> The Town of Ramesses II, the place known to the king, which he built for these Libyan people [*ṯk*], who had been living on the desert like jackals. He made them masters of the town, so that they would plant trees [*dgꜣ šn(wt)*]; so that they would work many orchards/vineyards [*kꜣmw*] in the countryside [. . .].
>
> Snape and Godenho, in press

The lack of significant non-Egyptian material within the enclosure at Zawiyet Umm el-Rakham makes it uncertain whether large groups of Libyan nomads stayed permanently within the fort, but the reference to the local nomadic population working on agricultural pursuits in the countryside surrounding the fort is highly pertinent considering the archaeological and ethnographic evidence discussed above.

2.1.4.3 Calorific and acreage requirements for the occupants at Zawiyet Umm el-Rakham

On the basis of an extensive ground and satellite survey of a 30 kilometres east-west by 15 kilometres north-south area of land south-west of Mersa Matrouh Vetter et al. (2009: 20) concluded that roughly 9 per cent (40.5 kilometres^2) of this area consisted of arable land, located primarily in the bottom of *wadis* or consisting of embanked fields on the *wadi* slopes. At maximum, this would provide 4,050 hectares of arable land within the investigated area. The authors (Vetter et al., 2009: 20) utilised a barley yield of 1 t/ hectare to calculate that the area could potentially feed 22,000 people. However, ethnographic data from similar environments in the Levant (Padgham, 2014: 132) suggests that a lower yield averaging 646.7 kilograms/hectare is a more realistic figure. According to figures from Pap. Vatican II (Applebaum, 1979: 99–100) an average annual barley yield in the area of Marmarica in the second century BC was on average 9.5 hectolitres, or 570 kilograms/hectare, and an annual emmer wheat yield of 7.25 hectolitres, or 521 kilograms/hectare. Recalculating the total yield of the arable land suggested by Vetter et al. (2009: 20) this suggests then that 2,308,500 kilograms of barley could be grown annually, assuming that no other crops were grown.

Table 2.1 Amount of arable land required to sustain 230 occupants at Zawiyet Umm el-Rakham

Food type	Amount of arable land (ha)	% of arable land (Vetter et al., 2009: 20)
Barley	116	3.63
Wheat	31	
Pulses	42	1.04
Fruits (fig)	5	0.13
Flax	1	0.03
Total	195	4.83

However, the ancient diet at Zawiyet Umm el-Rakham was more varied. While barley is a more reliable crop in the area than emmer wheat, and remains the predominant cereal crop grown even into modern times, other potential crops cultivated in the area in antiquity includes pulses, vines, olives, figs and dates (Johnson, 1959: 58–62). The lack of archaeobotanical analysis at Zawiyet Umm el-Rakham precludes firm conclusions regarding diet, but considering the evidence of large-scale imports of oils and wine to the site (Thomas, 2000 and Gasperini, 2016) the significance of locally grown olives and vines was lessened. Pulses as well as figs and dates may have provided the remainder of required calories (el-Barasi and Saaed, 2013: 50) supplemented by protein in the form of caprine meat and ostrich eggs (see Section 2.2). Padgham (2014: 21) estimates that cereals (barley and emmer wheat) provided 72.7 per cent of the annual calorific intake of New Kingdom Egyptians with a further 14.4 per cent provided by animal products (meat, dairy and fats) and the last 12.9 per cent provided by fruits, pulses and honey. Given this distribution it is evident that the majority of the available arable land would be dedicated to cereal growth.

At the average population estimate calculated above of 230 occupants and following the percentage mix of food types calculated by Padgham (2014: 21) the garrison would require 230 kilograms/year of barley for bread and beer and an additional 56 kilograms/year of emmer wheat per person or respectively 52,900 kilograms/year of barley and 12,880 kilograms of emmer wheat. Following Padgham (2014: 30) an additional 10 per cent seed corn for both types and 15 per cent loss from wastage produces a final requirement of 66,125 kilograms/year of barley and 16,100 kilograms/year of wheat required for the maintenance of the settlement at Zawiyet Umm el-Rakham. Considering the yield rates provided by Pap. Vatican II (Applebaum, 1979: 99–100) of 570 kilograms/hectare for barley and 521 kilograms/hectare for emmer wheat, a combined 147 hectares of land would need to be cultivated annually to provide the basic cereal requirement for the settlement. On the basis of the conclusions presented by Vetter et al. (2009: 20) these 147 hectares constitute 3.63 per cent of the total amount of potentially arable land within the surveyed area south of Mersa Matrouh.

Pap. Vatican II does not contain information regarding the yield rates of pulses or fruits, so the yield rates for area around Tel Gezer (Webley, 1972: 173 and 175) of 595 kilograms/hectare have been used as this area similarly relies on rain-fed rather than basin agriculture and has a comparable barley yield to

Table 2.2 Amount of arable land required to sustain 500 occupants at Zawiyet Umm el-Rakham

Food type	Amount of arable land (ha)	% of arable land (Vetter et al., 2009: 20)
Barley	320	7.90
Wheat		
Pulses	91	2.25
Fruits (fig)	11	0.27
Flax	3	0.07
Total	425	10.49

the one found in Marmarica. With a required 85 kilograms/year of pulses per person and a total population size of 230, 19,550 kilograms of pulses would be required at Zawiyet Umm el-Rakham annually. At the yield rate suggested for Tel Gezer of 595 kilograms/hectare, this would have required the cultivation of 33ha, and with the addition of 10 per cent kept for seed and an additional 15 per cent loss this would require an additional 42 hectares of land.

It is uncertain what fruits, if any, were grown locally to supplement the diet of the inhabitants although traditionally figs have been grown and continue to be grown in the Marmarica region successfully (Johnson, 1959: 58–62 and Mansour, 1995: 14). Data from 1993 suggests a yield rate for figs of roughly 13t/hectare or 30–40 kilograms per tree with between 400 and 1,111 trees per hectare (Mansour, 1995: 14). It is likely that ancient yield rates were considerably lower, but even considering a 50 per cent reduction of the lowest estimate of 400 trees per hectare, each hectare could nonetheless potentially provide 6,000 kilograms of figs per year with the average yield of 30 kilograms per tree (Mansour, 1995: 14). With a yearly requirement of 125 kilograms of fruits and vegetables on average per person (Padgham, 2014: 21), 28,750 kilograms of figs would be required to satisfy the requirements of the estimated 230 occupants of Zawiyet Umm el-Rakham. This would require a further 5 hectares of arable soil dedicated to the cultivation of fig trees. It should be noted however, that unlike grain, the cultivation of fig trees would require a waiting period of several seasons before the trees became sufficiently mature to bear crop (Table 2.1).

Considering the inherent uncertainty in calculating population size, a similar calculation for the garrison size of 500 (Table 2.2) suggested by Snape and

Wilson (2007: 128) has also been done. The acreage calculations presented show that the occupants of Zawiyet Umm el-Rakham had ample arable land located at a maximum distance of 15–20 kilometres and that they could – in particular by utilising the fertile *wadis* south of the fort such as Wadi Umm el-Ashtan (Rieger et al., 2012: 166–8) and Wadi Magid (Vetter et al., 2014: 50–3) – grow both the required variety and quantity of crops to sustain life. The predominant cash crop grown on the site was flax used to produce linen (see Section 4.1). By adjusting the estimated requirements of dry flax fibre (in kilograms) for a group of 100,000 Egyptians spread across five socio-economic groupings (Padgham, 2014: 64) and assuming a similarly stratified society at Zawiyet Umm el-Rakham, 254.2 kilograms of dry flax fibre would be needed annually for a population of 230 and 552.5 kilograms for a population of 500. Considering the possible utilisation of linen as a trade commodity, these figures have been adjusted up by a factor of 20 per cent to respectively 305 kilograms and 662.9 kilograms required annually. The acreage requirements to provide for this quantity of flax fibre has been calculated by using an estimated yield of 335 kilograms/hectare of dry fibre from Mesopotamia (Padgham, 2014: 65). Considering the poorer conditions of irrigation and the lower-quality soil in the Marmarica region, a 25 per cent loss has been estimated giving a yield of 251.25 kilograms/hectare. Considering the requirements suggested above, a population of 230 would require 1–2 hectares of land dedicated to flax cultivation while a larger population of 500 would require at most 2–3 hectares of land.

2.1.4.4 Labour requirements for agricultural production at Zawiyet Umm el-Rakham

The dryland agriculture, reliant primarily on the *c.* 150 millimetre average rainfall in the eastern Marmarica region (Vetter et al., 2009: 9) naturally differs from the inundation-based agriculture conducted in the Nile Valley. The calculation of labour requirement can nevertheless effectively utilise the recent methodology provided by Padgham (2014: 32–51) of calculating the labour rates (in work-days/hectare) of individual agricultural activities and using these to determine the labour requirements both for each individual step and the overall agricultural production.

Ethnographic evidence (Lyon, 1821: 44) suggests that local Bedouin prepared embanked fields similar to those found dating to the New Kingdom from Wadi Umm el-Ashtan (Rieger et al., 2012: 166–8) by ploughing using a wooden hoe, rather than an ard plough yoked to oxen. It is not clear whether the Egyptian occupants at Zawiyet Umm el-Rakham would have utilised this method, but considering the clear evidence of nomad agriculture in the area prior to the construction of Zawiyet Umm el-Rakham (Rieger et al., 2012: 167–8) this may suggest that the occupants relied on local knowledge of agricultural processes and adapted their methods to these. As Padgham (2014: 34) suggests, the exclusive use of hoes might also have been preferable to prepare smaller and dispersed tracts of land, such as the multiple embanked fields found in the region which were generally found to be between 0.1 and 0.4 hectares in size (Vetter et al., 2009: 12). In a study of the effectiveness of land preparation in Mexico on shrub-covered, rocky land unsuitable for ploughing, Lewis (1951: 154–7, Table 38) suggested a labour rate of 60 work-days/hectare using steel-bladed hoes.

Following Padgham (2014: 36) 10 work-days/hectare have been added due to the lessened efficiency of using wooden or bronze-tipped hoes. Twenty work-days/hectare have then been subtracted due to the lack of semi-decidous shrub forest in the investigated region, which characterised the area of Lewis' study (Padgham, 2014: 36) and would have complicated the preparation of the land.

Table 2.3 Labour requirements for agricultural production at Zawiyet Umm el-Rakham

Activity	Estimated labour rate (work-days/ha)	Competency index	People required (230 person estimate)	People required (500 person estimate)
Hoeing	50	1.17	36	77
Sowing and ploughing in seed	1.27	1.17	1	2
Weeding	34.2	1.17	25	53
Irrigation	39.9	1.17	29	62
Reaping (grain)	24.6	1.3	15	42
Harvesting (pulses and flax)	10	1.3	2	4
Transport	31.7	1.3	25	54
Threshing and winnowing	8.05		8	16
Tending fig trees	297	1.17	6	13
Total required	496.72	N/A	147	323

As such, the labour rate for the preparation of the land for sowing using hoes on previously fallow land in Eastern Marmarica has been calculated as 50 work-days/hectare. The process of hoeing was due to its physical intensity most likely conducted primarily by males, and a competency index of 1.17 (Padgham, 2014: 32–3) has been assumed. This provides the following calculation for 195 hectares of land for cereals, fruits, pulses and flax feeding 230 occupants at Zawiyet Umm el-Rakham: 195 hectares x 50 work-days/hectare = 9,750 x 1.17 / 314 work-days (following Padgham, 2014: 32) = 36 workers.

Sowing was most likely done by broadcasting, following trampling of the seeds into the ground by leading flocks of sheep or goat across the fields. Padgham (2014: 35) suggests an average labour rate for sowing of 0.37 work-days/hectare. To this has been added the estimated 0.9 work-days/hectare required to plough in seeds suggested by Padgham (2014: 36) to account for the added time it would take to lead herd animals across the newly sown fields. No direct ethnographic evidence exists for weeding of crops in the eastern Marmarica region so without more specific data the labour rate has been estimated at 34.2 man-days/hectare combined for three weeding cycles on the basis of ethnographic studies of weeding using hoes in Zimbabwe (Padgham, 2014: 37).

The labour rate for irrigation is more problematic to estimate. Due to the low annual rainfall, considerable effort would need to be expended in the construction of embanked fields, cisterns and other hydrological structures. A running maintenance would also be required to prevent these from falling into disrepair and wasting valuable water resources. At 100–150 millimetres annually, the rainfall in Marmarica is considerably lower than other agricultural communities in the Eastern Mediterranean (Padgham, 2014: 39). Given this increased need for irrigation and management of hydrological structures, the labour rate of Cyprus (with an average of 350–400 millimetres annual rainfall) of 13.2 work-days/hectare has been tripled to 39.9 work-days/hectare to account for lower annual rainfall and resultant increased labour requirements.

Using studies conducted by Steensberg (1943: 23) and Korobkova (1981: 340) of the effectiveness of reaping of cereals using flint sickle blades can establish the labour rate at 24.6 work-days/hectare (Padgham, 2014: 39). Depictions in the Tomb of Unsu from Thebes (Louvre Museum N1431, Potvin and Pierrat-Bonnefois, 2002: 24–5) suggests that both men and women took part in the reaping of cereals and a competency index of 1.3 has been assumed for this calculation. For the reaping of pulses and flax by pulling the stalks by hand, the labour rate of 10 work-days/hectare is suggested by Halstead and Jones (1997: 279).

Transport of the harvested material is a problematic calculation in the case of Zawiyet Umm el-Rakham. While it is clear that the dispersed nature of available arable land would have necessitated that the occupants exploited several of the fertile *wadis* south of the fort, as well as fertile strips on the littoral zone closer to the fort, the precise location of these fields cannot be determined, aside from the limited evidence at Wadi Umm el-Ashtan, located 2–5 kilometres south of the fort and Wadi Magid, located 8 kilometres southeast of the fort. The maximum extent of the surveyed area (Vetter et al., 2009) is roughly 15 kilometres from the fort.

However, given the lack of any further information, no certain labour rate can be determined. It is a reasonable assumption however, that the labour rate would be comparable to that calculated by Padgham (2014: 40) for Egypt considering the dispersed areas of arable land at Zawiyet Umm el-Rakham. As such, this labour rate of 31.7 work-days/hectare has been retained. The labour rates for threshing and winnowing estimated by Padgham (2014: 42–3) have been retained for this study considering the similarity of this process in the Nile Valley and at Zawiyet Umm el-Rakham as both areas were occupied by Egyptians. As such, the labour rate for grain is 5.55 work-days/hectare and for pulses 2.5 work-days/hectare (Padgham, 2014: 42–3). Similarly, the proposed labour rate of 297 work-days/hectare for the tending of fruit trees suggested by Padgham (2014: 46) has been retained (Table 2.3).

The calculations of labour requirements for the maintenance of the agricultural economy at Zawiyet Umm el-Rakham has highlighted that, even if assuming that different people were involved in each identified step of the agrarian work, the necessary product could be produced using between 62.2 per cent and 67.2 per cent of the occupants at the site. It is however more reasonable to assume that certain individuals were involved in multiple processes (such as a single individual participating both in hoeing, sowing and weeding for instance) which would considerably reduce the labour requirements of the population. The work required to process the harvested and winnowed cereal as well as prepare and weave the harvested flax fibres represents an additional labour requirement, but one which – certainly in the case of baking and brewing – was a less seasonal activity and most likely represented part of the daily life for those occupants not occupied with agricultural labour. This section has shown that despite the marginal location of Zawiyet Umm el-Rakham, it is reasonable to assume that the settlement had the necessary environmental and labour requirements to be largely self-sustaining, an interpretation also strongly suggested by the evidence of local craft production discussed elsewhere in this volume.

2.2 Proteins

Aside from the material related to the growing and processing of cereals discussed above, subsistence is also evidenced at Zawiyet Umm el-Rakham by an assemblage of animal remains found in Area K. Initial classification of this material was conducted by Louise Bertini and Salima Ikram who categorised the assemblage of 613 elements according to taxonomy (if possible), element, portion, side, sex and age (if possible) as well as noting secondary processes visible on the samples, such as butchery marks, gnawing and burning. The aged material initially formed a small portion of Bertini's MA thesis (Bertini, 2007) submitted to the University of Liverpool. These investigations form the basis of the discussion in this thesis of the implications of these identifications for a broader study of subsistence at Zawiyet Umm el-Rakham. The assemblage itself has degraded to a great extent in storage and a full re-investigation was not possible when the material was inspected again in 2014.

While the majority of the 613 elements could be taxonomically identified, a smaller subset (N=282) could only be identified according to size, such as large mammals (most likely horses or cattle), medium-large mammals (most likely donkeys, pigs or juvenile cattle), medium mammals (most likely sheep, goat) and small mammals (rodents, hares etc.). Due to this uncertainty, they have not been included in the analysis below. The faunal assemblage is generally poorly preserved due to the high ground moisture and salinity. Animal bones during the excavation were recovered by hand by the excavators, and primarily found in four clusters within Area K.

The most prominent of these is ZUR/K0,4 and ZUR/K1,4 (referring to the grid system utilised in the 1999 excavations) denoting a northern area of the courtyard KL against the wall of Space KQ in Building 4. The faunal cluster in

Table 2.4 Count of unidentified mammalian, avian and mollusc elements; the two former classified by size, the latter unidentifiable due to poor preservation (author)

Animal size	Amount
Small mammal	3
Medium mammal	239
Medium–Large mammal	17
Large mammal	12
Small bird	4
Medium bird	1
Large bird	1
Unidentified bird	2
Unidentified shellfish	3
Total	282

Table 2.5 Taxonomical classification for the Area K faunal assemblage (author)

Species	Amount	% identified	M. Ind. Identified	% M. Ind. Identified
Bos Taurus	12	3.6	3	10.3
Canis Familiaris	92	27.8	1	3.5
Capra Hircus	22	6.7	3	10.3
Ovis Aries	38	11.5	5	17.2
Ovis/Capra	115	34.8	9	31
Equus Asinus	2	0.6	1	3.5
Gazella	1	0.3	1	3.5
Sus Scofa	2	0.6	1	3.5
Tortoise	36	10.9	5	17.2
Oyster	11	3.3		
Total	331		29	

this area was found around an oven which also contained the complete skeleton of a dog (Bertini, 2007: 9, who interpreted the area as a room, although later excavations disproved this interpretation, Snape, pers. comm.). This cluster contains 308 of the elements analysed in this chapter.

A second cluster containing 160 elements was located in ZUR/K2,6 and ZUR/K2,7 constituting the south of the courtyard KL, lying against the northern wall of Building 1 and around the entrance to Building 2. A further 115 elements were found in grid square ZUR/K0,7, inside Space KKIII in Building 4. A final smaller cluster containing twenty-nine elements were located in ZUR/K5,6 spread across Space KE and Space KG. All of these clusters were either located in communal areas, in rooms directly abutting communal areas or – in the case of the smallest assemblage – in two spaces which had seemingly been blocked off. Deposits of ash and general collapse in Space KE may also indicate the purpose of the area for refuse deposit and explain the presence of the faunal elements as garbage (Table 2.4).

Butchery marks were identified on only eleven elements (though their precise type and direction was not noted), but the majority of the elements were either gnawed or burnt. The most likely explanation, in conjunction with the deposition of the material in communal areas, is that the assemblage constitutes a mixture of the material immediately discarded during the butchering of an animal (such as phalanges and possibly skulls, see below) and the material which had been cooked and eaten (long bones, ribs etc). Space KL may then have been employed as a combined butchering/refuse disposal area and the assemblage thus constitute the material associated with the final meals of the occupants before the site's abandonment.

292 of the 613 faunal elements recovered from Area K (47.5 per cent) have gnawing marks. While some of these may indicate the consumption of the meat directly off the bone by the human inhabitants of the fort, the majority reflect the disturbed nature of the deposit. Rodent bones (two femurs) found within the assemblage, along with a complete dog skeleton (see Section 2.2.1) testify the presence of various scavengers co-habiting with the Ramesside occupants and also disturbing the assemblage following the site's abandonment. This disturbance must be borne in mind, as it may have caused minor biases in the data, for instance by the removal or destruction of specific skeletal elements by larger scavengers.

Two methods have generally been employed in the statistical analysis of faunal data from archaeological sites in Egypt; Minimum Number of Individuals (MNI or M. Ind. Identified, cf. Legge, 2008 and 2012) or Number of Identified Specimens (NISP, cf. Bertini, 2007 and 2014). While MNI relies on the identification of the smallest possible number of individual animals identified in an assemblage based on the complete faunal record, NISP calculates the maximum possible number of individuals. Both of these methods have obvious failings, in that one underestimates the actual number of individuals and create inter-species ratios which do not take bone preservation into account.

The other overestimates the amount and often the importance of a specific species by ignoring the tendency of some skeletal components to fragment more easily than others, creating a larger assemblage and a large NISP count (see Grayson, 1984: 94–6 and Werschum, 2010: 25–6 for a criticism of both methods). Following the extensive work conducted by Anthony Legge on the faunal assemblages from the Main City and Grid 12 at Tell el-Amarna, as well as the nearby Stone Village (Legge, 2008 and 2012) this study utilises MNI. A primary issue with MNI, its tendency to create a bias when calculating inter-species ratios, is less significant in the Area K assemblage due to the dominance of caprine elements at the expense of both pigs and cattle, creating a far less varied assemblage than at contemporary sites, and downgrading the significance of calculating inter-species ratios to determine relative importance (Table 2.5).

2.2.1 Mammals

The taxonomically classified mammalian remains constitute 284 elements. Among these, the most significant are *ovis/capra* representing 53.0 per cent. A slight statistical bias can be attributed to the complete skeleton of a dog (*Canis Familaris*) found inside found inside an oven at the site, although how the animal ended up there is unclear. The influence of this complete skeleton on the overall percentile proportion of taxonomical categories is unfortunate but can be effectively combatted by considering the Minimum Individual Identified (% M.Ind Identified) which raises the caprine proportion to 58.5 per cent of the mammalian remains.

Cattle

Only twelve elements (3.6 per cent) of the identified assemblage belong to *Bos Taurus* or common cattle from Area K. However, as noted above the minimum number of identified individuals is consistent with at least three animals (10.3%) represented in the assemblage. All twelve elements of cattle are directly related to the skull, four are mandibles (three are left and one is unclear), a single fragment of hyoid and seven teeth (four molars, two pre-molars and one unclear). As noted by Legge, a small proportion of cattle remains by comparison to smaller animals such as pigs and *ovis/capra* and does not necessarily equate to a smaller significance of cattle in the diet (such as proposed by

Bertini and Linseele, 2011: 280), as their bulk make it possible for fewer individuals to contribute just as significantly to the local diet as a much larger group of smaller animals (Legge, 2008: 448). The very specific elements surviving in the Area K assemblage does suggest that cattle were not unimportant at the site by comparison to smaller domestic animals. However, it is clear that only very specific elements of the cattle were deposited in Area K, namely the animals' heads.

A possible explanation for this selective deposition may be that Area K only served as a butchering area for cattle. The butchering of cattle comprised the slitting of the animal's throat and possibly the deliberate pumping of the blood by applying pressure to the foreleg before the joints on the legs were removed either for consumption or preservation (Ikram, 1995: 44–52). At some point in the process the animal's head would most likely be entirely severed from the body (Luff, 1994: 166; Ikram, 1995: 48–9) and the usable parts such as horns, tongue and cheeks removed. As depicted on the butcher scenes from the Medinet Habu mortuary temple of Ramesses III (Epigraphic Survey, 1934: Pl. 173–4) the head could be deliberately removed from slaughtered bullocks and subsequently brought as offerings before the god.

The more desirable cuts associated in particular with the long bones were then removed from Area K entirely, and it is possible that these were taken to the quarters of the elite at the site who from their position at the top of the hierarchy were more likely to have received the better cuts of meat. The remains were then deposited elsewhere in a hitherto unexcavated portion of the site. Another possibility as noted by Legge (2008: 447) is the significance of the hind quarters and forelegs of cattle in religious depictions, and it is easy to envisage that a significant portion of these high-quality cuts were involved with the cultic activities conducted at the temple at Zawiyet Umm el-Rakham. The lack of animal bones in association with the temple itself or the adjoining temple magazines, make it impossible to ascertain whether these institutions participated in either storage and/or distribution of the most desirable cuts of beef at the site. Further investigation of Area N, which has been speculated to house the residence of the fortress commander Nebre, may further elucidate this point. However, at the present stage, it can only be concluded that the cattle remains at Area K do not represent complete or even partially complete animals, and that the preponderance of cranial elements most likely indicates the use of Area K as a butchering area, but not a disposal site, for cattle at Zawiyet Umm el-Rakham.

A further point is the origin of the cattle found in Area K. In her recent analysis of material from Kom Firin, Louise Bertini states that: '[...] cattle remains would be expected to be far more common than pig remains at a site that would have been supported by the central administration, where cattle parts would have been supplied to inhabitants' (Bertini, 2014: 308). Taken in conjunction with a previous statement regarding state provisioning: '[...] New Kingdom fort sites seem of have been provisioned by the state as seen at sites such as Tell Borg (Bertini, in press) and Zawiyet Umm el-Rakham (Bertini and Ikram, in press)' (Bertini, 2014: 306) Bertini argues that cattle were dispatched to fortress sites such as Zawiyet Umm el-Rakham by the central administration, either as living herds or as preserved cuts of meat. The evidence from Area K clearly argues in favour of living animals being brought to the area to be slaughtered, in particular the presence of mandibles, teeth and other parts associated with largely inedible portions of the animal.

Textual evidence from the Aswan/Philae stela of Thutmosis II also suggests that herds of domesticated animals were maintained by the garrisons at certain New Kingdom forts: '[...] Wretched Kush was rising in rebellion (*bšt*), those who were subjects (*ndt*) of the Lord of the Two Lands planning a plot (*k3t*) [...] to steal (*ḫnp*) the cattle (*mnmnt*) from behind (*ḥr s3*) the fort (*mnnw*) [...]' (*Urk* IV, 139.12–16, see also Lorton, 1990: 671). Two potential situations can be extrapolated from the text; firstly, *ḫnp* may not simply indicate the theft of the cattle for the reward of the theft in itself, but also as a potential way of starving the Egyptian garrison within the fort, which the Nubians may have been unable to physically conquer with a siege. Secondly, the reference to the rebels as 'those who were subjects' to Egypt suggests a similar situation as that in effect at Zawiyet Umm el-Rakham between the Egyptian garrison and the local Libyans who may have functioned in a supporting role to the Egyptian inhabitants. Cattle grazing freely near *mnnw*-forts in Libya are also mentioned on the Israel Stela of Merenptah (*KRI* IV, 18.10–11). As such, a herd of cattle were most likely maintained at Zawiyet Umm el-Rakham, although it is not possible to determine from where the original animals came. They may have been driven from fort to fort along the Marmarican coast or alternatively obtained by either trade or raiding from surrounding Libyans. The most likely scenario is perhaps that a herd of cattle was brought with the initial occupants of the fort and then allowed to breed freely thereby limiting the involvement of the central administration and making the site essentially self-sufficient with regards to cattle.

Sheep and goat

By contrast to the cattle elements found in Area K, the caprine elements more clearly represent whole animals. As with the cattle, the area was most likely used as a primary butchering area and immediate disposal site for horncores, phalanges and other inedible portions of the animal. Following consumption of the meat on the relevant elements (such as long bones and ribs) these were then added to the disposal pile. While the majority of the ovis/capra elements could not be sub-classified, Bertini (2007: 11–12) was able to determine a sheep to goat ratio of 5/3 using the minimum individuals identified above, although the sample is too small to support generalisations regarding the ratio of the entire assemblage. Although, Bertini (2007: 11–12) noted that the higher proportion of sheep over goats could be viewed as evidence of a wool industry at the site, she also suggested that the kill-off patterns did not support this notion as the sheep were generally killed young (<1.3 years) while the goats were noticeably older (three years). The slight preference for sheep over goats is both too uncertain and unclear to extrapolate on without a larger assemblage from the site.

However, it is clear that in comparison with contemporary material from the New Kingdom settlement site of Tell el-Amarna (Table 2.6 and Figure 2.4, Grid 12 and Workmen's Village: Legge, 2008: 446 and the Stone Village: Legge, 2012: 10), Kom Rabi'a (Jeffreys, Malek and Smith 1986: 8), Kom Firin (Bertini, 2014: 307) and Sais (Bertini and Linseele, 2011: 283) the proportion of ovis/capra is far more significantly represented at Zawiyet Umm el-Rakham, while pigs are almost absent and even cattle (*Bos Taurus*) has a far less significant representation. Note the reversed situation at the later Third Intermediate Period settlement of Tell el-Retaba where cattle and pigs are the predominant mammals at the site during most of the occupational phases (Grezak, 2020: Table 7). As with cattle, the type of remains found at the site show that living animals were butchered in Area K, rather than cuts of preserved meat arriving

Table 2.6 The Area K faunal assemblage in comparison with contemporary material from sites in the Nile Valley (data adapted from: Bertini and Linseele, 2011: 283 and Bertini, 2014: 307; Jeffreys et al., 1986: 8; Legge, 2008: 446 and 2012: 10)

% identified bones	Equid	Cattle	Pig	Caprine	Total
Area K	4.6	13.6	4.6	77.3	191
Grid 12, Amarna	1.8	18.2	45	35	407
Workmen's Village, Amarna	1	19.7	47.9	31.4	1725
Stone Village, Amarna	0	36.9	20.9	40.4	331
Kom Rabia'a 1984	0	26.4	46.5	27.1	156
Kom Firin	2.3	9.3	67.9	20.5	1054
Kom Rebwa, Sais (Phase II-V)	4.2	10.8	35.3	49.7	167

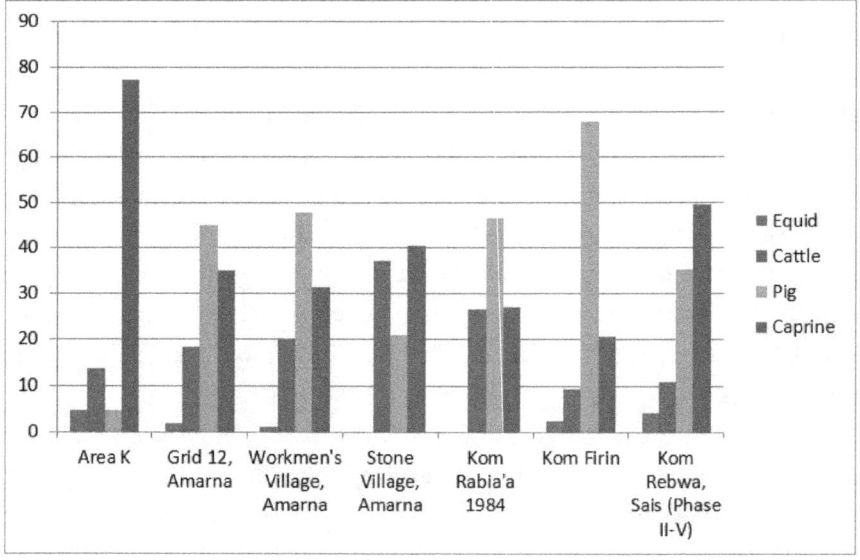

Figure 2.4 The Area K faunal assemblage in comparison with contemporary material from sites in the Nile Valley (data adapted from: Bertini and Linseele, 2011: 283; Bertini, 2014: 307; Jeffreys et al., 1986: 8; Legge, 2008: 446 and 2012: 10).

at the site from the Nile Valley. It is possible therefore that the Egyptian occupants also maintained a herd of sheep and goats, similarly to their Libyan pastoralist neighbours. Another possibility, considering the relatively young age at which the caprines were slaughtered may be that the animals were obtained alive from surrounding Libyans. This suggests either some level of

Libyan acceptance of Egyptian animals grazing outside the walls of the fort or alternatively an actual trade relationship based on the animals.

Dog

A single complete dog (*Canis Familiaris*) skeleton was found inside oven [1170]. Its deposition mixed with the fill from this oven suggests that it died contemporarily with the Egyptian occupation at the site, although the role of the animal at the site and whether it was wild or domesticated cannot be determined at this stage due to the degeneration of the skeletal elements. Neither can its species be identified. No other dog bones were found elsewhere at Zawiyet Umm el-Rakham.

Donkey

Only two elements belonging to *Equus asinus* were identified in Area K, both metacarpals. One was found in ZUR/K0,7 and the second in ZUR/K1,4. As stated above, the assemblage itself has been disturbed by scavengers and rodents and this may account for the lack of other equid elements found at the site. The use by the Egyptian army of donkeys as pack animals is substantiated by depictions in the Qadesh reliefs from Abu Simbel (Kuentz, 1928: Pl. XXXIV and Deroches Noblecourt, 1971: Pl. I) and the Memphite tomb of Horemheb (Martin, 1989: Pl. 29, E. Berlin 20363).

Gazelle

Only a single element from a gazelle (either *Gazella dorcas* or *Gazella gazella*) was found in Area K. This element is a horncore found in ZUR/K1,4. While it is possible that the garrison hunted local fauna such as gazelles it is more likely that the horncore may have been scavenged by a patrol from a deceased carcass, possibly with the intention of using the horn to fashion a tool or decorative object. Combined with an evident preference for domesticated caprines as a primary source of protein, this may explain the lack of wild fauna (or other gazelle elements) in the assemblage.

Pig

Pigs (*sus scofa*) are very scantily represented at Zawiyet Umm el-Rakham. Only two elements were identified, namely an orbit and a 3rd incisor both found in the ZUR/K0,7 cluster. As both these elements are associated with the skull, and considering their close deposition it is tempting to interpret this as a originating from the same animal. There is at least no evidence to suspect more than a single pig in the assemblage.

As Legge (2008: 452) has noted, the Egyptian pig is generally prone to heat stroke and requires good access to mud and water in which to wallow. With the heavy winter rains and a more moderate climate than that experienced at Tell el-Amarna during the summer, Zawiyet Umm el-Rakham would be a far more ideal location in which to maintain pigs. However, pigs are more difficult to transport long distances thus explaining their general absence from the faunal record at the remote settlement. Another possibility is that the occupants of Zawiyet Umm el-Rakham largely maintained their herds via cooperation and trade with the local Libyan pastoralists who herded exclusively caprines and cattle and as such that pigs were simply unavailable for them to obtain.

2.2.2 Fishing and hunting

As shown by the faunal assemblage presented above few remains of wild game have been found in the Area K, a state of affairs which is in agreement with research conducted by Linseele and Van Neer (2010: 71), which states that though remains of wild game are often present at settlement sites throughout the Dynastic period, they are rarely found in significant enough quantities to suggest heavy reliance on hunting as a method of subsistence. Caprines, cattle and pigs allowed the Egyptians to rely on a more stable source of protein in the form of their domesticated animals. To the inhabitants of Zawiyet Umm el-Rakham, living in relatively unfamiliar territory, the near-complete reliance on caprine remains as a primary source of protein may reflect an unwillingness to risk relying on hunting in an alien environment.

Despite the absence of much faunal evidence for hunting and fishing, a limited number of small finds nonetheless suggests at least limited exploitation of game animals and fish. Two arrow-heads were found in Area K, an unsurprising discovery considering the clear military character of the settlement. In fact, the paucity of weapons found throughout the site may show that the final garrison took care to bring their weapons with them when leaving the settlement. The salinity in the ground has also negatively impacted the preservation of metallic artefacts.

ZUR/K/156 (Plate 2) is an arrowhead chipped from a dull, light-brown chert and it was discovered in the area of Building 1 in the 1999 season. The shape of the arrowhead is typical of the New Kingdom and Late Period (Hikade, 2001: 124), with two barbs and a broad stem or tang for insertion into the shaft. After initial shaping, the object has been finely retouched along both cutting edges and along the tangs. ZUR/K/67 (Plate 2) is a metallic arrowhead, the only one discovered at the site. Its shape is unusual with little evidence of a defined tang, although the shape is not unattested in the New Kingdom (Huret, 1990: Fig. 7.63).

Overall, there is an extreme paucity of evidence of hunting from Zawiyet Umm el-Rakham. As stated above, it is likely that weapons also used for hunting – such as arrowheads – were collected by the final inhabitants before abandoning the site, but the lack of any significant assemblages of wild game within the faunal record clearly shows that hunting for the purposes of securing protein in the form of meat, as well as hide, bone and sinew for use as tools or raw material, was rare, although further excavation in different areas of the fort may in future lead to a re-evaluation of this interpretation. However, the relatively exposed situation in which the inhabitants of Zawiyet Umm el-Rakham found themselves, located in largely unfamiliar territory, appears to have been conducive to a more reliable food supply in the form of domesticated animals.

The significance of fish as part of the diet in Ramesside Egypt is by contrast undeniable (Loredana, 1988: 74–5). Janssen's (1997: 37–54) thorough investigation of fish and fishermen at the contemporary site of Deir el-Medina showed that specific fishermen were attached full-time to the village to maintain a steady supply. In the light of this prevalence of a piscine diet at contemporary sites in the Nile Valley, the rarity of piscine remains in Area K is curious. Only twelve vertebrae were found and considering their proximity within the same context, and similarity in size, they may have belonged to the same fish. The reason for this scarcity could be due to the decision of the excavators to sieve only some of the excavated matrix, potentially missing smaller faunal remains such as fish bones and additional vertebrae. Another possibility is that – like hunting – fishing was too uncertain a strategy to employ for basic subsistence and it was set aside in favour of domesticated animals.

A parallel to this preference for domesticated over wild animals is found at the contemporary mining camp at Timna on the Sinai Peninsula. The site is similar in its peripheral location to Zawiyet Umm el-Rakham, as is the reliance on caprine meat over fish – even though the Red Sea is within reach of the Timna encampment. Only ninety-two piscine remains were identified at Timna by comparison to 3,146 bones and bone fragments, belonging to caprines (Lernau, 1988: 245–6). Furthermore, the majority of the piscine remains from the site belong to fish imported either from fresh water sources, or from the Mediterranean (Lernau, 1988: 245) most likely in North Sinai.

The closest source of fish to Zawiyet Umm el-Rakham was the Mediterranean Sea, whose south coast lies only 1.5 kilometres north of the site. The bay north of the fort is however not conducive to fishing, as the sea floor is comprised exclusively of sand, with no rock formations or reefs to attract sea life. Rather, the larger shoals of saltwater fish are found, at least in the present day, north-east of the site, some 2 kilometres along the coast where a series of rocky islands jut into the water from the Marmarican plateau. A strong undercurrent goes from west to east, from the headland of Ras Abu Laho towards these rocky outcrops, making it difficult to manoeuvre small craft and the prevalent head-wind and accompanying heavy surf makes launching craft from the beach or even wading into the water problematic.

ZUR/K/21 and ZUR/KZ/11 (Plate 2) represent the only fish hooks discovered in Area K and Zawiyet Umm el-Rakham as a whole. They are both made from a copper-alloy and as a result of the high saline content in the ground, both are poorly preserved. They appear unlike the typical New Kingdom fish hooks, recognisable by clearly defined flanges and barbs (Brewer and Friedman, 1989: 29), although this may simply be due to the heavy corrosion of the artefacts. Line fishing is evidenced in the pictorial record from funerary contexts in Egypt although it is less well-represented in tomb depictions than net fishing (Brewer and Friedman, 1989: 29–30). By the New Kingdom, line fishing in tomb art is primarily conducted by the tomb owner within the confines of a garden, as opposed to in the Nile. In the context of Zawiyet Umm el-Rakham, line fishing may have represented the most practicable method for fishing around the rocky islands north-west of the site, where the jagged rocks and reefs immediately beneath the surface would snag nets.

ZUR/G4E/10 (Plate 2) represents an assemblage of sixty-five pierced ceramic barrel-shaped objects found within a locally manufactured beer jar. The ceramic objects were also manufactured from a local fabric, and were initially described as beads (Simpson, 2002: 190–2). However, further investigation has shown that the objects should instead be considered net sinkers. Used primarily for round cast-nets, net sinkers were secured around the circumference of the netting. When the net is thrown, the weights pull the edges down, trapping the prey. A thin cord around the circumference can then be used to close the net and a centrally placed thicker cord to pull the net and catch on land (Brewer and Friedman, 1989: 40–1).

A class of objects discovered in large quantities by Petrie at Tell el-Retaba were initially argued by him to be loom weights (Petrie and Duncan, 1906, Pl. XXXVIC.44–6), an interpretation also followed by the modern excavators at the site, where further examples of this object type have been recovered (Rzepka, Wodzińska, Hudec and Herbich 2009: 265). However, Petrie's initial interpretation was challenged by Oric Bates in his seminal article on ancient Egyptian fishing (Bates, 1917: 258, Pl. XXII.193–9), where the objects were designated as net sinkers, rather than loom weights. A close parallel to this assemblage was also found at Kom Firin (Spencer, 2014: Pl. 182) where they are described as 'net-floats'.

In the case of the ceramic beads from Zawiyet Umm el-Rakham, their function as net sinkers, as opposed to beads or loom weights, can be argued on the basis of an intact cast-net in the Louvre Museum (E.286) which is complete with ceramic net sinkers of similar size, shape and material as the artefacts discovered at Zawiyet Umm el-Rakham. As such, it can be argued that the inhabitants of the settlement at least attempted to use cast-nets in the nearby waters of the Mediterranean Sea, although the limited success they met with is shown demonstrated quite eloquently by the lack of piscine remains in the faunal record.

2.2.3 Birds and the ostrich-egg trade

Only eight elements belonging to birds were found in the Area K assemblage and all were too poorly preserved to taxonomically classify. Only half could be anatomically classified. Four of the elements belong to small birds, two long bones, a femur and a humerus. A further humerus could be classified as belonging to a medium bird, while a single fragment of femur most likely came from a large bird. Two long bone fragments could only be determined to have come from a bird, although their state of preservation made it impossible to classify either the anatomical element, the size of the bird or its taxonomy. The small amount of surviving material may be in part due to the relatively fragile nature of light-weight hollow bird bones and the clear evidence of scavenger activity at the site.

By contrast, large quantities of ostrich egg-shell were found in Area K, mostly associated with burnt deposits near ovens and ashy accretions. Fiona Simpson in her study of Libyan presence at Zawiyet Umm el-Rakham during the Late Bronze Age, conducted a comprehensive study into the significance of ostrich egg-shell to the Libyan nomads, and its role as a valuable trade commodity (Simpson, 2002: 416–41). As Simpson concluded, the lack of decoration on any of the dozens of fragmented ostrich eggs found at the site make it unlikely that they served a decorative purpose (like the incised ostrich egg shells found at Haua Fteah, Simpson, 2002: 438), but rather that they represented a further source of protein and nourishment to the Egyptian garrison (Simpson, 2002: 441). It is unlikely that the Egyptians themselves would venture far south in the search for ostrich eggs, instead, the eggs were most likely traded to the Egyptians by local Libyan tribesmen in exchange for metals and luxury objects (Simpson, 2002: 442) or potentially linen and bone pins (see Sections 4.1 and 4.3).

2.3 Subsistence at Zawiyet Umm el-Rakham

Perhaps the most obvious common trait in regard to the subsistence strategies employed by the inhabitants at Zawiyet Umm el-Rakham was the degree to which they seemingly relied on local knowledge and resources for their basic survival needs. The agricultural production at the site was directly dependent on local knowledge of water harvesting and climatic conditions, and while some grain was no doubt supplied to the site via transport vessels from the Nile Delta as proposed by Snape, the prevailing wind direction would have made east-west travel along the coast both difficult and time consuming.

Supply routes running from fortress to fortress overland along the Marmarican coast are also a possibility, but the prevalence of materials related to the harvesting of grain makes it more likely that the majority of grain was harvested locally.

In regard to meat, the faunal assemblage suggests that some live animals, notably cattle, were maintained at the settlement itself, most likely kept grazing on the plateau or in the *wadis* south of the fortress where some vegetation could be found. In addition to this herding, meat may also have been obtained in trade with local pastoralists, in particular younger, male caprines. Both of these strategies suggest a degree of security and surprisingly relaxed attitude for such a heavily militarised settlement, although it emphasises the dangers of focusing exclusively on the martial aspects of Zawiyet Umm el-Rakham and similar fortified New Kingdom settlements. In reality, as demonstrated through this investigation, the situation on the ground was considerably more complex than the military architecture and the bombastic contemporary royal monumental inscriptions would suggest at first glance.

3

Manufacture and Decoration of Pottery from Area K

Ceramic material in the form of diagnostic sherds represent the single-most common find from Area K, as is indeed the case with settlement sites throughout Egypt. Of the roughly 1,000 diagnostic sherds and whole vessels excavated in 1999–2002, 493 were re-examined in 2014 and this analysis is based predominately on this material (for a full catalogue of these vessels and diagnostic sherds, see Appendix I). Early on in the excavations it was realised that the ceramic material represented an avenue for a clear scientific provenance study which, by extension, could provide further evidence for the degree to which the Egyptian occupants at Zawiyet Umm el-Rakham relied on local resources for their basic survival at the site. This chapter presents the results of this provenance analysis alongside a broader discussion of the types of pottery produced and imported to Area K. Preliminary notes on this ceramic corpus were also published in 2016 by the author.

The ceramic material from Area K was classified using the Vienna System (Arnold and Bourriau, 1993) with the sherds being visually classified through the use of examination of a fresh break (created with steel clippers) in direct sun-light with the assistance of x10 and x20 magnification hand lens. The diagnostic sherds were then illustrated using the standard illustration conventions used for pottery in the archaeological record (Aston, 1998: 13–26). The diagnostic sherds were then typologically arranged on a hierarchical basis using three overall categories: Type I (open vessels), Type II (closed vessels) and Type III (non-vessel types such as ring stands). A complete typology of forms can be seen in Appendix I.

3.1 Macroscopic and microscopic classification of non-nilotic fabrics from Area K

Macroscopic examination of some of the diagnostic sherd material during the 1999–2002 seasons in Area K raised the possibility that at least some of the material did not appear to have been made from either Nile silt or marl, leaving the possibility that it was locally produced at or near the site (Snape, 2010: 285). A detailed examination of the 493 diagnostic sherds by the author in 2014 (note, only 454 of these were illustrated and included in Appendix I) showed that around 45 per cent of the material did not appear similar to any categories within the Vienna system, neither Nile silts nor marls. Instead, this material could be visually classified into three categories: ZUR A (14.23 per cent of corpus), ZUR B (26.63 per cent of corpus) and ZUR C (4.27 per cent of corpus, Figure 3.1).

ZUR A was found to be tempered with large quantities of fine white limestone along with smaller quantities of crushed shells and the occasionally small fragments of microfossil. The fabric is orange-brown throughout (5 YR 7/5) without any notable difference between the oxidised surface and the reduced section (see also a preliminary discussion of these fabric types in Nielsen, 2016).

ZUR B is more porous than ZUR A and tempered primarily with large quantities of rough, burnt sand as well as smaller amounts of straw and limestone. Its firing colour is similar, although not completely identical, to ZUR A (5 YR 6/5). ZUR C is the least prevalent local fabric. It is primarily tempered with small quantities of straw and appears to have been levigated prior to firing leaving very few inclusions and also making the finished sherds more friable and fragile than sherds made from ZUR A and B, possibly explaining the limited quantities of this fabric in the assemblage. It fires uniformly a light beige-brown colour throughout the section and on uncoated interior and exterior surfaces (5 YR 7/3).

All three fabric types were used to manufacture utilitarian pottery most commonly fabricated from Nile silt in the Nile Valley, and all three appear to have physical characteristics which suggest their origin as silt clay – rather than marl. All three are relatively soft and when broken or crushed they are easily reduced to a light silty dust. The macroscopic identification can therefore

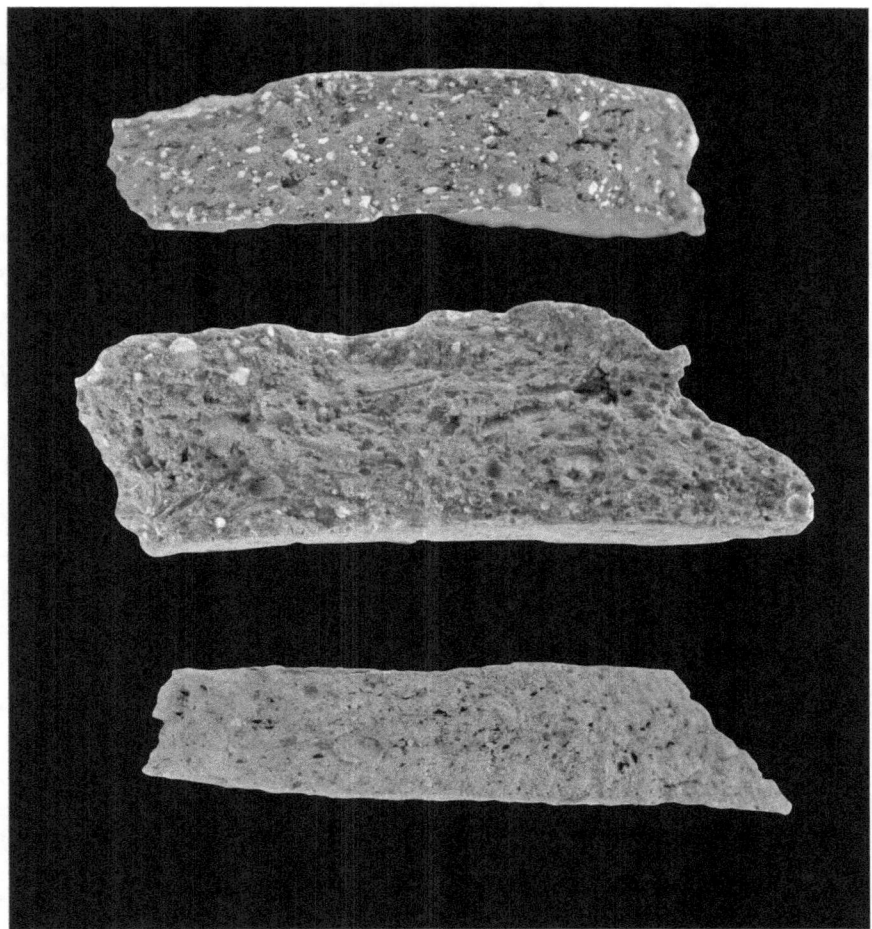

Figure 3.1 The main types of local ceramic produced at Zawiyet Umm el-Rakham, being (from top to bottom) ZUR A, ZUR B and ZUR C (S. Snape).

suggest that ZUR A–C are silt clays, but unlike in appearance to the known sedimentary silts from the Nile Valley.

To verify the results of the macroscopic examination, a limited-scale analysis of twelve selected sherds of ZUR A–C (Table 3.1) was undertaken with a portable NITON XLt-793W portable EDXRF (Energy Dispersive X-ray Fluorescence) spectrometer (for the use of pXRF in Egypt and the Near East (see for instance Morgenstein and Redmount, 2005, Ownby, 2006 as well as Forster, Grave, Vickery and Kealhofer, 2011 and Frankel and Webb, 2012). The spectrometer fires X-rays of a known energy into a sample, which causes the atoms in the material to emit fluorescent X-rays at energies characteristic of their elemental composition (Goren, Mommsen and Klinger 2011). These energies can be measured, and a chemical composition of the material determined. Readings were taken from small powdered samples of the relevant sherd material to avoid potential contamination from slips and other surface treatments and/or accretions resulting from deposition by measuring directly on the sherd surface.

The spectrometer was calibrated to measure a suite of eighteen elements, although only eight of these (Zr, Rb, Zn, Fe, Mn, Ti, Ca and K) provided consistent results above the instrument's detection level (both with the samples under analysis and the Standard Reference Materials, 'Lefkandi Brick' and 'Soil 7') and only these have been included in the discussion below. As discussed by Bourriau, Bellido, Bryan and Robinson (2006: 262) and also by Yellin and Killebrew (2010: 61) establishing the provenance of a fabric by comparing the fired ceramic to natural clay beds is a problematical process. The firing of the vessel and the human interaction with the raw clay (the addition of organic and inorganic tempers) manipulates the clay's chemical composition and can make direct comparisons uncertain. As such, the methodology of provenance

Table 3.1 Samples selected for pXRF analysis (author)

No.	Type	Reg. N0o.	Locus	Macroscopic Classification
1	Beer jar	ZUR/KE/28	KE	ZUR A
2	Bowl with direct rim	ZUR/K/140a	K1,4	ZUR A
3	Globular jar (body-sherd)	ZUR/KB/22	KB	ZUR A
4	Funnel-neck jar	ZUR/KZ/23	KZ	ZUR A
5	Globular jar	ZUR/KB/73	KB	ZUR B
6	Plate with direct rim	ZUR/KB/39	KB	ZUR B
7	Plate with modelled rim	ZUR/KZ/16a	KZ	ZUR B
8	Globular jar	ZUR/KE/19	KE	ZUR B
9	Dish with direct rim	ZUR/K/346q	K5,7	ZUR C
10	Plate with modelled rim	ZUR/K/336x	K1,2	ZUR C
11	Carinated bowl	ZUR/KZ/24	KZ	ZUR C
12	Plate with direct rim	ZUR/K/111b	K0,7	ZUR C

Table 3.2 Chemical composition of ZUR A–C (author)

Element	ZUR A		ZUR B		ZUR C	
	Mean	Standard deviation	Mean	Standard deviation	Mean	Standard deviation
Zr (ppm)	305.32	10.24	321.54	10.6	394.92	10.31
Rb (ppm)	45.52	4.43	42.65	4.42	46.65	4.27
Zn (ppm)	73.6	12.33	76.53	12.52	77.89	12.21
Fe (%)	3.38	0.03	3.72	0.03	3.35	0.03
Mn (ppm)	236.2	71.23	286.59	74.69	370.79	75.53
Ti (%)	0.56	0.01	0.66	0.01	0.61	0.01
Ca (%)	9.84	0.06	6.14	0.05	4.12	0.04
K (%)	1.86	0.04	2.28	0.04	2.24	0.04

determination follows the guidelines suggested by Yellin and Killebrew (2010: 61) of comparing instead with fired samples from known provenances.

The internal variance in the chemical composition of ZUR A–C is remarkably limited (Table 3.2). In particular the trace elements of rubidium (varying 8.57 per cent) and zinc (varying 5.51 per cent) as well as iron (varying 9.95 per cent) are present in nearly identical quantities in all samples. Other trace elements such as zirconium (varying 22.69 per cent) and manganese (varying 36.30 per cent) are less similar, although the fluctuations are expected, considering the minute quantities in which they are present. Even the fluctuation of the major elements of titanium (varying 15.15 per cent) and potassium (varying 18.42 per cent) is still limited. Combined, these close readings strongly suggest a common origin of all three fabrics, their differences in appearance and texture most likely caused by human manipulation.

One such manipulation is measurably present in the sample, namely the compositional proportion of calcium (varying 58.13 per cent). This variance can be explained with reference to the types of temper added to the raw clay. In ZUR A, the added limestone, marine shell and microfossils are all substances which are chemically classified as calcium; therefore, the proportion of calcium in ZUR A is comparatively high. In ZUR B, little to no limestone appears to be added as temper – although some small pieces are naturally present in the clay. ZUR C was levigated and any larger pieces of limestone were removed prior to firing, thus accounting for the very low quantity of calcium in the samples. ZUR B, which appears to have no limestone added or taken away from its matrix, may register the amount of calcium closest to that which naturally occurred in the clay. It appears from the internal comparison of ZUR A–C that all three fabrics may share a common origin and that major differences in their chemical composition were caused by human agents prior to firing.

Research conducted on contemporary material from sites in Canaan with Egyptian occupation such as Aphek (Martin, 2004: 276–7, see also Martin, 2007 and 2008 and Martin and Ben-Dov, 2008) has demonstrated that Egyptian potters at these sites who manufactured common Egyptian shapes would deliberately chose a the local clay source most similar in appearance and qualities to Nile silt and add specific inclusions in imitation of Nile silt fabrics. It is likely that similar strategies were employed at Zawiyet Umm el-Rakham, although there is no local clay source which is greatly similar to Nile silt due to the difference in geo-environment. As such, the primary similarity is in the types and quantities of inclusions. ZUR A, with its multiple inclusions of limestone is reminiscent of Nile D. ZUR B with its inclusions of sand and chaff is more similar to Nile B2, while the relatively friable and levigated ZUR C is more similar in appearance to Nile B1. This indicates that the potters at the fort were most likely Egyptians who had sufficient experience as craftsmen to prefer specific inclusion types – most probably determined by the 'feel' of the clay – in informal ratios.

A great number of chemical analyses of Nile silt, Egyptian ceramics, foreign ceramics found in Egypt as well as elsewhere in the Eastern Mediterranean have been conducted since the foundational work of authors such as Kaplan (1980) and Artzy and Asaro (1977). This includes the work of Bourriau, Bellido, Bryan and Robinson (2006) which analysed 150 Nile silt sherds and 193 marl sherds using Neutron Activation Analysis.

In addition, extensive work by Ownby using petrographic analysis (see for instance Ownby and Brand, 2019 for a discussion of recent advances in this method) has also added greatly to the information about provenance of imported vessels from Egyptian New Kingdom sites (see for instance Ownby, 2010 and 2012, as well as Ownby and Bourriau, 2009, Ownby and Smith, 2011, and Ownby, Franzmeier, Laemmel and Pusch, 2014, as well as Ownby, 2016a for a study of earlier Middle Bronze Age Canaanite imported jars from Kom Rabi). Additionally, Ownby had also utilised this petrographic analytical method to investigate the composition of fabrics within the Vienna System,

Table 3.3 Chemical composition of ZUR A–C and measured samples of Nile silt (adapted from Bourriau et al., 2006: 264)

Element	ZUR A		ZUR B		ZUR C		Bourriau et al., 2006: 264	
	Mean	Standard deviation	Mean	Standard deviation	Mean	Standard deviation	Mean	Standard deviation
Zr (ppm)	305.32	10.24	321.54	10.6	394.92	10.31		
Rb (ppm)	45.52	4.43	42.65	4.42	46.65	4.27	45.3	14
Zn (ppm)	73.6	12.33	76.53	12.52	77.89	12.21		
Fe (%)	3.38	0.03	3.72	0.03	3.35	0.03	6.43	0.89
Mn (ppm)	236.2	71.23	286.59	74.69	370.79	75.53	1214	660
Ti (%)	0.56	0.01	0.66	0.01	0.61	0.01	0.87	0.16
Ca (%)	9.84	0.06	6.14	0.05	4.12	0.04	3.84	2.3
K (%)	1.86	0.04	2.28	0.04	2.24	0.04		

arguing that the addition of petrographic analysis can add to the existing visual classification of fabrics based on fineness and inclusions (2016: 460) as well the technological production aspects of, for instance, marl vessels (Ownby and Griffiths, 2009). In addition to these studies, further chemical analysis (using, for instance, pXRF) has also been conducted on other ceramic artefacts from Egypt, such as unfired clay figurines (cf. Braekmans, Boschloos, Hameeuw and van der Perre, 2019) as well as ceramic coffins (cf. Ibrahim and Mohamed, 2019). For the purposes of this comparison, the chemical characterisation of Nile silt sherds published by Bourriau et al. (2006) has been used (see Table 3.3) to provide a point of comparison between a 'typical' Nile silt assemblage and the ZUR A–C samples from Zawiyet Umm el-Rakham to form the basis of an external comparison.

The 2006 study of Bourriau highlights the generally high quantities of iron in Nile silt, while the quantity of calcium is generally present at only around 3% (Bourriau, 2006: 264, referring also to the work of Fitton Hughes and Quirke, 1998: 123). By contrast, the quantity of calcium in ZUR A–C is far higher than what is common for Nile silt fabrics and also fluctuates more unpredictably, a result of human interaction with the raw clay. The quantity of iron is more consistent in ZUR A–C and is far lower than iron quantities measured by Bourriau (2006: 264).

The ratio between calcium and iron in ZUR A–C is in fact inverted by comparison to contemporary Nile silt fabrics strongly indicating that ZUR A–C is non-Nilotic in origin. The large difference in relative quantities of manganese between Nile silt fabrics and ZUR A–C also support this notion. Furthermore, the quantity of manganese in ZUR A–C is also lower by nearly half in comparison to contemporary Egyptian marl clays (Bourriau, 2006: 265) further supporting the hypothesis that ZUR A–C are neither Nile silt nor marl clay fabrics.

Without locating a kiln in or nearby the site of Zawiyet Umm el-Rakham it is problematic to conclude with complete certainty that local manufacture of pottery was conducted by the fort's inhabitants. However, the macroscopic and chemical analysis have demonstrated clearly that ZUR A–C are non-Nilotic in origin, are not marl clays and considering the use of marine shells and microfossils in the temper of ZUR A, are most likely the products of local manufacture.

3.2 Egyptian ceramics in Area K

While a perhaps surprisingly large amount of ceramic material from Area K was manufactured locally as discussed above, the majority of the material was manufactured in the Nile Valley and imported to the site (Table 3.4). Both the vessels which were locally produced, as well as those that were imported to the site from the Nile Valley are overwhelmingly Egyptian in shape and decoration (see Appendix I). Even with an evidently well-developed local production of pottery, it is nevertheless clear that the inhabitants in Area K depended, to some extent at least, on material manufactured in the Nile Valley. This raises the question of how and under what conditions such material travelled nearly 300km from the Nile Valley to Zawiyet Umm el-Rakham.

It is unlikely that shipments of empty ceramic vessels would be despatched from the Nile Valley to Zawiyet Umm el-Rakham. The local production of pottery was most likely capable of supplying the basic needs of the local occupants. Closed vessels from Egypt could have been used to send required supplies, but the presence of open vessels – unsuitable for long-range transport – made from Nile silt can most easily be explained by discussing the provisioning of expeditionary forces and the army in general (see also Heagren, 2007: 142–3 for a discussion of ceramic materials brought with campaigning armies).

The eighteenth-Dynasty tomb of Horemheb from Saqqara contains several depictions of a military force in camp (Berlin 20363 as well as Bologna 1888 in Martin, 1989: Pl. 28–9). Berlin 20363 shows the upper right-hand corner of a structure, interpreted by Martin as a command tent (Figure 3.2, Martin 1989: 36 and Pl. 28-29). Inside the tent is a small assemblage of ceramic vessels, two types of which are found in the Area K corpus, funnel-neck jars and two round-based

Table 3.4 Egyptian Nile silt and Marl fabrics from Area K

Fabric type	No. of sherds	% of Area K corpus
Nile B1	2	0.40%
Nile B2	132	26.83%
Nile C	3	0.60%
Nile D	114	23.17%
Marl D	22	4.47%
Marl F	1	0.20%

dishes placed in pot-stands. The command tent shown on Bologna 1888 (Figure 3.3, Martin, 1989: 36 and Pl. 28–9) contains similar material, although a pair of two-handled Egyptian amphorae are also shown leaning against the wall of the structure. Immediately above them is a flat-based bowl with a direct rim filled with food-stuffs. To the right of the command tent, a soldier is hurrying forward carrying a yoke across his shoulders. From the yoke are two nets one of which holds a tall ovoid jar. Above the tent, another carrying net is shown containing what may be interpreted as a flat-based jar.

The two blocks show that ceramic vessels of types similar to material found in Area K were found in military encampments, in this case probably serving as storage receptacles and eating utensils for the supplies of an officer, but they also elucidate a method for the transportation of closed vessels – by utilising a similar yoke system found on Bologna 1888. A similar system is also seen on a

Figure 3.2 Berlin 20363 (Martin, 1989: 36 and Pl. 28–9).

Figure 3.3 Bologna 1888 (Martin, 1989: 36 and Pl. 28–9).

continuation of the scene on Bologna 1889, where a soldier is transporting two Egyptian amphorae secured to the yoke by strings pulled through their handles (Martin, 1989: Pl. 32).

Depictions of the royal camp at Qadesh from Luxor and Abu Simbel provide further evidence (Figure 3.4, Kuentz, 1928: Pl. XXXIV and Desroches Noblecourt et al., 1971: Pl. I). In the upper-right hand corner of the camp in both depictions, two soldiers can be seen sitting next to a round bottomed bowl and engaged in a meal. In the lower left-hand corner of the encampment in both depictions are a series of storage vessels secured to yokes similar to those depicted in the Horemheb encampment. The iconographic evidence supports the notion that ceramic material was brought into the field by commanders, both finer material such as marl amphorae for wine, as well as more common open forms (such as round-bottomed bowls) which functioned as ration bowls for the soldiery. This is also evidenced at Haruba and Bir el-Abd where both open and closed forms made from Nile silt and local marls were recorded (Goren, Oren and Feinstein 1995).

The short occupation of Zawiyet Umm el-Rakham, potentially less than fifty years, makes it likely that some of this material would have been in use for

Figure 3.4 The royal camp at Qadesh (Desroches Noblecourt et al., 1971: Pl. I).

almost the entire occupation of the structure. Similarly, once broken, it is likely that at least some of the material was deposited within middens in Area K. It is unknown whether any kind of rotation system functioned at Zawiyet Umm el-Rakham in order to relieve troop detachments, although some rotation of troops would further explain the presence of the open vessels made from Nile silt; as it is likely that each rotation would bring more ceramic material with them. Taken together with the material brought to the area by the forts' builders and original garrison and deposited once broken within Area K, this explains the presence of Nile silt ware in the area. The local production of pottery was most likely established as a way of supplementing an already existing corpus of both closed and open shapes part of which was subsequently partially deposited within Area K providing the significant division between Nile and local silt-ware.

3.3 Manufacture and decoration

3.3.1 Wheel-made pottery

The majority of the Area K pottery – both the vessels imported from Egypt and those locally produced – are wheel-made. Distinguishing this manufacturing technique in the field is aided by the parallel lines or grooves visible on the interior surfaces and created by the potter manipulating the clay while it is rotated. While several types of wheel manufacture were used throughout Pharaonic history, the fast wheel was most commonly used during the New Kingdom, and it is most likely that this was also the case for the Area K pottery (Aston, 1998: 29).

3.3.2 Hand-made pottery

While not as common as wheel-thrown pottery certain vessel types within the Area K corpus are clearly hand-made. This is most noticeable in the case of Type I.7, the bread plates (see Appendix) which are manufactured simply by pressing a lump of clay in a flat circular shape and the pinching and pushing the edges upwards leaving a carination beneath the rim which can often be observed to contain the potter's finger-prints, or alternatively using a coil technique. Another wholly handmade vessel is the small marl clay cosmetic flask (Type II.5.3), attested by its unevenness and lack of any evidence of wheel-throwing in the form of wheel-marks.

3.3.3 Composite manufacture

A smaller number of vessel types found at Zawiyet Umm el-Rakham could be manufactured using several different shaping techniques. These include the pilgrim flasks which could either be manufactured from two wheel-thrown dishes placed together with a handmade spout and handles added (as noted by Gallorini, n.d., see also Knudsen, 2003 for an overview of the manufacturing methods used on pilgrim flasks found at el-Ahaiwah) or alternatively, the body could be manufactured in a single piece on the wheel before a handmade spout was pushed through and handles were added (as seen in contemporary examples from Beth Shean, see Frances and McGovern, 1993: 94–102). The Egyptian amphorae found at Zawiyet Umm el-Rakham (such as ZUR/K/280 K1,8, see Appendix no. 451) were also most likely made in stages using different manufacturing techniques with the base being manufactured in a mould and the body wheel-thrown (see for instance Aston, 2004 and see also Budka, 2015: 301 for examples of oasis amphorae from Abydos).

3.3.4 Slips

A slip has been described by Aston (1998: 30) as consisting of '[…] pigment (paint) + water + clay […]'. Discoveries of nuggets of blue, white, yellow and red pigments in the Temple Magazines (Thomas, 2000: 20–38) at Zawiyet Umm el-Rakham shows that the local potters had access to all three materials. The Area K corpus silt ware show great similarity in its choice of slips with contemporary material from the Nile Valley, primarily in the form of the heavy reliance on red (or reddish-orange) and cream slips covering either interior, exterior or both surface or applied in bands. In most cases, it appears that the slips were applied with a brush or by hand, rather than by dipping or pouring prior to firing (Aston, 1998: 29). Seven distinct types of slip were distinguished within the Area K corpus:

- Type 1: Red slipped on interior surface
  This surface treatment is present on 3.87 per cent of the entire corpus, and found both on the silt ware imported from the Nile Valley (47.36 per cent) but is slightly more commonly found on the locally produced material (52.63 per cent). The style is exclusively found on open vessels.
- Type 2: Red slipped on exterior surface
  This types of decoration is present on 5.70 per cent of the Area K corpus. The treatment is found on open vessels, on closed vessels, and also on both the imported Nile silt ware (60.71 per cent) and the locally manufactured ceramics (39.29 per cent).
- Type 3: Red slipped on interior and exterior surfaces
  This treatment was the most popular type within the repertoire of slips, both for imported Nile silts (49.32 per cent) and locally produced material (50.68 per cent). This style of decoration is found exclusively on open vessels, most commonly on the plates, dishes and bowls.

- Type 4: Cream slip on exterior surface
  Primarily closed vessel types within the Area K corpus were treated with cream slips on their exterior surface, comprising 12.58 per cent of the corpus – imported and local. Out of the sixty-two diagnostics and whole vessels decorated with a Type 4 slip, 74.19 per cent are imported Nile Silt (primarily Nile D), whereas the local silt wares are much less commonly decorated in this way (25.81 per cent).
- Type 5: Cream slip on interior and exterior surface
  As with Type 4, Type 5 is almost exclusively found on imported Nile silt vessels (88.00 per cent) as opposed to the locally manufactured examples (22.00 per cent). Overall, this particular style of slip is uncommon at the site representing only 5.33 per cent of the silt vessels in total.
- Type 6: Band of red slip on interior surface
  This type is only found on two vessels in the entire Area K corpus, one made from Nile D, and a locally produced example made from ZUR A fabric. Both are open shapes.
- Type 7: Band of red slip on exterior surface
  As with Type 6, Type 7 is only found on two vessels from the Area K corpus, both made from Nile silt (Nile B2 and Nile D). Both vessels are open shapes.

Slips of the various types listed above are common both on the imported silt wares and the locally produced pottery in Area K. Similar styles are represented in both the imported Nile silt ware and the locally produced material, and even though there is more prevalent use of cream slips in the imported material, the style is nonetheless represented in the locally produced pottery from the site and the preference for red over cream slip by the local potters may be due to the firing colour of the local fabrics which naturally fire cream- to light brown as opposed to the greyish-black and brownish-red firing colour of Nile silts. It may have been viewed as unnecessary to place a cream-coloured slip on an already cream coloured vessel. Another possibility is made clear by the overall prevalence of slipped vessels; 53.39 per cent of the imported Nile silt vessels are slipped, whereas only 35.78 per cent of the local vessels are. This may reflect a lack of resources (primarily pigments) to produce the slips at Zawiyet Umm el-Rakham due to its relative isolation.

3.3.5 Polychrome decoration

During the excavations of Area K, fifteen rim- and body-sherds of polychrome – or blue-painted – pottery were discovered. These vessels are painted exclusively with blue, red and black pigments. Four categories of decorative schemes or motifs are present in the corpus, namely: 1. Geometric Motifs, 2. Floral Motifs, 3. Faunal Motifs and 4. Uncertain Motifs (Figure 3.5). The first category is by far the most common and is present in some form on nearly all vessels. The common denominator of this decorative scheme is the use of horizontal bands (1.a), mainly of red, black or dark blue to separate the vessel's decoration into several horizontal zones. While used occasionally in the eighteenth Dynasty to create borders between zones of distinct decoration such a faunal motifs or hieroglyphic depictions (Takamiya, 2007: 1764), the horizontal bands and lines on the nineteenth-Dynasty pottery from Zawiyet Umm el-Rakham are decoration in their own right as opposed to borderlines for more intrinsic decorative patterns, whose use had diminished by the early nineteenth Dynasty (Aston, 1998: 354). This use of horizontal bands and lines in blue, red and black can also be found on vessels from other nineteenth-Dynasty contexts, such as Deir el-Balah (Gould, 2010: 19–20).

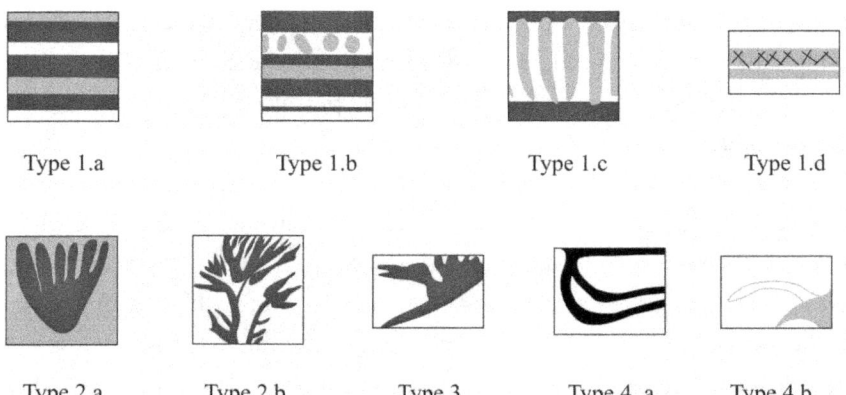

Figure 3.5 The different types of decorative scheme utilised on the polychrome pottery from Area K, Zawiyet Umm el-Rakham (author).

A variety of the horizontal bands and lines appear in the form of horizontal rows of dots (1.b), usually red, or oval shapes (1.c) of blue or red paint, which in the latter's case are reminiscent of the more detailed vertical lotus petals or overlapping petals found on some eighteenth-Dynasty blue-painted pottery (Takamiya, 2007: 1763, see also Type AId in Hope, 1991: 68–70). A single example also preserves thin black lines creating a band of cross-hatching (1.d) comprised of inverted V-shapes above a horizontal red line.

The simplification of blue-painted pottery from the eighteenth to the nineteenth Dynasty has been recently explored by Takahashi (2020) on the basis of a corpus of blue-painted sherds from four sites, Saqqara, Dahshur North, the tomb of Amenhotep III (KV 22), and the tomb of Userhat (TT 47), spanning a chronological horizon from the reign of Amenhotep II to the reign of Ramesses II. Takahashi demonstrates that not only does the complexity of the decorative schemes decrease from the eighteenth to the nineteenth Dynasty (2020: 10–13), the clay utilised for blue-painted ware also changes from marl clays to silt clays, an observation very much supported by the blue-painted assemblage from Zawiyet Umm el-Rakham which consists exclusively of silt-ware.

Floral motifs are uncommon within the Zawiyet Umm el-Rakham assemblage, as would be expected following Takahashi (2020: 10) with the move from 'graphic' to 'stylised' decoration style, and are found exclusively in the form of either a highly stylised free-floating lotus blossom (2.a) or an entire stem of lotus flowers rising vertically on the vessel (2.b). Faunal representations are even rarer and are only found with complete certainty on a single vessel in the form of a flying duck with an open beak depicted in blue on the interior surface of the vessel. While the geometric motifs can usually be found as the exclusive decoration (in varying combinations) on a vessel, the floral and faunal motifs are usually found in combination with the geometric designs and one-another.

ZUR/KM/13 (Figure 3.6) is an excellent example of this combination of motif types; thick horizontal bands of blue paint on a red slip provide the background for the representation of a flying duck located immediately in front of several free-floating lotus blossom, the whole scene to be interpreted as a duck flying into the air from a pool or pond, a motif found elsewhere on blue-painted pottery from the New Kingdom such as the jar fragment FOS

Figure 3.6 ZUR/KM/13, a blue-painted plate depicting a duck or other waterbird taking flight over a pond with waterlilies (S. Snape).

31.1101 from the University of Cambridge (Hope, 1991: Pl.1.c), on ovoid jars in the Cairo Museum (Hope, 1987: Pl. XXXIII) (SC 12073 and SC 12072) and on a tall jar found by Brunton and Engelbach at Saqqara (1927: Pl. 34). Types 4.a and 4.b may potentially represent further faunal or figurative motifs, but in both cases, the decorations were too poorly preserved to be securely identified.

Overall, the quality of the decoration found on the blue-painted pottery from Zawiyet Umm el-Rakham is far from as fine as that which is so representative of the eighteenth Dynasty from Saqqara and Tell el-Amarna with its thin lines, careful decoration and wider repertoire of designs (For the eighteenth-Dynasty blue-painted pottery repertoire from Saqqara see for instance Takamiya, 2007: 1766, Takahashi, 2014, 2017 and 2019 as well as Aston, 2011; see also Rose, 2007 for the blue-painted pottery from Tell el-Amarna as well as Hope, 1997 and 2016 for the Memphite corpus). Instead, the Zawiyet Umm el-Rakham material, as well as contemporary material from

Qantir (Aston, 1998: 354–5) and Saqqara (Bourriau and Aston, 1985: 36), is more crudely executed and displays a limited variety of figurative and floral designs.

Despite the presence of materials required for the manufacture of blue-painted pottery at the site, such as cakes of Egyptian blue pigment found in the temple magazines (Thomas, 2000: 20–38), no locally manufactured material has so far been located. Instead, this particular sub-group of material seems wholly imported from the Valley, most likely from the region around Memphis where Nile B2 and Nile D are the most common material types (Bourriau, 2010: 23–4). This is in agreement with the hypothesis proposed by Aston (1998: 56) that blue-painted pottery production was primarily centered in major settlements with royal residences within Egypt such as Memphis and Qantir although it should be noted that this hypothesis has been partially challenged by the discovery of locally manufactured blue-painted pottery from the relatively isolated site of Deir el-Balah (Yellin and Killebrew, 2010: 73). The decorative scheme is primarily geometric with lines of blue and red colouring with two types of lotus-blossom decoration and a single example of figurative decoration, namely a duck found on ZUR/KM/13.

3.3.6 Incised and applied decoration

While by no means as common as slips, 'string-line' decoration is found in a small amount of open shapes, exclusively plates, dishes and bowls. This decorative style is achieved by looping and pressing a twisted coil of string into the vessel during its leather-hard stage, creating a series of impressions running the entire circumference of the vessel. In addition to decoration, the string also afforded potential structural support to vessels while drying prior to firing. In many cases, such as the spinning bowl ZUR/2014(K)/1, multiple parallel lines of decoration are present (cf. Aston, 1998: 328–9 for examples of this decorative style). This style of decoration is found both on vessels manufactured locally and those imported from the Nile Valley. Applied decorations – that is the application of extra pieces of clay to serve an aesthetic or functional purpose – are less common and are primarily found in Area K in Type I.3.4c and Type III.1.2.

3.3.7 Pot marks

Few examples from the Area K corpus have pot-marks, a term which encompasses geometric or – more rarely – hieroglyphic marks on the surface of the pottery, either incised into the vessel after firing, cut into the vessel prior to firing or drawn with a finger or a tool in the slip of the vessel prior to firing (Aston, 1998: 33; see also Ditze, 2007: 275–81 for a comprehensive overview of types of pot marks used during the Ramesside period and potential interpretations). Three types of pot marks have been found on the Area K pottery, two geometrical and one hieroglyphic. All were scored into the vessels pre-firing.

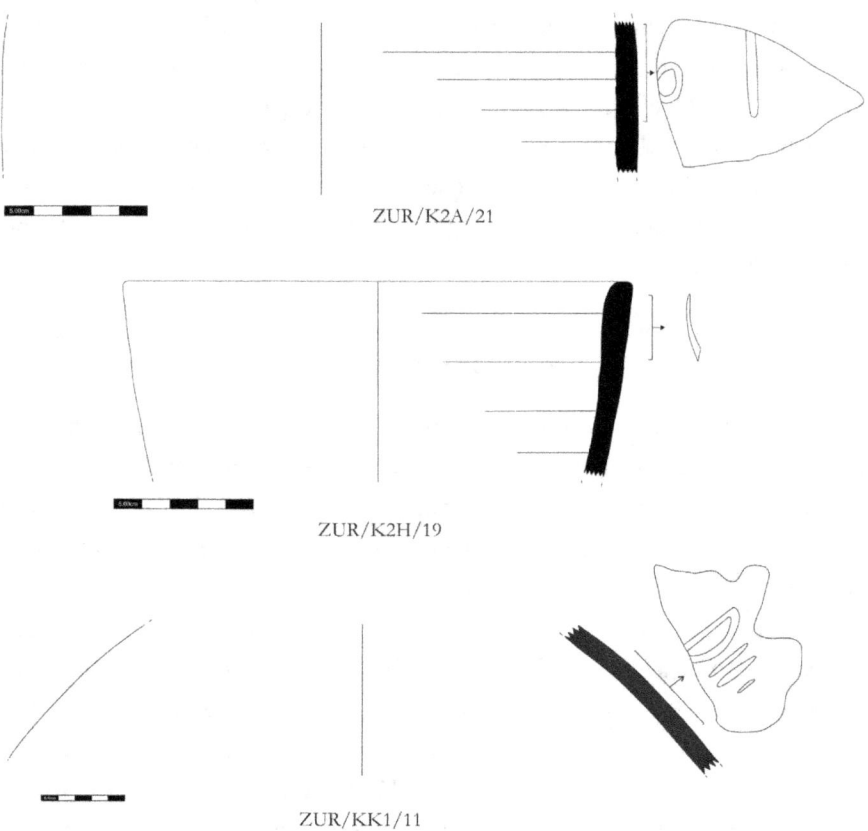

Figure 3.7 Illustrations of the three pot marks found in Area K at Zawiyet Umm el-Rakham on ZUR/K2A/21, ZUR/K2H/19 and ZUR/KK1/11.

Vessel ZUR/K2A/21 is a body sherd from an Egyptian amphora made from Marl D and covered with a thick white slip on its exterior surface. The pot mark comprises a post-fired geometric design consisting of a single line and a round 'loop' made by moving a finger in a semi-circular motion on the wet slip. The design is a composite of two common designs found in contemporary corpuses, namely that of a single line (Ditze, 2007: 290, Group A01) and the 'U-shape' or loop (Ditze, 2007: 290, Group C02).

ZUR/K2H/19 is a locally produced (ZUR B) funnel-neck jar with a line- or crescent shaped pre-fire pot mark on its external surface. The mark is too poorly preserved for a definitive interpretation although it is most likely similar to Ditze's category A01 (2007: 290). The only hieroglyphic pot mark is found on ZUR/KKI/11, a body sherd from a locally produced (ZUR A) globular storage jar in the form of the incised phrase *nb t3wy* ('Lord of the Two Lands') on its external surface. This type is generally rare and is only paralleled by a single example from the contemporary Qantir corpus (Ditze, 2007: 435, Group G05).

3.4 Discussion

The ceramic corpus from Area K evidences a number of significant facts about local production and import of materials within and to Zawiyet Umm el-Rakham. Though no kiln installation inside or outside the fortification has yet been located, it is clear from both the macroscopic and microscopic analysis of the ceramic corpus that a substantial quantity of vessels were manufactured locally, most likely using silt from the *wadis* south of the fort or along the coast (such as Wadi Agiba located around 2 kilometres west of the fort). It is also clear from the lack of any significant difference between the locally produced and the imported corpus, that the potters working at Zawiyet Umm el-Rakham were very familiar with common Ramesside pottery shapes, both open and closed.

Despite a clearly well-developed local production of pottery, the occupants nevertheless relied on material from the Nile Valley which had either been brought to the site by its original builders, or as part of rotations of military personnel in and out of the area. The most likely mechanism by which Nile pottery was brought to the site was most likely as a combination of both, and perhaps also on shipments of grain and other material sent to the site on ships along the coast to resupply the outpost, in particular in the early years of its occupation.

While the production of ceramics is the most extensively evidenced craft production conducted at the site, it is not the only one. The production of textile, stone working as well as the manufacture of bone pins are also all evidenced from the archaeological assemblage within Area K. The following chapter will discuss these industries and place them in the broader context of Egyptian self-sufficiency and import of material at Zawiyet Umm el-Rakham.

4

Craft Production

The fortress at Zawiyet Umm el-Rakham was not occupied for a lengthy period of time. Its abandonment may also have been relatively sudden as a great deal of materials were left within Area K, in particular tools related to craft production, as well as the products of the manufacture themselves. It is also possible that these tools and materials were not deemed important enough to bring away from the settlement upon its abandonment. The material predominately evidences three types of industry conducted within Area K during the early Ramesside Period: (1) the production of flax linen, (2) stone production (including chipped stone) and (3) the manufacture of bone pins. Very little of the excavated material evidences any kind of metal-working at the site, although this may in part be due to later gathering of material from the site by Libyan pastoralist nomads, and also the high ground salinity which militates against the preservation of copper-alloy artefacts.

4.1 Textile production

The textile production (Plate 2) within Area K is evidenced by four distinct archaeological artefact types, namely spinning bowls, spindle whorls, loom weights and a potential loom found in Area G (see Section 4.1.2). The corpus of material is sufficiently extensive to suggest a fairly industrious production of linen conducted within the confines of the fortification. The production of linen from the flax plant (*linum usitatissimum*) is among the earliest evidenced industries conducted within the Nile Valley, with evidence for its cultivation and manufacture dating from the Predynastic Period onwards (Brunton and Caton-Thompson, 1928: 634). However, the natural environment among the Marmarican coast is very different to that which prevailed within the Nile

Delta and Nile Valley and the flax plant's sensitivity to highly saline soil (Hayward and Spurr, 1944) would perhaps suggest that its cultivation in the environs of Zawiyet Umm el-Rakham could not have been successful.

However, this interpretation ignores the *wadis* south of the fortress which, as discussed above, were also utilised to grow grain. The *wadis* provide not only the silty loam and good drainage needed for the successful cultivation of the flax plant (Kemp and Vogelsang-Eastwood, 2001: 27), the winter rains in the area also lead to frequent floodings of the *wadis* and the deposition of new loam. The growing of flax outside the immediate vicinity of the fortress also suggests, as with the cultivation of grain in the same area, that the Egyptian garrison did not consider themselves in a state of siege while in the area, nor does it suggest that the local inhabitants in the area were overtly hostile to the Egyptians.

It may even be that the production of flax linen at Zawiyet Umm el-Rakham directly benefitted the local Libyan population. On the basis of the Egyptian iconographic record from the New Kingdom, it seems likely that many Libyans wore what has been interpreted as either raw-hide cloaks or kilts with only some sections of society, potentially the elite, wearing garments made from linen (O'Connor, 1990: 63). The same preference for rawhide over linen is also noted by both Holscher (1955: 32–3) and Bates (1914: 121–2) at least during the earlier New Kingdom. However, by the late Ramesside Period it appears based on the quantities of linen garments taken by the Egyptians as spoils-of-war after the Libyan war of Merenptah, that rawhide clothing had gradually been replaced by linen clothing contemporarily with Egypt's New Kingdom (O'Connor, 1990: 63). If nothing else, this may suggest that there was a desire within sections of Libyan society to possess linen clothing and in that light, the production of flax linen at Zawiyet Umm el-Rakham may have furnished the Egyptian occupants not just with clothing (which could of course also have been imported as finishing clothing from Egypt) for themselves, but also with a valuable and desired trade commodity (see also a discussion of the value of linen as a trade good for the Egyptians in the Near East in Kemp and Vogelsang-Eastwood, 2001: 436–7).

Not all the steps involved in the manufacture of flax linen is evidenced at Zawiyet Umm el-Rakham (for a detailed overview of the process see Vogelsang-Eastwood, 1992 and 2000). The harvesting process itself leaves few traces, and the process of softening the hardened outer fibres of the plant (retting) could have been conducted in still pools of water in the bottom of the *wadis* and so may not have left any archaeological traces either. It is possible that the large limestone trough found in KD could have been used for the retting process, though given its dimensions, it is unlikely that a very large quantity of flax could have been contained there at a time. The earliest stage of the manufacturing process evidenced at the site is the spinning of the retted fibres into thread using spinning bowls and spindle whorls.

4.1.2 Spinning

Spinning-bowls are evidenced in both Middle and New Kingdom funerary art (Newberry, 1895: Pl. XXVI and Davies, 1929: Fig. 1A, see also Crowfoot, 1931 for an ethnographic study of hand spinning methods utilised in Egypt and Sudan with parallels to ancient spinning methods). These bowls, made either from ceramic or stone, are generally identified by the presence of one or (more commonly) two vertical loops attached to the bottom. The bowls would be filled with water allowing the flax fibres to be wetted as they were passed trough the loops onto a handheld spindle. The ten spinning bowls, fragments or diagnostic sherds recovered from Area K were predominately made in clay with only one larger example made from limestone (ZUR/KC/14). The ceramic bowls were either manufactured in Egypt and imported to the site, or made locally (see Appendix I, I.4 for full details) and all bar one of the ceramic examples contained two internal loops, similar to examples found at Tell el-Amarna (Kemp and Vogelsang-Eastwood, 2001: 291–306, see also Rose, 2007: fig. 148–9) and also from the site of Deir el-Medina (Deir el-Medina, Nagel, 1938: Pl. XI: Type XVI) and Deir el-Ballas (Schwartzer, 1990: 6–8).

Only three spindle whorls were recovered from Area K (for an overview of the usage of spindle whorls see Kemp and Vogelsang, 2001: 265–7) two made from local biosparite limestone and one from ceramic. The ceramic spindle whorl (ZUR/K/12, Plate 2) was most likely made from the repurposed base of a vessel with the whole for the spindle drilled out post-firing. The vessel was manufactured from local ceramic (ZUR A) as evidenced by its pale colour and the large quantities of marine shells in the matrix. Both the typical shapes of Late Bronze Age Egyptian spindle whorls – disc-shaped and domed – are represented, and while it may appear odd that only so few spindle whorls have survived by comparison to spinning bowls, this is most likely because the majority of the spindle whorls used at the site were carved from wood. Due to the high water table and ground salinity on the coastal plain, no significant wooden artefacts have survived from Area K or other areas of Zawiyet Umm el-Rakham. Both the limestone spindle whorls (ZUR/KB/62 and ZUR/KH/8, Plate 2) were of the domed type, decorated with incisions radiating from the central hole and paralleled by finds both from Tell el-Amarna (Kemp and Vogelsang-Eastwood, 2001: 287) as well as fortified settlements similar to Zawiyet Umm el-Rakham (such as Tell Heboua I, el-Maksoud, 1998: 255 and Kom Firin, Spencer, 2014: Pl. 262).

4.1.2 Weaving

Following the spinning of the flax fibres to thread, weavers would manufacture the thread into cloth of differing quality. In the absence of many loom installations surviving in the archaeological record, the clearest evidence for the weaving process is in the form of so-called loom-weights. While this particular type of artefact has been identified since at least the early twentieth century (Petrie and Duncan, 1906), their precise function has caused debate (Giddy, 1999: 193–5). The function of such weights would have been to hold the threads in an upright warp-weighted loom, but they could also have been utilised in other industries, as weights for scales and even net-sinkers. The potential loom weights from Area K numbering five in total are all of a flat oblong perforated type very similar to contemporary material excavated at Kom Rabi'a (Giddy, 1999: Pl. 41.2709, Plate 2). And while these weights could have been utilised in other industries, it is significant all five loom-weights from Area K were found in clusters either in KN, KKII or KB surrounded by other tools related to spinning and weaving (Figure 4.1). As such, while the shape of the artefact is evidently multifunctional, their context suggests a function within the textile industry.

A more tenuous and problematic piece of evidence for the weaving of flax linen at the site comes, not from Area K, but from G6, a stone circle which is most likely the only architectural remains of Libyan squatter activity at the site shortly following its abandonment (Simpson, 2002: 201–2). Excavations in the area revealed a square limestone block (ZUR/G6E/5, Figure 4.2) with a central depression which was initially classified as a grinding stone. However, closer examination of the artefact shows that it is dissimilar to other querns and mortars found at the site. It is instead identical to artefacts found, for instance at Tell el-Amarna (Kemp and Vogelsang-Eastwood, 2001: 373–81) and described as socket-blocks which most likely functioned as supports for upright looms. ZUR/G6E/5 was most likely moved to Area G by the later inhabitants of the settlement, and may indeed have been used for a brief time as a mortar. It is possible that it was originally located with a twin within Area

Figure 4.1 Spatial overview of tools related to textile production (triangle: spinning bowls; circle: spindle whorl; square: loom weight) (S. Thomas and author).

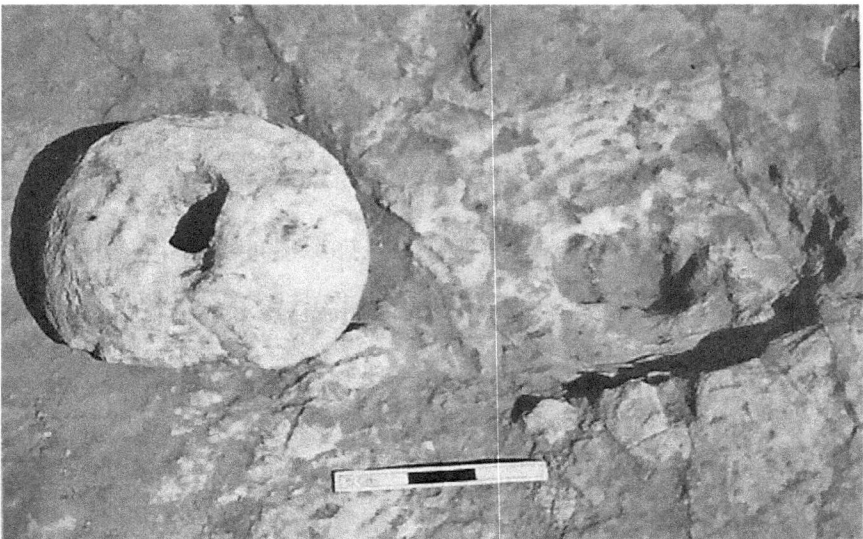

Figure 4.2 Possible loom support found in Area G, scale bar in picture is 15.0 cm (S. Snape).

K, potentially in one of the areas where most of the textile manufacturing tools were found, where it supported a weight used by weavers in the area to turn the flax thread produced there into cloth.

4.1.3 Discussion

The most notable feature of the assemblage of material related to linen production from Area K is its spatial arrangement. Aside from three of the spinning bowls, badly broken and clearly deposited in areas of garbage disposal (Space KE and KG), the remaining material can largely be classified into four groups, Group 1, found in Space KKII and KN and comprising loom-weights and spinning bowls, and Group 2 found in Space KC, KB and KAB and comprising spinning bowls, loom-weights and a spindle-whorl. A spinning bowl found next to a second loom-weight can also be found in Space KH (Group 3). Two spinning bowls were also found in Building 5 (Group 4). The groups of material may denote areas where weaving was conducted, although, considering the unfinished state of several of the loom-weights, it may simply be areas of manufacture (spinning and stone-working) overlapping.

Most of the tools involved in this industry are locally produced, aside from a small number of spinning bowls brought from Egypt. The local pottery production helped to either replace broken examples or expand the production by producing more vessels made locally; similarly, an attempt was clearly made to make a more durable spinning bowl from local limestone. The local limestone was also used in the production of the loom-weights and two of the spindle-whorls. As such, two local industries – pottery manufacture and stone-working – directly contributed to a third, the local production of cloth. The basic raw material (flax) was also locally grown. Textile production was clearly conducted at the site, and it seems likely that its primary function was to achieve self-sufficiency in cloth and secondarily, to produce a small surplus intended as high-value barter goods for trade with local Libyan tribesmen.

4.2 Stone working

The Marmarica Formation constitutes a substantial stretch of limestone and dolostones running along Egypt's northern coastline (Aref, el-Khoriby and Hamdan, 2002: 182; el-Shahat, 1993: 75). The limestone itself is overwhelmingly a mixture of reefal (Abdallah, 1966) and fossiliferous components (Abdallah, 1965). The primary allochem component is fossil material. The ortchochem component of the material is in the form of sparite, meaning visible crystals of calcite spar (Trudgill, 1985: 10–11). Robert Folk (1965: 166) suggests that the term for the local limestone should be 'biosparite', meaning a sparite-based limestone with a high content of biological (fossil) inclusions (Trudgill, 1985: 10–11). The biosparite limestone in the area surrounding Zawiyet Umm el-Rakham is sub-mature, in that wave action and time has not yet rounded the fossils making the material mature or supermature (Folk, 1965: 166–7). For practical purposes, the high content of fossil inclusions and its crystalline structure weakens the limestone considerably, and as such the basic stone material available to the occupants was highly crumbly and friable. Hard stones, such as granite and basalt are also rare in Egypt's Western Desert (with the exception of basalt sources near Bahariya, Rizk and Davis, 1991: 233) and entirely absent along the coast

4.2.1 Local limestone production

This geology placed both opportunities and limitations on the occupants at Zawiyet Umm el-Rakham (Plate 3). On the one hand, large clay deposits were less prevalent than in the Nile Valley, though still substantial enough to furnish raw material for Zawiyet Umm el-Rakham's enclosure walls. On the other hand, limestone in the form of cobbles was readily available and used in place of mudbrick in the construction of domestic structures within Area K. These cobbles and fragments of limestone also formed the basis of a substantial production industry at the site, the end products of which are readily identifiable through macroscopic examination due to the presence of biological fossil inclusions and the general substandard quality of the stone. In the absence of hard stone, the occupants manufactured architectural components (such as lintels and door jambs), furniture and even vessels from the local limestone, using largely imported hard stone tools, notably pounders and hammer stones as well as bronze chisels.

Twenty-three pounders or hammerstones were found in Area K, eleven of which could be more closely examined by the author in 2014 (Plate 3). Among the assemblage imported hardstone pounders dominate (only ZUR/K/338 is made from local limestone) with ten out of the eleven either made from diorite (two, ZUR/KM/2 and ZUR/KQ/5) and the remainder from quartzite neither type being present naturally along the Marmarican coast. The pounders were easily identifiable by their shape being spherical (rather than the broader range of shapes displayed at other sites, for instance Kom Rabi'a, (Giddy, 1999: 212–14). As noted by Giddy (1999: 211–12) the publication of pounders from Egyptian New Kingdom sites is generally poor, with relatively few published examples (such as Boyce, 1995: 98–104; Schneider, 1996: 52 but also Kemp and Stevens, 2010b: 402–11 and Spencer, 2014: 153–5).

The pounders from Area K were most likely used to roughly shape the soft local limestone, and may also have functioned as hammers for use with bronze chisels, one of which was found in Area G, the area of the site associated with later Libyan squatter activity (Simpson, 2002: 193–4). It is possible that wooden mallets were also used in the manufacture of stone artefacts, but due to the poor preservation of wooden artefacts at the site no such item has survived in the archaeological record.

Figure 4.3 Overview of Area K showing the main structures, architectural type as well as some of the uncovered door jambs and lintels (S. Snape).

By far the most plentiful stone product manufactured within Area K were architectural components for the structures found in the area, namely lintels and door jambs. These could not be re-examined in 2014 and some were left *in situ*. The following descriptions are based on plans and excavation notes (Figure 4.3). While inscribed lintels and door jambs from domestic settings are commonly found in published corpora (Peet and Woolley, 1923: 37; Kitchen, 1993b; Giddy, 1999: 301–2; Budka, 2001; Gabolde and Fahid, 2003), uninscribed examples are almost entirely lacking. This may be in part because non-elite structures utilised wooden or brick jambs and lintels (cf. Tell el-Amarna, Kemp and Stevens, 2010a: 354–61), or simply because these uninscribed artefacts were not deemed significant by early excavators. By contrast to Tell el-Amarna all of the jambs and lintels within Area K were manufactured from local limestone, all of them uninscribed. Five lintels were recovered in total, either complete or fragmentary. They are roughly formed, rectangular in shape, but the lack of polishing and lack of symmetry may suggest that they were roughly made, most likely with a broad chisel, indicated by the chisel marks present on their worked surfaces.

Thirteen whole or fragmented door jambs were also excavated from Area K. All six doorways identified in Area K were found with either a whole or a fragment of both doorjambs still *in situ*. As with the surviving lintels, the door jambs were roughly made and all were roughly rectangular in shape. In place of solid threshold stones, the structures in Area K generally had thresholds made from limestone cobbles held in the silt-matrix, the exception being roughly shaped, rectangular limestone slabs in the threshold of Buildings 1, 2 and 3. Within these structures the solid threshold stones are only found in areas that connect the interior and exterior environments.

The most notable feature of these architectural components is their sheer quantity. As noted by Giddy (1999: 302), such components are generally absent from most domestic sites. This is most likely due to the isolated nature of Zawiyet Umm el-Rakham. Less liminal sites would be periodically quarried from stone material for subsequent build phases or structures in neighbouring settlements, and so such elements were removed after a structure was abandoned. This, however, did not occur at Zawiyet Umm el-Rakham as the only substantial post-Ramesside occupation of the fortification was in the form of transient Libyan occupation which most likely lasted only a short time.

Aside from the architectural components, local limestone was also used to manufacture furniture. Six rectangular tables (similar to examples from Tell el-Amarna, see Kemp and Stevens, 2010b: 10) were located within Area K along with two fragments of low stools. Sadly, these could not be re-examined in 2014 or photographed. In addition, two headrests were also recovered from the same context (KZ, one of which can be seen on Plate 3) close to two pounders (ZUR/KZ/6 and ZUR/KZ/16, Plate 3) suggesting perhaps that the artefacts were in the process of being manufactured when they were abandoned. They are of an unusual trapezoidal shape paralleled only from the site of Qau, most likely from a New Kingdom burial reusing an earlier Old Kingdom grave (Brunton, 1927: 62, Pl. XLI.28).

In addition to the furniture, two stone vessels were also uncovered from Area K, ZUR/K/30, a flat plate with a raised lip and a ring base, and ZUR/KC/13, a thick-walled bowl, both made from local biosparite limestone (Plate 3). Similar types were discovered at the site of Deir el-Balah (Klein, 2010: Figs 25.3.14 and 25.3.16) and the plate in particular is of typical Canaanite manufacture (Sparks, 2007: 126–7) perhaps suggesting that at least one of the manufacturers living and working at Zawiyet Umm el-Rakham was either Canaanite or had knowledge of how to produce typical Canaanite stone vessels.

4.2.2 The chipped stone assemblage

A small assemblage of chipped stone tools, debitage and cores (n=92) was excavated from across Area K between 1999 and 2001. The assemblage is small by comparison to a far larger assemblage of chipped stone materials (n=2565) found in Area H (Simpson, 2002: 239 and 284) which may either suggest that Area H had been designated as an area for chipped stone production or, perhaps more likely that the later Libyan occupants of the area made an effort to collect all useful tools and materials from across the site and bring it to Area H for storage and re-working where necessary (Simpson, 2002: 355–6). This is also suggested by the large amount of exhausted cores in Area K (see Table 4.1) by comparison to the amount of debitage and tools.

The Area K flint was divided into Simpson's (2002: 367–82) existing material categories based on the material from Area H (Table 4.1). The Area K assemblage confirms Simpson's (2002: 385) hypothesis that the mined flint type E (for a full description of the various flint types identified at Zawiyet Umm el-Rakham, see Simpson, 2002: 367–82 and Table 4.2) arrived at the site most likely in the form of cores. Five of the nine cores found in Area K are of this material. Furthermore, four of these cores were partially exhausted, and only one (ZUR/K2A/11) was still relatively complete and unworked. The largest proportion of material within Area K is Type E, although the majority of the remaining material is in form of pebble flint brought from the Western Desert, including some of the locally collected poor quality flint FDS2/2 and FDS2/3.

The tool assemblage from Area K consists of fifty-three tools, of similar categories to those found in Magazine 6. The most prevalent types are sickle blades (most either heavily used or with evidence of sickle sheen) accounting for a quarter of the tools found. Aside from the more common tools, such as scrapers and notched blades, a small assemblage of lance points was also located at the site. The small amount of these weapons may indicate either that they were taken away from the site by squatters that the last garrison took care to bring their weapons with them when abandoning the site.

Table 4.1 Area K assemblage divided by material type (see Simpson, 2002: 367–82)

	Debitage	Cores	Blade blanks	Borers	Notched blades	Points	Scrapers	Sickle blades	Total
Type A*									2
Type B*	3	3	1	1					8
Type C									
Type D					2				
Type E*	2	5		3			2	9	21
Type F				1					1
Type G		1							
Type H					8		4		13
Type I									
Type J	2		6	1		3		1	14
Type K									
Type L	5								5
Type M									
Type N*								1	1
Type O									
Type P									
Type Q									
Type R*	3					1		4	7
Type S								2	3
FDS2/2	15			1					16
FDS2/3							1		2
FDS2/5									
Total	30	9	7	7	10	4	7	17	92

Table 4.2 Types of lithic material found in Magazine Six (adapted from Simpson, 2002: 367–82)

Group	Type	Description	Debitage % in Magazine 6	Amount tools	Amount cores	Proposed origin
1	A	Pale pink to dark pink; polished appearance and texture.	50.4	16	0	Egypt/Dakhla
	B	Pink-brown-white flint; pale brown, weathered cortext.	10.25	19	0	Not known
	C	Grainy opaque pale red.	1.62	6	2	Not known
	D	Dark red; possibly identifcal to Type A.	0.21	9	0	Not known
2	E	Pale grey/green; smooth, glassy texture; thin weathered brown cortex (smaller quantities show white, clean context).	20.7	8	1	Egypt/Dakhla
	F	Pinkish-white type; cortext varies from grey to reddish-brown.	0.85	11	1	Not known
	G	Brownish-yellow translucent.	0.56	5	0	Not known
3	H	Brownish-grey with a grainy texture.	5.3	1	1	Not known
	I	Opaque pale-brown; grainy surface; dense texture.	0.3	7	0	Not known
4	J	Smooth white-grey flint; light brown cortex.	4.9	7	0	Not known
5	K	Smooth brown flint with white patches.	1.5	3	0	Not known
	L	Dark brown with a smoothe texture; white patches.	1.26	1	0	Not known
6	M	Smooth white flint; pale brown cortext.	1.4	3	0	Not known
	N	Pale yellow.	0	1	0	Egypt
7	P	Opaque black flint; smooth, polished surface.	0.21	0	0	Not known
8	Q	Dusky red; grainy texture.	0.56	2	0	Not known
9	R	Dark grey opaque flint.	0	6	0	Egypt
10	S	Opaque mid-brown flint; matt surface; probably chert rather than flint.	0	2	0	Egypt
11	FDS2/2	Greeny-grey type; smooth, polished surface; cortex weathered reddish-brown; similar to Type E.	0	1	0	Local
	FDS2/3	Reddish-brown weathered cortex; ranges from orangey red to matt browny red.	0.2	1	0	Local
	FDS2/5	Opaque to semi-translucent; light brown to pink; matt surface with fossil inclusions.	0.06	0	0	Local

Out of the seventeen sickle blades (Plate 1) found in Area K, twelve show evidence of gloss or microwear and can then be qualified as true sickle blades following Rosen's definition (1997: 57), although the remaining five blades will also be discussed in this section as they are morphologically similar to typical Egyptian sickle blades, although they lack micro-wear or sheen and may as such have been in the final stages of manufacture and as yet unused when the site was abandoned. Seven of the sickle blades showing signs of sheen or microwear are terminal blades, with the remaining five being middle blades. Of the non-glossy sickle blades, three are terminal and two are middle blades. As a single terminal blade is generally required per sickle bow, there are sufficient terminal blades to equip seven sickle bows (ten if the non-glossy sickle blades are counted).

However, as with the sickle blades in Magazine 6 (Simpson, 2002: 326–7) there is a discrepancy in the ratio between terminal and middle blades. With eight terminals to only six middle blades overall, there are too few middle blades to equip eight sickle bows, which would each have required between eight and ten middle blades (Simpson, 2002: 326). This, as Simpson (2002: 326) has suggested, may indicate that Libyan squatters collected blades at random from various points at the site, or brought certain blades away with them or that a larger number of terminal blades were manufactured and stored as replacements.

Notched blades (Plate 3) are relatively crude implements, consisting of a flake or blade with either one or multiple man-made notches along the cutting edge. These notches are occasionally retouched around the edge to make them sharper. Notched blades and flakes were also found in Magazine 6 (Simpson, 2002: 338–42). Simpson (2002: 339–40) notes that while they could have had multiple uses, one possibility is that the examples found in Magazine 6 were of Libyan manufacture and possibly used as crude sickle blades (based on a hypothesis suggested by Caton-Thompson, 1952: 41).

However, considering the presence of similar notches blades during the Egyptian occupation and the prevalence of actual sickle blades, this interpretation is unlikely. A more likely use for the notched blades within Area K is as the preliminary manufacturing tool in the process of bone pin manufacture (see Section 4.3). The striations going across the length of the several of the bone pins indicate that a sharp implement was used to 'shave' out their preliminary form before a polishing stone was used to finish the object. The notched blades were most likely used for this purpose.

Eight blade blanks (Plate 3) were found in the Area K assemblage. As a type of object, these are problematic. Three of them are small, fragmented pieces which may have originally been middle section sickle blades although they are too poorly preserved to determine this accurately. The remaining five blades are longer and slimmer and most likely had multiple uses as cutting implements.

Seven small scrapers (Plate 3) were found in the Area K assemblage. In appearance they are similar to the eleven scrapers found in Magazine 6 (Simpson, 2002: 342–6). Their appearance is curious; unlike the remaining flint tools, they are distinctly non-Egyptian in appearance and as discussed by Simpson (2002: 344–6) they are more similar to probable Libyan scrapers found on Bate's Island. If these scrapers are indeed Libyan, and not simply crude tools made quickly by a member of the Egyptian garrison, they may indicate the presence of at least a small group of Libyans working within Area K simultaneously with the Egyptian occupation. Seven borers (Plate 3) were found in the Area K assemblage. As with the scrapers, these are simple, low-expertise objects, most likely held directly in the hand rather than attached to a haft. As discussed by Simpson (2002: 346–53) is similar to material from other sites in the Western Desert (Midant-Renyes, 1998: 18 and Pl. 8), but near-identical objects also appear across the Near East (Rosen, 1997: 68–71) and as such it is problematic to determine their precise origin. As with the blade blanks and notched blades, they had multiple uses, including the working of leather and sewing of clothes, which is also evidenced at Area K by the presence of a bone needle or awl.

Two lance heads (Plate 3) were also found in Area K. Both are similar in shape to weapons found in Middle Kingdom-Early New Kingdom layers at Mirgissa (Dunham, 1967: Pl. XCII), although with a distinctly more pronounced serration on both edges of the blade. Both lance heads are broken, which may explain why they were left behind when the fort was abandoned, as the general paucity of weapons indicates that the final garrison brought their weapons with them. Both lances are made from Flint Type J (Table 4.2. and Simpson, 2002: 367–82) a good-quality material possibly stemming from a flint mine rather than collected as pebble flint. It is possible that these weapons were manufactured in the Nile Valley and brought to the site by members of the garrison rather than being manufactured locally.

The chipped stone assemblage from Area K is in many ways a fragmentary corpus. The scavenging activity by Libyan squatters following the site's abandonment and their targeting of flint objects above other object types have created an unfortunate bias due to disturbance of the original context, as well as the re-working of objects and the potential introduction of new flint materials into the assemblage in Magazine 6. However, despite these hinderances, the corpus nonetheless clearly shows some production of certain types of tools (including sickle blades) was conducted at the site. While some of these tools were brought finished to the site from elsewhere, the presence of exhausted cores within the Egyptian occupational phases clearly shows that manufacture at the site was also conducted. While some of these tools required well-developed skill, others, such as the scrapers and notched blades, are indicative of a more low-expertise industry. It seems likely that craftsmen with varying skills worked within the same areas making a variety of objects, mostly for use as tools in other industries.

Some of the material from the site, notably that stemming from the Western Desert and oases, furthermore indicates a potential trade with local Libyans, or at least enough local good-will to allow members of the garrison to travel great distances from the fort to obtain raw materials. Considering the possible Libyan nature of certain of the tool types, especially the scrapers, it is possible that local Libyans engaged directly in the local chipped stone industry, both by providing material, but also by manufacturing tools within the Egyptian fortification. This, along with the availability of local resources located a great distance from the fort within Libyan territory, is another indication of relatively peaceful, possibly even cooperative conditions between the Egyptian garrison and the local Libyan tribes in the area.

4.2.3 Discussion

As with other industries at the site, the working of stone relied both on local materials and imports from Egypt. Despite the poor quality of the local limestone, the occupants at Zawiyet Umm el-Rakham used it extensively for lintels, door jambs and thresholds, tools, vessels, cultic objects, such as stelae, as well as the buildings themselves. The working of this local material was conducted largely with imported tools – hard stone pounders and copper-alloy chisels.

The chipped stone assemblage presents a similar picture with a mixture of imported and locally acquired materials, and also some evidence of local Libyan production both during and following the Egyptian occupation of the site. As with the cultivation and processing of linen discussed in section 4.1 above, it seems probable that the stone working industry relied to a certain extent on the goodwill of local inhabitants who permitted the Egyptian occupants to range freely to collect the vast quantities of limestone cobble required for structures and materials at the site, and even traded and worked pebble flint alongside the Egyptian garrison at the fort.

4.3 The production of bone pins

Long, tubular bone, wood or metal pins with blunt edges and sometimes with decorated handles appear frequently associated with hairdressing and personal adornment in the ancient Egyptian pictorial record (such as depictions of hair-dressers using such implements to fix wigs in place in reliefs from the First Intermediate Period, Riefstahl, 1956: Pl. IX and XIII). These hairpins have also been found associated with hair in the archaeological record, such as in a tomb from Abadiya which contained several bone hairpins still placed in the surviving tresses of hair (Tassie, 2008: 132, see Ashmolean Museum, E1035).

An assemblage of several bone hair pins from a New Kingdom context at Gurob was also published by Petrie (1927: 24–5 and Pl. XIX.11-16, see also Thomas, 1981: 61–2 and Pl. 17.416-19) and a similar assemblage from a wider selection of sites currently held in the Louvre Museum was published by Vandier (1972: 152–4). Further examples have also been more recently excavated from the Egypt Exploration Society's work at Memphis (Giddy, 1999: 170 and Pl. 36.2140 and 2876).

Twenty-four whole or fragmented tubular bone pins and needles were found during the excavation of Area K. This assemblage can be subdivided into four categories: (1) Locally produced hairpins; (2) Imported hairpins; (3) needles or awls; and (4) possible pin-beaters (Plate 4).

The locally produced hairpins are by far the largest group, representing twenty-one of the objects. In general, the state of preservation of these objects is poor. In section they are roughly circular and one (ZUR/K/123) shows some crude decoration in the form of parallel incisions on the handle of the pin, most likely made using a notched flake. The objects are made from long-bones, most likely of the dominant caprine species found at the site. ZUR/KKIII/4 is the only obviously imported hairpin in the assemblage. It is not only made with more skill than the others, with a delicately carved head and a polished surface, it was also manufactured from ivory rather than long-bone. No other ivory objects have been found at the site, nor has any evidence of ivory manufacture. It is possible that future excavation may locate such evidence, but at the present, it is more prudent to interpret ZUR/KKIII/4 as an import from the Nile Valley.

ZUR/KN/40 represents the only needle or awl discovered at the site. It is well-preserved with the remains of decoration around its perforation in the form of geometric incisions. While the body of the needle is round, its head is square, possibly to make the perforation easier. Bone needles have been found in Egypt since the Predynastic (see Petrie Museum of Egyptology UC9053 from Badari), and while metal needles are more commonly found in the New Kingdom (such as twelve examples from Kom Rabi'a, Giddy, 1999: 178 and Pl. 39 and from Tell el-Amarna, Kemp and Stevens, 2010b: 348 and Fig. 20.3), bone needles were evidently still in use (see for instance an eighteenth-Dynasty example from Tell el-Amarna, British Museum 1921, 1008.22).

ZUR/K2J/40 is the only pin or pin-like object not made from a long bone. Instead, it was manufactured by polishing the edges of the rib from a caprine (the curve and shortness of the bone rules out a larger animal, such as cattle). It is roughly circular in section, and is generally dissimilar to the other hairpins in the assemblage. It is possible that this object should be interepreted as a 'pin beater', generally found in association with linen production (Kemp and Vogelsang-Eastwood, 2001: 358–73, see also Braulinska, 2012: Figs 3–8 for similar objects from Tell el-Retaba). However, while the curve of ZUR/K2J/40 is reminiscent of the pin-beaters, its general shape is not. The pin-beaters are exclusively flat objects, much thinner than they are wide (Kemp and Vogelsang-

Eastwood, 2001: 368–9). It is possible that the object was only half-finished and that the maker intended to flatten the object by carving or polishing away the excess bone, but this interpretation is uncertain.

Giddy describes briefly the potential methods of manufacture for the bone hairpins found at Kom Rabi'a, noting in particular the 'lightly incised line' (Giddy, 1999: 170) which runs down the length of the object. Similar sets of parallel lightly incised lines are apparent on some of the hairpins from Area K. Others, such as ZUR/K/123 have small incisions reminiscent of the '[...] fine cross-hatched lines [...]' (Giddy, 1999: 169) described by Giddy on the material from Kom Rabi'a. In the case of the hairpins from Area K, these cross-hatchings have often been nearly erased by subsequent polishing of the object, especially noticeable on ZUR/KQ/1.

On this basis it is possible to suggest that the manufacturing process consisted of two stages; a rough shaping of the objects by whittling or carving the bone, most likely using a notched or straight blade, which created a series of incisions perpendicularly across the pin's body. The second stage involved polishing and while this may have been achieved with a number of the polishing stones found at the site, or simply with sand, a discovery in Area N suggests a specific method.

When excavating Space N34, the excavators noted that one of the blocks (ZUR/N34/8, Figure 4.4) made from local limestone and used to construct the walls of this small residential area was covered in a series of grooves or striations. The block was lifted free of the wall and examined. Six grooves were found on one surface, between 6.00 and 11.00 centimetres in length and with an average breadth of 1.00 centimetre. The shape of the grooves suggests that thin objects were pressed towards the surface and pulled or pushed across it. The differing depth of the grooves (deeper in the middle, shallower towards each end) suggests that the maximum amount of downwards force was employed towards the middle of the grove, consistent with a person pulling a long, thin object across the surface. The block is too large and heavy to have been used as a hand-held polisher, but the grooves are identical in appearance to grooves found on sanders from Tell el-Amarna (Kemp and Stevens, 2010b: 439–40).

Figure 4.4 Polishing stone ZUR/N34/8 (S. Snape).

4.3.1 Discussion

The most notable feature of the assemblage of hairpins and needles from Area K is the sheer quantity of the locally produced bone examples. The amount far outweighs the amount discovered at contemporary settlement sites such as Kom Rabi'a (Giddy, 1999: 170) and suggests a well-developed and extensive production. The spatial arrangement of the objects shows significant clusters around spaces KM, KL and KKIII (Figure 4.5), suggesting a possible area of manufacture. The objects are however commonly found throughout the area.

Figure 4.5 Spatial arrangement of locally produced bone pins (S. Thomas and author).

The most pressing question is naturally the reason for this extensive manufacture. Soldiers during the New Kingdom are generally thought to have been shaved, or at least have short hair (see for instance depictions in the tomb of Userkaf, Hodel-Hoenes, 2000: 73). As such, it is unclear whether the garrison would have required hair pins, although it is possible that some of the soldiers brought their wives with them or had relations with local women, and inscriptional evidence suggests that Nebre, the fort's commandant lived at the fort with his wife (Snape and Godenho, in press). This may in part explain the production, although another possibility also presents itself: ZUR/KL/11 is a bone hairpin similar in manufacturing technique and shape to the others found at the site, and almost certainly the product of local manufacture. However, it was deposited in the fill of Space KL, after the site had been abandoned by the Egyptian garrison and possibly even somewhat later than the brief Libyan squatter occupation which followed the fort's abandonment. It is likely therefore that the object was dropped by the Libyan squatters, possibly indicating that they had the object before the site was abandoned. Depictions of contemporary Libyan tribesmen with intricate hairstyles are common in the Egyptian pictorial record (Bates, 1914: 134–7). The hairpins could as such tentatively be considered as objects which the Egyptian inhabitants of Zawiyet Umm el-Rakham manufactured as possible trade objects for the local Libyans, most likely representing a less formalised and organised barter trade than the possible linen trade discussed above.

4.4 Craft production in Area K

When considering the crafts discussed above, textile production, stone working and the production of bone pins, the most obvious factor is the degree to which the inhabitants of Area K (and Zawiyet Umm el-Rakham more widely) relied on local materials, whether naturally occurring in the immediate landscape such as the biosparite limestone cobbles that surrounded the site, or grown locally, such as the flax used for linen manufacture. This reliance on local material is more complex than simply utilising a specific material for a single stage of production. These different industries, and others less well evidenced in the archaeological record, were intertwined. Flax was grown locally and spun using spindles carved from local limestone. Threads were woven into cloth most likely using pin beaters also produced locally from the widely available bones of caprines and other animals consumed at the site. The finished textile may then have served a final function in ensuring the continuation of these production strategies by being traded or gifted to local inhabitants in exchange for peaceful co-existence.

As with the production of local pottery discussed in Chapter 3 and the agricultural industry evidenced in Area K discussed in Chapter 2, these local productions were not small-scale or opportunistic operations. In particular the use of local limestone in everything from furniture to vessels to the walls of the structures in Area K themselves, evidence the capacity of the Egyptian garrison to range far beyond the immediate environs of the fortress. By extension, this further reinforces the sense that the Egyptian occupants were well-integrated within their environment.

The evidence of craft production from Area K substantiates to a great extent the evidence supplied for the ceramic industry and the subsistence strategies employed by the occupants at the site. The Egyptians living and working in Area K were not a militarised rump, trapped behind heavy fortifications in a state of permanent siege, living in fear of hostile Libyan tribes surrounding them on all sides. They had the capacity to fully utilise the, to them, somewhat alien natural landscape and to develop a degree of self-sufficiency, lessening their reliance on stretched supply lines from the Nile Valley. In addition, both the production of textile, chipped stone manufacture and potentially also the production of bone hairpins, evidence the levels to which the garrison relied on trade and peaceful cooperation with their Libyan neighbours.

5

The West Delta and Marmarican Fortresses

5.1 Introduction: The Western Delta and Marmarica in the Ramesside Period

Urban expansion during the Ramesside Period is predominately associated with the Eastern Nile Delta, in particular the site of Qantir-Piramesses. The site was greatly expanded by the early Ramesside rulers and the location selected as Egypt's *de facto* capital until the silting up of the Pelusiac branch of the river Nile made continued occupation at the site untenable. However, while much urban activity was focused in the Eastern Nile Delta during the Ramesside Period, a number of sites in the Western Nile Delta were also either built or substantially altered, in particular during the reign of Ramesses II.

Chief among these is a number of fortified structures which stretch from the Western Delta west along the Marmarican coast terminating at Zawiyet Umm el-Rakham (Figure 5.1). The settlements which comprise this so-called 'fortress chain' contain a number of shared architectural features, notably substantial fortification walls and additional fortification architecture such as buttresses, towers and gateways, along with triparte temples. In terms of physical layout and appearance, they are similar both to the 'temple towns' built in Nubia during the late eighteenth Dynasty as well as the fortified settlements built in Nubia during the nineteenth Dynasty, such as Amara West and Aksha. The purpose of this chapter is to examine the textual and archaeological evidence for these structures and suggest what their role may have been within the wider context of the early Ramesside Egyptian foreign policy.

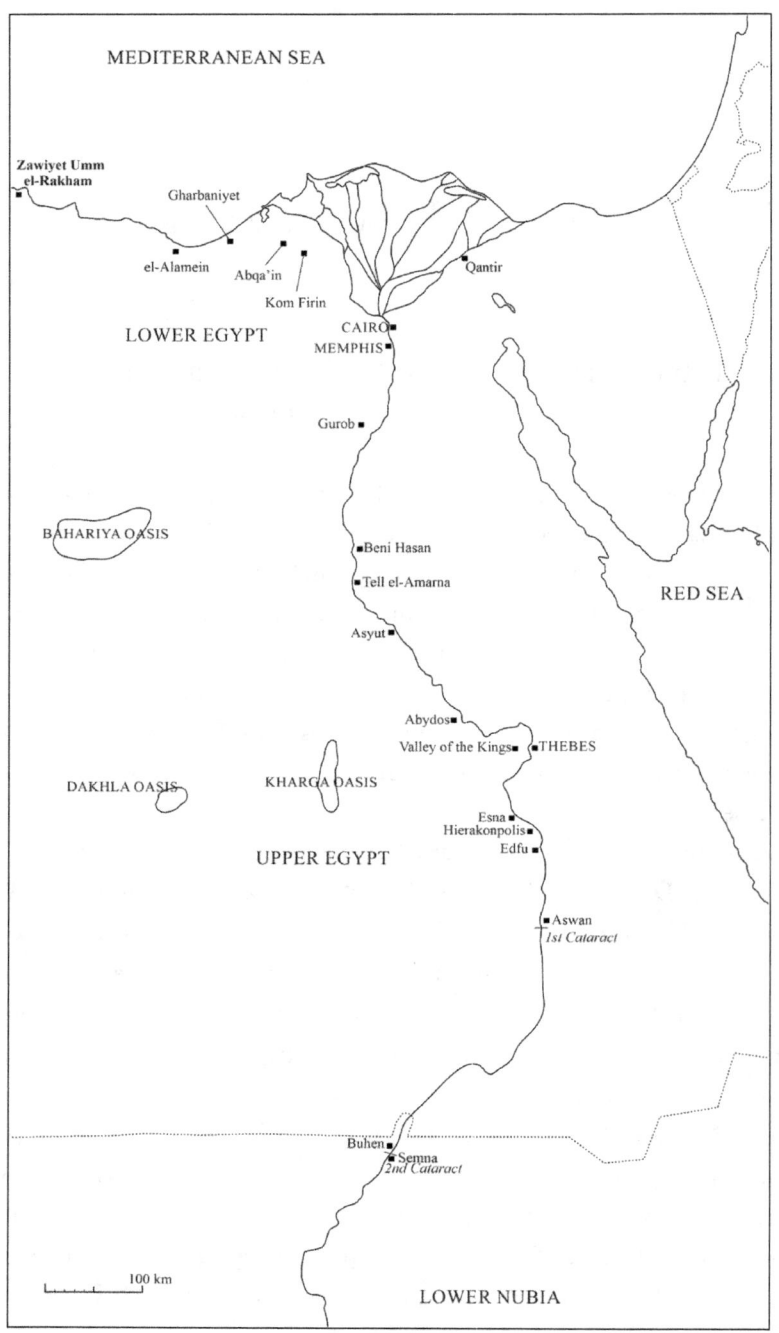

Figure 5.1 Map showing the location of the Marmarican and West Delta fortresses (author).

5.2 The Marmarican and West Delta fortifications in the written record

Unlike the Middle Kingdom fortifications in Nubia, there is little in the way of textual evidence which describes the day-to-day running, construction or organisation of the fortified settlements on the edge of Egypt's Western Delta and along the Marmarican coast, and no texts at all which predate the reign of Ramesses II. From the reign of Ramesses II, the Abu Simbel inscription makes a vague reference to structures of some kind built possibly to house prisoners-of-war: '[...] he has placed the Shasu in the western land [...]' (*rdi.n=f Šзsw r tз imnty*, KRI II, 206:15). A second inscription from the reign of Ramesses II makes a brief reference too to Libyans (*ṯhnw*) being settled in '[...] towns bearing his name [...]' (*dmiw ḥr rn=f*, KRI II, 406:3). A third inscription makes reference to the fortifications or fortified settlements (*mnnw*) being constructed upon the 'foreign land of Tjemeh' (*hзswt n ṯmḥ*, Snape, 1995: 171). Finally, the inscription of Nebre itself contains a reference to Zawiyet Umm el-Rakham itself, referring to it as the town (*dmiw*) of Ramesses II (Nielsen, 2017: 1569).

During the reign of Merneptah the Libyans invasion attempts of the Egyptian Nile Delta and the subsequent Egyptian military campaigns against the Rebu and Meshwesh invaders is described in some detail in the Great Karnak Inscription of Merenptah as well as in the so-called Israel Stela of Merenptah. The Karnak Inscription contains several references to fortified structures in the Western Nile Delta being plundered by the invading Libyan forces ([///] *r ḥwrc nn n mnnw*, Manassa, 2003: 27). Manassa (2003: 27) argues that this reference can be taken as proof that the fortifications on the Marmarican coast, including Zawiyet Umm el-Rakham, were not abandoned during the reign of Ramesses II as the Egyptian troops would have destroyed the forts prior to abandonment so they could not fall into enemy hands and as such there would be nothing left to plunder (2003: 30). However, as demonstrated in this publication, there does not appear to have been any deliberate attempts by the Egyptians (or indeed the Libyans) to destroy the structure at Zawiyet Umm el-Rakham. Rather, there is indeed evidence of later Libyan squatter occupation occurring at some point after the Egyptians abandoned the fortification, possibly in connection with the raids or occupations alluded to in this section of the Karnak inscription.

A later section of the Great Karnak Inscription of Merenptah contains a reference to another fortified structure either in the Western Delta or more likely on the Marmarican coast, the 'fortress of the West' (*mnnw imnty*, Manassa, 2003: 47). The identity of this structure is not known. Manassa (2003: 48–9) argues that this structure could potentially be Zawiyet Umm el-Rakham although in the absence of any evidence of occupation at the fortress after the reign of Ramesses II, it is perhaps more likely that the Fortress of the West was one of the fortified structures closer to Egypt (discussed below) such as Tell Abqa'in, el-Alamein or el-Gharbaniyat, all of which could be argued to be on Egypt's western border. A brief reference in the Israel stela of Merenptah may be describing the state of the remaining western fortifications after the king had defeated his Libyan enemy: 'The forts (*mnnw*) are left to themselves [. . .] The (high)-walled battlements are undisturbed; it is the sunlight that (alone) awakens their guards' (Sagrillo, 2012: 441).

Also dating to the reign of Merenptah is Pap. Louvre N 3136 which contains reference to a fortified settlement described as 'the city upon the western bank' (*p₃ dmi nty [ḥr p₃ r] wḏ imnty*, Manassa, 2003: 128) as well as 'great stronghold' (*nḫtw ꜥ₃*, Manassa, 2003: 128) partly manned by Sherden mercenaries who were despatched against the Libyans. The precise location of this structure is not clear, although it seems likely to be one of the fortresses located in the Western Nile Delta.

Both the Karnak inscription of Merenptah and the Kom el-Ahmar stela from the reign of same ruler makes reference to several other locales which may be identifiable as one or more of the fortified settlements located along Egypt's western borders, respectively the 'house-of-truth of Merenptah Hotephirmaat, destroyer of the Tjehenu-Libyans' (*p₃ pr-m₃ꜥt n mr-n-ptḥ ḥtp-ḥr-m₃ꜥt [ḥtm] ṯhnw*, Morris, 2005: 630, although as noted by the author the word *ḥtm* was reconstructed by Brusch and due to further wear neither inscription today preserves that portion) located near *pr-irw* (for a discussion of the precise location of this toponym, see Manassa, 2003: 103–6) as well as the more encompassing term 'the upper towns of the desert/ foreign lands' (*n₃ dmiw ḥryw n smt/ḫ₃st*, Morris, 2005: 630) which surely must refer to the string of fortifications located on the Marmarican coast, such as el-Gharbaniyet and el-Alamein. Finally, the Karnak inscription also contains reference to the 'mountain of the opening of the land' (*wp-t₃*) but again, the precise location of this toponym cannot be ascertained, although it has been speculated by Manassa (2003: 25) to refer to the area around the Wadi Natrun.

The Medinet Habu inscriptions of Ramesses III which also record the battles fought as part of the Libyan Wars of this ruler also contain a number of toponyms which may be identifiable as one or more fortified structures in the westernmost edge of the Nile Delta and the along the Marmarican coast. As with the Karnak inscription of Merenptah, the battle reliefs of Ramesses III specifically mention the 'town' (*dmi*) known as 'Ramesses-ruler-of-Heliopolis' (*rꜥ-ms-s ḥkꜣ iwnw*) which was located close to the previously mentioned 'mountain of the opening of the land' (*wp-tꜣ*) (KRI V, 43: 9–10). The accompanying reliefs (for an extensive discussion of these reliefs see Morris, 2005: 778–82) also depict several fortified structures notably the 'town' (*dmi*) of 'Ramesses-Meryamun-the-repeller-of-Tjemeh-land' (*wsr-mꜣꜥt-rꜥ mry-imn ḫsf ṯmḥ*) as well as the 'town House-of-Sand' (*dmi ḥwt-Šꜥ*).

Overall, the cursory mentions and toponym lists which are all that remains within the textual record which references the fortifications in the Western Delta and along the Marmarican coast makes it impossible to directly identity the names of any individual structures. Without clear archaeological evidence, such as inscriptional evidence from one or more of the potential fortress locations which bear clear mentions of one or more of these toponyms, it is impossible to identify which name was carried by which location, and indeed if these names were altered depending on the reigning king. It is noteworthy for instance that two structures from the reigns of Merenptah and Ramesses III bear strikingly similar names (respectively the 'house-of-truth of Merenptah Hotephirmaat, destroyer of the Tjehenu-Libyans' and the 'town of Ramesses-Meryamun-the-repeller-of-Tjemeh-land') both located within the vicinity of the mountain of Wep-Ta. Perhaps the two names denote the same structure which may not even have been built during the reigns of neither Merenptah nor Ramesses III but was simply renamed as rulers came and went ensuring that it always carried the name of the reigning king.

Rather than rely on scant textual evidence alone, it is therefore necessary to examine the – sadly – equally fragmentary archaeological evidence for the most well-documented of the fortified structures located along Egypt's western border, namely Tell Abqa'in, Kom Firin and Kom el-Hisn in the Western Nile

Delta and Kom el-Nogous, el-Gharbaniyat and el-Alamein located west of Alexandria along the Marmarican coast.

5.3 The West Delta fortifications of Ramesses II: Tell Abqa'in, Kom Firin and Kom el-Hisn

The notion of a series of fortified structures, a fortress chain, located along Egypt's Western Delta and the Marmarican coast and providing a parallel to the better evidenced Walls of the Ruler located along the edge of the Eastern Nile Delta and along the northern coast of the Sinai Peninsula was first proposed by de Cosson in his 1935 publication *Mareotis: Being a Short Account of the History and Ancient Monuments of the North-Western Desert of Egypt and of Lake Mareotis*. de Cosson argued that the coastal road leading from Alexandria west toward Cyrenaica was barred during the Late Bronze Age by 'fortifications dating from Ramses II' (de Cosson, 1935: 26) and later elaborates that he believed the fortifications at Khashm el-Eish near Borg el-Arab could be identifiable with the previously mentioned location of Wep-Ta mentioned in the Kom el-Ahmar stela of Merenptah and in the Medinet Habu battle reliefs of Ramesses III (121). He also includes a brief description of the potential fortification at el-Gharbaniyat (128).

Building on the work of de Cosson and also Brinton (1942), Alan Rowe, lecturer of Near Eastern Archaeology at the University of Manchester and a director of the Graeco-Roman museum in Alexandria published two seminal pieces containing a broad overview of archaeological remains in the Mariotis region and the Marmarican coast (Rowe, 1953 and 1954). Based both on the examination of textual evidence along with superficial archaeological surveys, Rowe identified what he believed to be several Ramesside-era fortifications in the Western Delta and immediately west of Lake Mariotis. Among these were el-Bordan where Rowe found a number of red granite blocks bearing inscriptions dated to the reign of Ramesses II, as well as el-Gharbaniyat (Rowe, 1953: 134). In his 1954 paper Rowe identified a total of six fortifications built by Ramesses II along the Marmarican coast stretching from Alexandria to Mersa Matrouh (from east to west: Marea, el-Gharbaniyat, el-Bordan, el-Alamein and Zawiyet Umm el-Rakham as well as an un-named fortress located between el-Bordan and el-Alamein). In addition to the Marmarican fortresses, Rowe also identified six fortifications on the edge of Western Delta (Ezbet Abu-Shawish, Kurum el-Tuwal, Kom Abu-Girg, Tell Abqa'in, Kom Firin and Kom el-Hisn) (Rowe, 1954: 498).

Of the fortifications in the Western Delta identified by Rowe, no significant evidence is provided for any Ramesside activity at Ezbet Abu-Shawish. Nor has any later excavation in the area suggested the presence of any New Kingdom fortifications and it is not entirely clear from Rowe's publication why it was included in his list of West Delta fortresses. As for Kurum el-Tuwal, excavations by Eilmann, Langsdorff and Stier (1930) in the late 1920s revealed primarily Classical and Late Antique remains. The excavators did note the presence of Pharaonic sculptural material built into the walls of later Coptic architecture, including fragments of columns and limestone blocks bearing fragmented inscriptions in hieroglyphs (including the phrase 'the great god', $n\underline{t}r$-$˓_3$ commonly used to describe the King). It is possible that these inscriptions originally came from a Ramesside temple built in a fortified enclosure at the site as speculated by Rowe (1954: 498) although no further archaeological evidence for such a structure has been found at the site.

As with Kurum el-Tuwal, the primary evidence of a hypothetical Ramesside fortress at Kom Abu-Girg is in the form of a few inscribed blocks identified in the area by E. Breccia in his annual *Rapport sur la Marche du Service du Musée en 1912* (Breccia, 1913 see also a discussion of Breccia's discoveries in de Cosson, 1935: 148ff). While Breccia's report on archaeological work at Karm Abu-Girg primarily focuses on Classical and Late Antique architecture, including a Coptic church and cemetery, the author also briefly describes a fragment of an inscribed red granite obelisk and several other inscribed, but heavily damaged, stone blocks dated by inscriptions to the reign of Ramesses II (Breccia, 1913: Fig. VI). As with Kurum el-Tuwal, it is essentially impossible at this stage to clearly evidence whether or not a Ramesside fortress existed at Karm Abu-Girg. The inscriptional material could well have been moved from the site from elsewhere in order to recycle it in the construction of the Late Antique church found at the site, or the blocks could have originated from the site.

Far better evidence survives from the site of Tell Abqa'in. First identified as a potential Ramesside site by Darresey (1905), the site was later excavated by Labib Habachi (1954) who identified a number of inscribed blocks dating to the reign of Ramesses II as well as a number of wells at the site. Tell Abqa'in was further investigated by a University of Liverpool mission in the 1990s under the direction of Susanna Thomas (2000, 2002 and 2011) identifying not only further inscribed materials (including a fragmented door jamb mentioning both Ramesses II and the Levantine deity Anath, Thomas, 2011: 525–7) but also Ramesside ceramics and evidence of local industries such as weaving (Thomas, 2011: 528–9). Further investigation of the area was conducted by Trampier in 2007–8 (Trampier, 2014: 89–108) and the site was subsequently excavated by the Ministry of State for Antiquities from 2014 onwards.

Using a combination of remote sensing surveys and field walking, Trampier identified a number of unexcavated features at Tell Abqa'in with clear parallels to structures found at Zawiyet Umm el-Rakham, including a potential tripartite temple (Trampier, 2014: 94) as well as defensive features (Trampier, 2014: 92–4). The surface collection of pottery conducted on the site by this author identified a mixture of Ramesside ceramics as well as later Ptolemaic and Roman materials (Trampier, 2014: 99–103).

Visited first by Petrie in the late 1880s as part of his work for the Egypt Exploration Fund (Petrie, 1886), the site of Kom Firin received relatively limited attention from the archaeological community until the 2000s. Excavators in the 1970s noted the site's impressive mudbrick surviving mudbrick walls (Coulson and Leonard 1979) as well as the presence of inscribed blocks dating to the reign of Ramesses II (159) though much of the material from the site was, as also noted by Petrie (1886: 94–5) datable to the Late Period rather than the New Kingdom. A comprehensive re-investigation of the site by a British Museum mission under the direction of Neal Spencer from 2002 onwards have aided the understanding of the site and proved beyond a doubt that while the site was certainly occupied during the Late Period, a substantive Ramesside-era fortified settlement also existed at Kom Firin (Spencer, 2008: 23–4). In addition to a wealth of material related to Ramesside occupation and industry (Spencer, 2014) the site also hosted a modest tripartite Ramesside temple broadly architecturally similar to the one located at Zawiyet Umm el-Rakham and potentially Tell Abqa'in as well (Spencer, 2008: 36–54).

The final site in Rowe's hypothetical 'line' of fortifications in the Western Delta is the site of Kom el-Hisn. Occupation at this area of the Western Delta predates the New Kingdom as evidenced by the presence of both Old Kingdom and Middle Kingdom settlement remains and cemeteries (see Wenke, Buck, Hamroush, et al., 1988 for an overview of the Old Kingdom settlement at the site and Hamada and el-Amir, 1946; Brunton, 1947; Hamada and Farid, 1947, 1949 and 1950 for the First Intermediate Period, Middle Kingdom and New Kingdom cemetery from the site) while Ramesside remains (including a potential enclosure wall and a potential temple) was first identified by Griffith in the mid-to late 1880s (Gardner, 1888: 77–80, see also Kirby, Orel and Smith, 1998 for a more recent survey of the archaeological remains at the site). The long-lived occupation of the site and its location on the edge of the Western Delta certainly makes it likely that the site was among those fortified during the reign of Ramesses II. As such, while the archaeological evidence recovered from the site is not as clear as the material recovered from Kom Firin and Tell Abqa'in it is nevertheless reasonable to assume that Kom el-Hisn, while not – like Zawiyet Umm el-Rakham – constructed during the reign of Ramesses II, certainly received increased royal attention during this period both in the form of increased defences and potentially also the construction of a small temple structure.

5.4 The Marmarican fortresses: Kom el-Nogous, el-Gharbaniyat and el-Alamein

In regard to the sites identified by Rowe along the Marmarican coast as being potential Ramesside fortresses, little evidence exists from Marea and el-Bordan aside from a few blocks of red granite which may or may not have originated from a Ramesside temple structure at the sites (Rowe, 1953: 130 and 134). Slightly more substantive evidence exists from both el-Alamein and el-Gharbaniyat. During the North Africa campaign of the Second World War, a corps of Canadian soldiers stumbled upon fragments of a Ramesside granite stelae at an unclear location south of the old el-Alamein train station (Brinton, 1942). Following the discovery of the stela (and a nearby mudbrick wall), it was moved to Burg el-Arab while another inscribed stone slab was left *in situ* (Habachi, 1980: 19).

The nearby site of el-Gharbaniyat was first identified as a potential Ramesside settlement by de Cosson (1935: 31 and 127–8) who described a granite column inscribed with the cartouches of Ramesses II found at the site along with some mudbrick architecture though de Cosson's evidence for dating this to the Ramesside period is unclear. The inscription on the granite column makes reference to Ramesses II as being one 'beloved of [the Canaanite deity] Houron' (Habachi, 1980: Fig. 6). This parallels the inscription found at Tell Abqa'in where Ramesses II is described as 'beloved of Anath', another Canaanite deity, is clear. This may suggest that at least some of the Ramesside-era temples built in the Western Delta and Marmarican coast specifically included shrines for Canaanite deities. The reason for this is unclear, but may perhaps be a direct result of including Canaanite troops in the garrisons of these fortifications as discussed in Section 1.5.

The most recent discovery of a potential fortress site west of Alexandria is at the site of Kom el-Nogous. During a magnetometry survey conducted by the French archaeological mission to Taposiris Magna and Plinthine in 2015 at the site of Kom el-Nogous, a number of buildings dating to the Third Intermediate Period and later were identified (Dhennin and Somaglino, 2022). In the foundations of a Roman-era building, the team uncovered a number of highly fragmented limestone blocks dating to the reign of Ramesses II (Dhennin and Somaglino, 2022: Figs 6–17) as well as private stela (2022: Figs 18–25) similar to those found in the chapels at Zawiyet Umm el-Rakham. These blocks most likely represent the remains of an earlier temple structure at the site, and given its location and the similarity between these inscribed fragments and those found for instance at Tell Abqa'in, el-Alamein and Zawiyet Umm el-Rakham itself, it seems likely, although not completely certain, that a fortified settlement stood at this site during the Ramesside Period

5.5 Via Libyca?

On the basis of the evidence, it is reasonable to conclude that while some of the sites identified by de Cosson, Rowe and Habachi contain very limited evidence to suggest Ramesside occupation, let alone the presence of a Ramesside fortress, other sites – notably Kom el-Hisn, Kom Firin and Tell Abqa'in in the Western Delta and Kom el-Nogous, el-Gharbaniyat, el-Alamein and of course Zawiyet Umm el-Rakham itself along the Marmarican coast – contain sufficient archaeological evidence to suggest that they were either built as fortified settlements or that they were earlier structures fortified during the reign of Ramesses II. The logical question is of course to wonder why these sites were so heavily fortified during this particular period. Against what enemies were they built or re-fortified?

Several potential candidates have been suggested. Rowe argued that the fortifications could have been employed against incursions of Sea People during the reign of Ramesses II and later, as well as against the Libyan invasions of the later Ramesside Period (Rowe, 1954: 486–8). Habachi in his seminal article on the military posts of Ramesses II in western Egypt (1980) saw the structures, in particular Zawiyet Umm el-Rakham as direct responses to piratical incursions by the Sea People, similar to those evidenced in the Tanis II stela dated to the reign of Ramesses II which describes an attack on the Egyptian Nile Delta by Sherden pirates (*KRI* II, 290: 1–4). Later scholars, notably Snape (2003) has suggested that at least Zawiyet Umm el-Rakham may have functioned as both a strategic bottle neck to prevent eastward movement of Libu and Meshwesh warriors, and also that the site may have protected water supplies for foreign merchants landing on the Marmarican coast *en route* to Egypt. A complimentary function of Zawiyet Umm el-Rakham, one of providing an economic interface for Egypto-Libyan contact in the area, was also proposed by the current author (Nielsen, 2017).

While each fortification no doubt served its own purpose defined by its location, political and cultural context, it seems clear that many of the structures were constructed in the same chronological period with shared architectural features. This suggests that the fortress construction and re-fortification of existing settlements was part of an overall political plan spearheaded by the Egyptian state during the early part of Ramesses II's reign. The purpose of this plan, and the events which inspired it, are problematic to identify, but it is possible that a potential answer lies not in the reign of Ramesses II himself, but in the truncated reign of his father, Seti I. Not only did Seti's reign see the refortification of fortresses along the Ways of Horus in the Eastern Delta and along the north Sinai coast (for instance at Tell Heboua I, Xekalaki, 2021: 3943), it also witnessed the construction of new fortified settlements in Nubia, for instance at Amara West (Spencer, 2012: 21), fortresses which are remarkably similar in architectural layout to structures such as Zawiyet Umm el-Rakham and Kom Firin. In addition, Seti himself also campaigned along the Marmarican coast during the latter part of his reign (see Section 1.2.2).

Taking this information together, it is possible that the fortification of the Marmarican coast was not a policy created by Ramesses II or his advisors, but rather part of a broader policy of refortification along all Egypt's three frontiers – Sinai, Nubia and Libya – first launched during the reign of Seti I. The purpose of this campaign may have been to underline the shift of Egyptian priorities from the chaotic end of the eighteenth Dynasty, or further legitimise the Ramesside family as powerful and worthy rulers of Egypt by emulating the more warlike tendencies of eighteenth-Dynasty pharaohs such as Thutmosis III and Amenhotep II. Seti having included an amalgam of the throne names of Thutmosis III and Amenhotep III into his own throne name (Nielsen, 2018: 80) was certainly eager to underscore his family's connection, in terms of demeanour and priorities in the absence of actual blood-links, to the rulers of Egypt during the Golden Age of the mid-eighteenth Dynasty. The fortification of the Marmarican coast, the first time this area had received significant attention from the Egyptian state during the entirety of Pharaonic history, may have been simply one facet of this much broader policy of militarisation.

Did the fortresses along the Marmarican coast then represent a western counter to the *Via Maris*? A *Via Libyca* perhaps? Almost certainly not. Via Maris represented one of the busiest trade routes of the Eastern Mediterranean during much of the Bronze Age. The Egyptians, despite their short-lived presence on the Marmarican coast, seemed to have little interest in trading substantially with the Libyan tribes living further west towards Cyrenaica. The fortresses in the Western Delta and along the Marmarican Coast should not be viewed as a 'road to somewhere', but rather a series of fortified settlements which served a multiplicity of purposes, from providing information on and safe harbour for passing merchant ships, to information about the movement of hostile Libyans (in particular during the later Ramesside Period as evidenced by the report sent by the 'Fortress of the West' informing Merenptah about the flight of the Libyan chief Meryre [Davies, 1997: 161]), to providing a, somewhat smaller, stage for trade and contact between Egyptians and Libyans.

6

Subsistence and Production Strategies at Early- to Mid-Ramesside Forts

6.1 Introduction

Along with the best-evidenced sites discussed in Chapter 5 (Kom Firin and Tell Abqa'in in particular), the archaeological material from Area K at Zawiyet Umm el-Rakham finds a number of useful parallels at other fortified centres either built or substantially (re-)fortified during the early years of the Ramesside Period and the reigns of Seti I and Ramesses II, namely Amara West in Upper Nubia as well as Tell Heboua I, Tell Heboua II, Tell el-Borg, Tell el-Retaba, Haruba A-289/Bir el-Abd and Deir el-Balah located on the edge of the Eastern Delta and along the north Sinai coast.

The aim of this chapter is to provide an overview of the evidence for subsistence and production strategies employed at these nine Ramesside fortified settlements in order to place the material from Area K into a broader context. This discussion will also allow broader conclusions with regards the survival strategies employed by the Egyptian state (and local inhabitants) in liminal zones, such as the eastern and western frontiers of Egypt's New Kingdom area of control. The nine sites (Figure 6.1) make a suitable assemblage of comparison not only because of their chronological (and in some cases architectural) similarity to Zawiyet Umm el-Rakham, but also because they have all been excavated relatively recently, and as such have yielded sufficient amounts of relevant archaeological comparanda. It is also for this reason that a site such as Aksha in Upper Nubia has been excluded from the comparison because insufficient material pertaining to provisioning or production has been published, in favour of a focus on inscriptional evidence (Fuscaldo, 1992 and 1994).

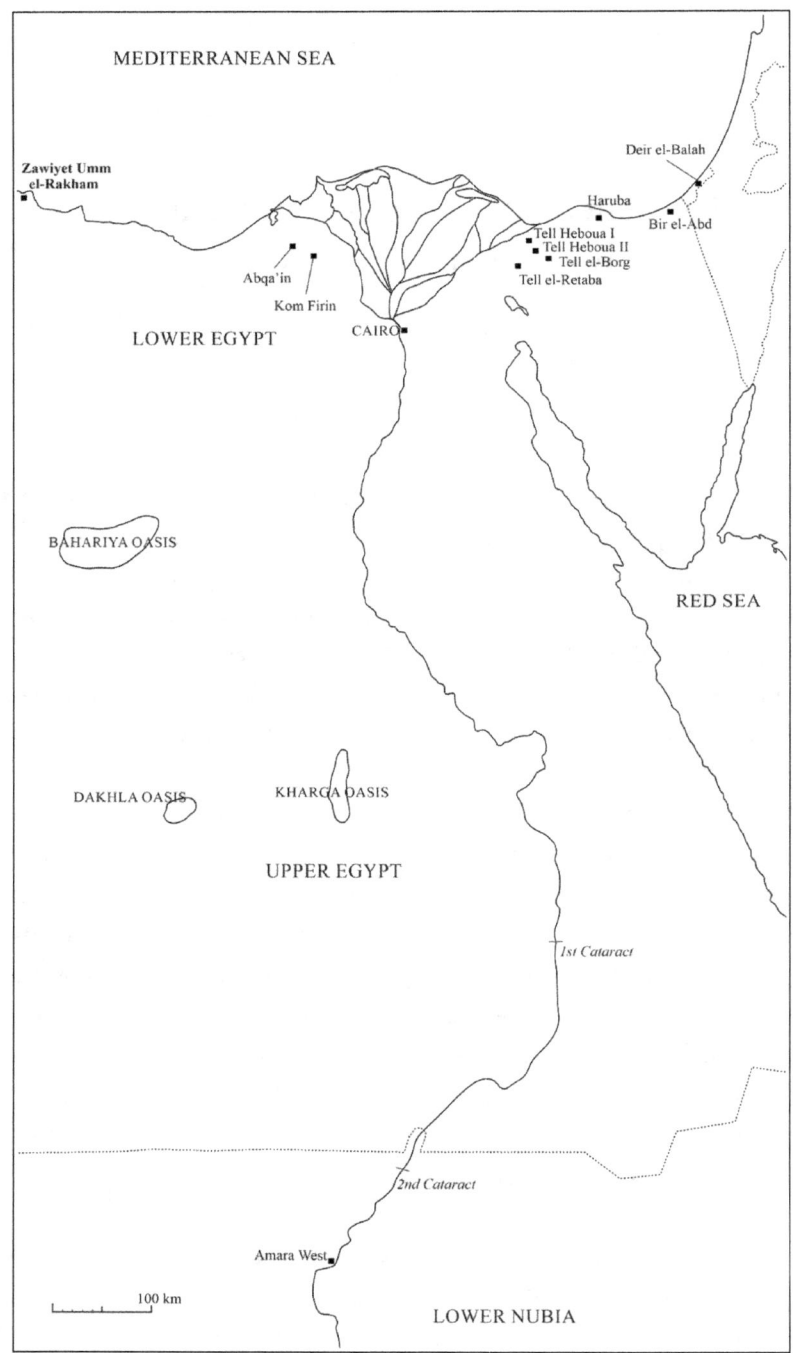

Figure 6.1 Ramesside fortified settlements discussed in Chapter 6 (author).

Similarly, sites such as Sai Island and Sesebi have been excluded from comparison due to the limited amount of Ramesside material recovered from these sites by comparison to earlier eighteenth-Dynasty material (for an overview of work at Sai Island see in particular Budka, 2017 and 2020 and for Sesebi see in particular Spence et al., 2011).

6.2 Subsistence strategies

As discussed in Chapter 2, evidence of agricultural production (in the form of tools for the harvesting and processing of grains, along with tools used to bake bread and brew beer) as well as animal husbandry, is among the most common material from Area K at Zawiyet Umm el-Rakham. Given the absolute imperative of ensuring sufficient supplies of food not just at fortified sites but at all settlements, this is not surprising. It is also mirrored by the relatively vast amounts of evidence from contemporary parallel sites in the Eastern and Western Nile Delta and Upper Nubia.

6.2.1 Agriculture

The clearest evidence of grain production at a given site is the presence of the sturdiest tools involved in the harvest, sickle blades with sheen or gloss, or alternatively archaeobotanical evidence of processing waste. Evidence from the site of Kom Firin in the North-western Delta is in the form of assemblages of sickle blades (Spencer, 2014: 56 and Figs 269, 272 and 274) from the Ramesside enclosure, although the presence of sheen or gloss is difficult to determine from the available photographic material. A contemporary assemblage of lithic tools from Tell Heboua I were published by Caneva (1992) who interpreted 86 per cent of the assemblage as sickle blades and noted evidence of lustre and sheen on many of the blades, evidencing use. Much of the assemblage however was obtained from surface collection and as such a precise date was problematic to achieve for all examples in the assemblage (Caneva, 1992).

Another contemporary assemblage of sickle blades the majority of which displayed lustre was collected at the site of Deir el-Balah and dated to the fourteenth and thirteenth century BC (Rosen and Goring-Morris, 2010, see also Morris, 2005: 518–19). The presence of sickle blades at these sites in the Western Delta and the Sinai Peninsula indicates that local production of grain was undertaken, similarly to Zawiyet Umm el-Rakham, by the military garrison although its extent is uncertain and it is possible that the production was merely intended to supplement centrally distributed supplies, in particular at the larger sites such as Tell Heboua I, which may have served as a grain reserve and arsenal for Egyptian armies crossing into Canaan and would therefore require considerably more grain than would be needed to merely feed its garrison (Morris, 2005: 711).

Archaeobotanical analysis conducted with bucket flotation has produced a series of preliminary results regarding plant use at the site of Tell el-Retaba (Rzepk, Hudec and Jarmuzek, 2013). The chronologically relevant samples were obtained from Area 3, including a large mudbrick wall from the reign of Ramesses II (Rzepka et al., 2013: 84) and Area 9, a series of three 'barracks' (Rzepka et al., 2013: 87–9) datable to the reign of Ramesses II. Emmer wheat and barley dominates the assemblage with additional weed species most likely employed for fuel, although this usage is less marked in the nineteenth-Dynasty assemblage than in earlier eighteenth-Dynasty samples from a settlement underlying the later fortress (Rzepka et al., 2013: 91). The nineteenth-Dynasty material constitutes primarily the remains of cereal processing waste (Rzepka et al., 2013: 92) indicative of local production. Supporting the notion of local grain production is also the discovery of an assemblage of typical New Kingdom sickle blades found in the area of an eighteenth-Dynasty settlement and the nineteenth-Dynasty fortress (Rzepka, el Din, Wodzińska and Jarmuzek, 2012–13: 267–9). The use of locally grown grain as well as various fruits is also evidenced at the *mnnw*-fort at Amara West (Ryan, Cartwright and Spencer, 2012: 105–6 and Ryan, 2017).

Grain processing in the form of ovens, quern stones, mortars and handstones are nearly universally found at all the relevant sites (Tell Heboua I: el-Maksoud, 1998: 72, Tell Heboua II: al-Ayedi, 2006: 37, Tell el-Retaba: Rzepka, Wodzińska, Malleson, et al., 2011: 148–50 and 163–4, Deir el-Balah: Klein, 2010: 280–7, Kom Firin: Spencer, 2014: 56, Tell Abqa'in: Thomas, 2011: 523 and Amara West: Spencer, 2009: 53). The hierarchy under which the grain was processed differs from site to site. At Zawiyet Umm el-Rakham (see Section 4.2), as well as Tell Heboua II (al-Ayedi, 2006: 37) and Tell Heboua I (el-Maksoud, 1998: 72) there are no smaller granaries located within or in conjunction with the domestic units wherein the grain processing was conducted. By contrast, smaller granaries or grain bins were found in conjunction with domestic architecture at Tell el-Retaba (Rzepka et al., 2009: 253–5) and Amara West (Spencer, 2009: 53). The former strategy, of requiring the producers to obtain the required grain from centralised storage facilities, as opposed to maintaining a small stock within domestic units, indicates a higher level of centralised control over grain processing. This may also be the case at Kom Firin where the uncovered granaries could potentially hold far more grain than a single household would require (Spencer, 2014: 32, see also an extensive discussion of storage fascilities found at contemporary fortified settlements in Spencer, 2014: 31–2).

6.2.2 Proteins

Analysis of faunal remains from the Ramesside enclosure at Kom Firin revealed that the inhabitants at the site relied predominately on pigs maintained locally, with a much more limited representation of cattle and caprines on the site (Bertini, 2014: 310). This stands in stark contrast to the results from Tell el-Borg (Bertini, 2019) where the faunal assemblage, similar to the the one found at Zawiyet Umm el-Rakham, shows a heavier reliance on sheep, goat and some cattle, whereas pigs are far less represented. This may be a reflection of the fact that Tell el-Borg, like Zawiyet Umm el-Rakham, is located in a far more arid environment than Kom Firin, where rearing pigs is simply not practicable. The evidence from the site suggests a heavy reliance on cattle, rather than pig, which makes up only 5 per cent of the assemblage (Bertini, 2013: 109) and caprines, which constitute just over 20 per cent (Bertini, 2013: 210). A substantial amount of evidence for ovicaprine husbandry has also survived in the form of both faunal remains and dung pellets from Amara West (Dalton and Ryan, 2020).

The presence of several ceramic scrapers inside the magazine-turned-workshop of Ramesses II in Area 9 at Tell el-Retaba (Rzepka et al., 2011: 148–50) suggests that tanning and curing of animal hides was conducted at the fortress as well. By extension, this industry suggests that butchery was conducted at the site, which in turn suggests some level of self-sufficiency and possibly the maintaining of a local herd of animals. Data from additional fortified settlements, notably at Amara West and the final publication on material from Tell el-Borg, would help to further elucidate this issue. However, the existing data, alongside textual evidence discussed elsewhere in this book (for instance Urk IV, 139.12–16 and KRI IV, 18.10–11), strongly suggests that rather than relying on centralised distribution of preserved meat, early Ramesside fortified settlements maintained herds of caprines and cattle, in some cases in conjunction with pigs when the environment was found to be suitable such as it was at Kom Firin (Bertini, 2014: 310).

With regards to fishing and hunting, the most extensively published corpus comes from Kom Firin. Within the Ramesside levels, a small proportion of fish (primarily cat fish) as well as ducks and molluscs were identified (Bertini, 2014: 307). There are no wild mammals such as gazelle represented within the assemblage. As such, the primary non-domesticated source of meat at the site came from fish most likely caught in the nearby river or estuary (Bertini, 2014: 310). Fish bones were also found within the Ramesside enclosure at Tell el-Borg, although these may predate the Ramesside occupation (Hoffmeier, Knudstad, Frey, Mumford and Kitchen, 2014b: 213). However, taken in conjunction with the discovery of net sinkers at the site (Moshier, 2014: 75), it is indicative that while great reliance was placed on domesticated animals, primarily cattle, some foraging strategies were also employed, mainly in the form of fishing in order to supplement the food stores of the settlement.

6.3 Pottery production

Extensive evidence for local pottery production was discovered in the 1980s in conjunction with the North Sinai Survey at Haruba A-289, A-345 and Bir el-Abd (Oren, 1987 and Goren et al., 1995). Thin-sections were collected from four-hundred sherds from the major sites excavated by Oren and his team and used to investigate the amount of locally produced material (primarily of two types, Haruba Marl and Bir el-Abd Marl) in comparison with imported Nile silts and marls and materials imported from southern Canaan (Goren et al., 1995: 110). An intense study of these sites show that they were most likely part of a nucleated workshop environment (Oren, 1987: 103), producing both open and closed vessels for several sites in North Sinai, not merely the closest settlements.

Concerning this internal distribution within the Ways of Horus, Tell el-Borg provides further evidence. An extensive corpus of pottery from the site has been produced by Hummel (2014 and 2019a–d) and while the majority of the vessels from the nineteenth Dynasty were produced from Nile silts or are in the form of imported Marl amphorae, a smaller number were produced in Northern Sinai, from Bir el-Abd and Haruba marl (Goren et al., 1995: 110 and Hummel, 2014: 368) and provides evidence for Oren's interpretation of the nucleated pottery workshops at Haruba A-345 in particular as providing pottery to other sites on the Sinai Peninsula (Oren, 1987: 103). Further petrographic analysis of the Tell el-Borg pottery to determine possible sources of the clay and distinguish which portions of the corpus were locally manufactured, if any, has not so far been attempted and no local clay sources or kilns have been identified near Tell el-Borg (Hummel, 2014: 368).

An administrative quarter located outside the walls of Tell Heboua II in conjunction with a group of nine 'furnaces' (al-Ayedi, 2006: 38) or kilns bears some architectural similarity to the rambling administrative unit and potter's workshop found at Haruba A-345 (Oren, 1987: 98–106) which included both granaries (Oren, 1987: 98–9 and al-Ayedi, 2006: 38) as well as a complex of kilns for the manufacture of pottery (Oren, 1987: 98–106). Considering the description provided by al-Ayedi (2006: 38) that '[l]arge quantities of pottery sherds were found' in the area of the nine furnaces, and given the striking architectural similarity with contemporary structures at Haruba A-345, it is a reasonable assumption that production of pottery was conducted in the area.

Instrumental Neutron Activation Analysis (INAA) was also conducted on a sample of Egyptian-style ceramics from Deir el-Balah (Yellin and Killebrew, 2010). The investigation demonstrated that the majority of ceramics found at the site were locally manufactured, a fact also confirmed by the discovery of a Canaanite-style kiln (Dothan and Brandl, 2010: 282–3) associated with the thirteenth-Dynasty BC occupation at the site. Only specific types of vessels (notably storage jars and white-slipped flasks, Yellin and Killebrew, 2010: 73) were imported to the site from Egypt. A more recent study of selected ceramics from Amara West (Spataro, Millet and Spencer, 2014) using Scanning Electron Microscopy-Energy Dispersive X-Ray Spectrometry (SEM-EDX) similarly determined that the majority of Egyptian-style pottery at the site was locally manufactured, most likely in the same workshops as Nubian pottery of the same period, despite the differences in manufacturing techniques (wheel-made and hand-moulded), an interpretation also supported by the discovery of a single pottery kiln at the site (Spataro et al., 2014).

6.4 Textile production

The most convincing assemblage of data from Tell Heboua I evidencing the existence of not only flax cultivation, but also most of the final steps of the process of spinning and weaving is a series of three loom weights, three spindle whorls and a spinning bowl all found in close proximity to each other within MS. X (el-Maksoud, 1998: 255). Another double-looped spinning bowl was also found in BAT. II, a Ramesside administrative and industrial building (el-Maksoud, 1998: 215). The evidence from the contemporary site of Tell el-Retaba is more problematic: Flax-linen production was conducted certainly during the eighteenth-Dynasty occupation of the site as evidenced by a spindle whorl found in the area of an eighteen- to nineteenth-Dynasty settlement as well as several typical New Kingdom spindle whorls and loom weights found at the site by Petrie and Duncan (1906: Pl. XXXVIc). One in particular (Petrie and Duncan, 1906: Pl. XXXVIc.32) even bears identical decoration to the complete limestone spindle whorl ZUR/KB/62 found in Area K. It is possible that this production may have continued during the nineteenth Dynasty.

A large collection of typical Egyptian 'double-looped' spinning bowls were also found at Deir el-Balah (Gould, 2010: 42–7). While these were absent from the Seti I fortress foundation strati (Strata VII), they were nonetheless present during the occupation of the fort contemporary with Ramesses II (Gould, 2010: 46). The vessels were locally manufactured and Gould argues (2010: 47) that they may have been primarily involved in the manufacture of linen for use in the nearby cemeteries, as well as for the use of the site's living inhabitants. Several ceramic spindle whorls (Spencer, 2014: 55) and one example made from limestone (Spencer, 2014: Pl. 262) as well as possible loom weights (such as Spencer, 2014: Pl. 213, Pl. 223 and Pl. 231) have been found along with spinning bowls (Smoláriková, 2014: Fig. 63, No. C815) at Kom Firin. Flax linen production is also evidenced at the site of Tell Abqa'in by the discovery of a single spinning bowl (Thomas, 2011: 528 and Fig. 10).

6.5 Stone working

As demonstrated by Spencer (2014: 5) many fortified settlements during the New Kingdom were equipped with stone temples. Along with the maintenance of the temple, the manufacture of tools required for grain processing, weaving and other industries, stone-working might be envisaged as a corner-stone industry within these settlements, required both for the manufacture of buildings and architectural elements which glorified elements of the state and the king, and also for maintenance and everyday objects. Evidence for stone working is primarily the results of the process; objects manufactured from local stone, inscriptions and buildings, but also the tools used by stone masons, such pounders and metal chisels (although the latter category tends to survive poorly or simply have been moved deliberately once a site was abandoned due to the value of the copper).

A great deal of inscribed material has been uncovered from the site of Tell Heboua I (presented by el-Maksoud and Valbelle, 2005). Some evidence from MS. XI indicates some degree of stone working at the site, mainly the presence of several hard stone pounders (described by el-Maksoud [1998: 418–19 and 426] as weights, although considering their similarity to contemporary examples of pounders from Zawiyet Umm el-Rakham and Tell el-Retaba, and lack of any piercing make this interpretation unlikely). Due to the sporadic publication of material from the site, no evidence of further stone working has been so far presented, but considering the lack of flint working at the site, it is tempting to interpret these pounders as primarily engaged within a stone-working industry whose precise limit and intensity remains unknown.

The most persuasive evidence for stone working at the contemporary site of Tell el-Retaba is a series of spherical stones made predominately from quartzite but also from flint and limestone (Rzepka et al., 2009: 257–8). Rzepka's (2009: 257) interpretation of these objects is that they were most likely sling shots. However, an overview of contemporary sling shots from the Eastern

Mediterranean, as well as earlier examples (Vutiropulos, 1991), show that the average weight of a sling-shot was around 30.00 grammes. The weight of the nineteen spherical stones found at Tell el-Retaba range from 125.00 to 300.00 grammes (Rzepka et al., 2009: 257). It seems unlikely that Egyptian sling shot would be between four and ten times heavier than contemporary material from other cultures, especially considering the pressure it would place on a leather sling to fire a 300.00gr projectile and the strength required to hurl it any distance at all. The material, size and appearance of the spherical stones are instead identical to the collection of pounders and hammer stones from Zawiyet Umm el-Rakham and the eighteenth-Dynasty assemblage of pounders from Tell el-Amarna (Kemp and Stevens, 2010b: 409–11) and Memphis (Giddy, 1999: 212–14).

The construction of the Temple of Atum by Ramesses II on the site (Rzepka et al., 2009: 153) would have required a large contingent of stone masons to carve the limestone blocks, much like the temple at Zawiyet Umm el-Rakham, although a small amount of more specialised sculptural material was most likely imported to the site (such as a granite dyad statue and a granite stela of Ramesses II, Petrie and Duncan, 1906: XXXII), much like the statue of Nebre from Zawiyet Umm el-Rakham which was most likely only inscribed at the site but carved near the Tura quarries in Memphis (Snape and Godenho, in press). The presence of lower-quality limestone stela most likely belonging to elite members of the fortress (Fuller, Retaba 1978) along with the pounders indicates a similar craft production of stone as at Area K, namely that a group of specialist masons were attached to the site where they both provided objects for the state and the elite (such as temple carving and private stela) and most likely also aided other crafts at the site for instance by manufacturing stone tools needed for grain processing and weaving.

At Deir el-Balah, the majority of stone-objects related to daily life at the site, notably quern stones, were locally manufactured (Klein, 2010: 280) although, as at both Tell el-Retaba and Tell Heboua I, the tools utilised by the stone masons, such as pounders and chisels were primarily manufactured from imported hard stone such as basalt (Klein, 2010: 286–8). An assemblage of stone working tools such as pounders, hammerstones, grinders and rubbers were also found at Kom Firin (Spencer, 2014: 56), primarily manufactured from limestone, quartzite and granodiorite.

Less material has been published pertaining to the production of chipped stone tools. As described above, a catalogue of lithic tools found during field walks in the area surrounding Tell Heboua I, and the satellite sites of II, III and IV were presented by Caneva (1992). Caneva concluded that the assemblage was mostly fashioned from non-local material, an interpretation also supported by the lack of any cores found at any of the relevant sites. As such, it seems likely that very little chipped-stone production took place, and that any production was mainly focused on modification and tool-repair rather than a large-scale industry.

A similar situation was in effect at the site of Deir el-Balah (Rosen and Goring-Morris, 2010: 273–7). Within the assemblage of 658 recovered flints dating primarily to the fourteenth and thirteenth centuries BC are 107 pieces of debitage, as well as a series of smaller blade cores (Rosen and Goring-Morris, 2010: 275). As none of these cores were of a sufficient size or type to have produced the prevalent sickle blades found in the assemblage, Rosen and Goring-Morris (2010: 275) concluded that these tools were brought finished to the site. Tool manufacture at the site itself was primarily limited to the manufacture of a smaller number of simple tools (such as blades and notches) with more complex tools (such as sickles) imported finished from another site or possibly from Egypt.

6.6 Conclusion

This chapter was intended to provide a review of the available archaeological data related to subsistence strategies and craft production industries at fortified settlements in Nubia, Libya and Sinai constructed or occupied during the early Ramesside Period. The intention was to investigate the degree to which these structures were dependent on centralised distribution of materials and secondly, whether significant differences in strategies existed between individual sites.

The immediately notable feature is the degree of reliance on local resources and the local landscape at the majority of the sites investigated. Several are dependent on locally grown crops, both cereal crops, but also fruits and even flax as the basis of a linen manufacturing industry conducted within several of the settlements. The prevalence of local pottery manufacture, and the complex internal distribution system evident in North Sinai and possibly also Nubia, indicates great familiarity with the local landscape and also an ability to construct and successfully run manufacturing architecture (such as kiln structures) outside the immediate control of the fortifications themselves (such as at Deir el-Balah and Haruba A-345).

The omnipresence of stone masons and the reliance on local stones suggests a relatively good working knowledge of local geology (evidenced by the deliberate import of hard stone tools when none were locally available for instance) and also the ability to mine resource in the settlement's hinterland, outside the immediate protection of the fortifications. Other industries are less well-evidenced, primarily chipped stone manufacture, which relied primarily on imported tools, and was to a great extent confined to modification and repair of existing tools rather than large-scale production. Similarly, metal working is almost entirely absent from the archaeological record at these sites, and when present is primarily in the form of limited crucible-based repair and re-casting of smaller objects (such as at Kom Firin, Spencer, 2014: 58). This agrees with the evidence of large-scale, state-controlled industrial manufactures of metal objects, especially weapons, within larger settlements in the Nile Valley such as Pi-Ramesses and Thebes (Pusch, 1990 and 1994 and Prell, 2011).

Aside from at least a partial reliance on locally grown grain, the maintenance of herds of domesticated animals (cattle, caprines and pigs primarily) further suggests that stable conditions in the hinterland of the settlements were required for the survival of the inhabitants. The forts contain evidence for a partly autonomous economic system whose expression differs little from site to site, despite their geographical and architectural differences. Well-developed subsistence strategies – focused on the control of domesticated species with a smaller addition of 'safe' foraging, such as fishing, alongside local grain production – was the foundation of survival at most of the relevant settlements. Craft industries were reflections of major industries conducted at any population hub in the Nile Valley, such as Qantir, Memphis and Tell el-Amarna (Spencer, 2014: 33).

Conclusion

Living and Working at Zawiyet Umm el-Rakham

Zawiyet Umm el-Rakham was not a long-lived settlement. The occupants of the site abandoned it most likely less than fifty years after it was founded and, aside from some later temporary occupation by local pastoralists, the site lay largely forgotten and ignored for the better part of 3,200 years. The material found within it does not represent a time-capsule though, but an assemblage of archaeological artefacts which were either forgotten or deliberately abandoned by the last Egyptian occupants of the fortress, as well as that material which was not considered valuable enough to remove by later temporary residents. It is important to bear this fact in mind when considering the implications of the material: It is not a comprehensive sample of material as was present during the Egyptian occupation of the fort. Depositional processes, human agency – both ancient and modern – have no doubt reduced the original materials that were imported to, or produced at, the site during its brief history.

However, the material that remained to be excavated in Area K nevertheless provides a fascinating, if fragmentary, insight into the strategies employed by the Egyptian inhabitants of Zawiyet Umm el-Rakham in order to ensure their survival in what for them must have been a decidedly alien environment. Firstly, as discussed in Chapter 1 it is worth noting that the composition of the garrison is not known, and it is likely that both individuals who previously lived in the Nile Valley as well as other groups, such as individuals from the Sinai Peninsula and Canaan also made up part of the population of the site.

In addition, a great deal of the material either directly suggests, or strongly hints, at a well-developed coorperative relationship between the occupants of Zawiyet Umm el-Rakham and the semi-pastoralist nomads living for part of the year along the coast. It is possible that this relationship was built initially on subjugation and even on the continued threat of violence, but given the mobility of the local inhabitants, it is perhaps more likely that the relationship involved a degree of mutual benefit. Certainly, the agricultural industry conducted with implements found in Area K would most likely not have been possible without the help, both in terms of knowledge and labour, of local inhabitants. The complex and sophisticated methods needed in order to successfully grow crops based on a combination of rainfall and basin agriculture was almost certainly not something the Egyptian inhabitants of the area could have learned on their own.

Other industries evidenced within Area K similarly hint at an element of cooperation and trade between the occupants of the fortress and local groupings: It is possible that the production of linen was entirely for the consumption of the Egyptian inhabitants of Zawiyet Umm el-Rakham, but it seems more likely perhaps that some of the material was produced for bartering purposes. Similarly, the plethora of bone hairpins both imported and locally manufactured may also reflect the manufacture of an items which was primarily intended as trade goods, albeit most likely fairly low-value ones.

Among the most frustrating aspects of the research into the assemblage of archaeological material from Area K is the complete absence of any material that can definitively be said to evidence occupation of local pastoralists within the fort. As discussed in Section 1.2, part of the reason for this dearth is that very little material that can clearly be said to have been manufactured by the Late Bronze Age inhabitants of Marmarica has been found anywhere at all. It may also be that any locally produced non-Egyptian material was simply removed from the site by local inhabitants when the Egyptians left the area. This lack of evidence makes it impossible to state with certainty whether or not the Egyptians who built Zawiyet Umm el-Rakham and who most likely comprised the majority of its occupants not only worked and traded with local inhabitants of the area, but also lived with them inside the walls of the fort. Future excavations outside the walls of the fort may shed further light upon this fascinating question and help to further elucidate the details of the Egypto-Libyan relationship at the site.

In the present circumstances however, a number of threats militate against the continued preservation of Area K and Zawiyet Umm el-Rakham as a whole. New builds, hotels and holiday bungalows primarily, along the coast have claimed a lot of the area immediately around the site, as has agricultural expansion. In addition, the site has flooded several times in recent years due to strong winter rains.

As such, while the material from Area K may not be a time-capsule, it can nevertheless help us begin to understand what life was like for those men and women who lived, worked and – most likely – died in the rickety stone buildings, cramped alleyways and small communal spaces that made up Area K and which almost certainly stretched far further than the area that has so far been excavated, maybe even comprising the majority of the space within the walls of the fortress. These individuals and those few materials they left behind represent the on-the-ground expression of Egypt's foreign policy during the Ramesside Period, the real people behind the royal rhetoric and the triumphant depictions both in Egypt and at the site itself, such as the line of Libyan prisoners of war being drawn behind a chariot which are depicted on the fortress' gateway. Was that how the Egyptian inhabitants saw those pastoralists with whom they worked and traded? As vanquished enemies kept down by the threat of Egyptian retaliation. We will likely never know the answer to this question, but this investigation of material from Area K, not material belonging to the elite sphere, but to the ordinary occupants of the settlement, may suggest that a far more complex and multi-layered situation existed within this tiny community of Egyptians existing on the very margins of Egypt's sphere of influence, hundreds of kilometres from their homes towards the end of the Late Bronze Age.

Appendix

Catalogue of Area K Ceramic Vessels

I.1 Plates

The prevalent types of open vessel – plates, dishes and bowls – were categorised initially by mathematical formula (Aston 1998: 43–4; Holthoer, 1977 and Traunecker, 1981). The formula for sub-dividing open vessels was calculated by dividing the MBD (Maximum Body Diameter) by the height of the vessel (H) and multiplying by 100, giving a value denoted as VI. Aston (1998: 43) suggested that if VI is less than 125, the vessel is a beaker, if it is between 125 and 275, the vessel is a bowl, if it is between 275 and 500, the vessel is a dish and if it is above 500, the vessel is a plate. In many cases, the height could only be ascertained by reconstructing the vessel following the curve of the preserved rim portion and some uncertainty always exists in these cases, an uncertainty which was limited by the introduction of parallel vessels.

While not as common across New Kingdom sites as dishes and bowls, plates are nonetheless found at a series of New Kingdom sites, such as Qantir (Aston, 1998: no. 15–16, 116 and 2473), Memphis (Bourriau, 2010: Fig. 60/1.8.4), Saqqara (Bourriau et al., 2005: 24–5), Thebes (Dziobek, 1992: Pl. 68.11/15) and in Nubia (Williams, 1993: Fig. 129b; Budka, 2019: Pl. 8). At Area K group I.1 (including its sub-groups, see above) represent the third most common type of open vessel following I.2 Dishes and I.3 Bowls. The plates with direct rims (I.1.1) have where possible been divided into two categories according to the shape of their base (I.1.1a and I.1.1b).

I.1.1 Plates with direct rim

1 ZUR/K/16b K1,8
Nile B2 Diam. 23.0cm

2 ZUR/K/140k K1,4
Nile B2 Diam. 28.0cm

3 ZUR/K/344l K4,5
Nile B2 Diam. 41.0cm

4 ZUR/K/336m K1,2
Nile D Diam. 26.0cm

5 ZUR/K/134e K0,5
ZUR B Diam. 38.0cm

6 ZUR/K/116d K1,4
ZUR B Diam. 34.0cm

7 ZUR/K/16s K1,8
ZUR B 23.0cm

8 ZUR/K/345(1)e K5,6
ZUR B Diam. 24.0cm

9 ZUR/K/289p K0,8
ZUR C Diam. 16.0cm

10 ZUR/K/111b K0,7
ZUR C Diam. 40.0cm

11 ZUR/K/116f K1,4
Nile B2 Diam. 44.0cm

12 ZUR/K/345d K5,6
Nile B2 Diam. 25.0cm ht. 3.5cm

13 ZUR/K/108c K0,7
ZUR A Diam. 62.0cm ht. 6.1cm

14 ZUR/K/134c K0,5
ZUR A Diam. 34.0cm ht. 3.3cm

15 ZUR/K/289y K0,8
ZUR A Diam. 26.0cm ht. 3.2cm

16 ZUR/K/278a K0,8
ZUR C Diam. 20.0cm ht. 2.5cm

17 ZUR/K/278c K1,8
Nile D Diam. 38.0cm ht. 5.2cm

18 ZUR/K/215g K0,4
ZUR A Diam. 22.0cm ht. 4.2cm

19 ZUR/K/320i K4,0
ZUR A Diam. 23.0cm ht. 3.3cm

20 ZUR/K/320j K4,0
ZUR A Diam. 17.0cm ht. 3.1cm

21 ZUR/KE/31 KE
ZUR A Diam. 24.0cm ht. 3.7cm

22 ZUR/K/289u K0,8
ZUR B Diam. 22.0cm ht. 3.8cm

23 ZUR/K/215c K0,4
ZUR B Diam. 30.0cm ht. 2.2cm

24 ZUR/K/194f K1,4
ZUR B Diam. 34.0cm ht. 4.0cm

Appendix: Catalogue of Area K Ceramic Vessels 137

25 ZUR/K/336u K1,2
ZUR B Diam. 30.0cm ht. 2.5cm

26 ZUR/KB/39 KB
ZUR B Diam. 40.0cm ht. 3.2cm

I.1.1a Plates with direct rim and flat base

As Aston (1998: 148) notes, Type I.1.1a was not commonly found at the nineteenth-Dynasty site of Qantir, but was well-represented at the eighteenth-Dynasty site of Tell el-Amarna. Despite this rarity, the vessel types are nonetheless represented at contemporary sites in the Nile Valley, such as examples of Type I.1.1a found both in Memphis (Bourriau, 2010: Pl. 213, 1.1.1), Thebes (Dziobek, 1992: Pl. 68.11/18), Saqqara (Aston, 2011: Fig. VI.7, no. 63), Deir el-Medina (Nagel, 1938: Pl. IX.1164.54), Tell el-Borg (Hummel, 2014: Pl. 213/1.1.1) and in Nubia (Williams, 1993: Fig. 115.b–c).

27 ZUR/K/344m K4,5
ZUR B Diam. 13.0cm

29 ZUR/KAB/34 KAB
ZUR B Diam. 28.0cm ht. 4.2cm

28 ZUR/KA/30 KA
ZUR B Diam. 26.0cm ht. 5.1cm

I.1.1b Plates with direct rim and round base

This type of vessel is usually crudely manufactured on a wheel, and the walls are generally thick and occasionally asymmetrical. Parallels for this type are common within the corpus of Ramesside pottery both in Egypt – such as at Qantir (Aston, 1998: nos. 687–9 and 1108), Deir el-Medina (Nagel, 1938: Pl. VII, K.2.137), Thebes (Dziobek, 1992: Pl. 67.11/9), Memphis (Bourriau, 2010: Pl. 60, 1.2.4), Saqqara (Aston, 2012: Fig. VII.18, no. 107) – but also at Egyptian settlements in Nubia (cf. Williams, 1993: Fig. 101m) and the Levant (Gould, 2010: Fig. 2.1.10).

30 ZUR/K/16t K1,8
Nile D Diam. 23.0cm ht. 3.2cm

31 ZUR/KB/67 KB
ZUR B Diam. 40.0cm ht. 5.8cm

I.1.2 Plates with modelled rim

32 ZUR/K/49a K4,4
Nile B2 Diam. 44.0cm

33 ZUR/K/116m K1,4
Nile B2 Diam. 28.0cm

34 ZUR/K/289s K0,8
Nile B2 Diam. 22.0cm

35 ZUR/K/336p K1,2
Nile B2 Diam. 26.0cm

36 ZUR/K/339a K1,4
Nile B2 Diam. 26.0cm

37 ZUR/K/344i K4,6
Nile B2 Diam. 29.0cm

38 ZUR/K/346e K5,7
Nile D Diam. 47.0cm

39 ZUR/K/346g K5,7
Nile D Diam. 26.0cm

40 ZUR/K/215d K0,4
ZUR B Diam. 50.0cm

41 ZUR/KB/70 KB
ZUR B Diam. 32.0cm

42 ZUR/K/16j K1,8
ZUR B Diam. 19.0cm

43 ZUR/K/16k K1,8
ZUR B Diam. 23.0cm

44 ZUR/K/108j K0,7
ZUR B Diam. 26.0cm

45 ZUR/KB/20 KB
ZUR B Diam. 18.0cm

46 ZUR/K/336x K1,2
ZUR C Diam. 24.0cm

47 ZUR/K/336i K1,2
ZUR C Diam. 30.0cm ht. 4.3cm

48 ZUR/K/116k K1,4
Nile B2 Diam. 22.0cm ht. 4.1cm

49 ZUR/K/346b K5,7
Nile B2 Diam. 45.0cm ht. 5.8cm

50 ZUR/KE/17 KE
Nile B2 Diam. 60.0cm ht. 5.2cm

51 ZUR/K/346n K5,7
ZUR A Diam. 40.0cm ht. 6.2cm

52 ZUR/K/134b K0,5
ZUR A Diam. 32.0cm ht. 4.2cm

53 ZUR/K/16ad K1,8
ZUR A Diam. 31.0cm ht. 4.5cm

54 ZUR/K/215f K0,4
ZUR A Diam. 46.0cm ht. 7.1cm

55 ZUR/K/261a K1,5
ZUR B Diam. 36.0cm ht. 3.8cm

56 ZUR/K/16c K1,8
ZUR B Diam. 26.0cm ht. 1.8cm

57 ZUR/K/344k K4,5
ZUR B Diam. 27.0cm ht. 3.30cm

58 ZUR/K/263c K1,2
ZUR B Diam. 38.0cm ht. 4.5cm

59 ZUR/K/336o K1,2
ZUR B Diam. 40.0cm ht. 5.5cm

60 ZUR/K/289i K0,8
ZUR B Diam. 32.0cm ht.4.2cm

61 ZUR/K/346b K5,7
ZUR B Diam. 45.0cm ht. 6.3cm

62 ZUR/K/336v K1,2
ZUR C Diam. 28.0cm ht. 5.0cm

I.1.2a Plates with modelled rim and flat base

Type I.1.2a is generally rare at contemporary sites such as Qantir (Aston, 1998: 148), a rarity reflected in Area K. It is not however without parallels in Egypt despite its rarity (cf. Aston, 1998: nos. 722–7, 1166 and 2405, Bourriau, 2010: Fig. 60, 1.8.4 and Nagel, 1938: Pl. VI, 1142.8).

63 ZUR/K/345a K5,6
Nile B Diam. 24.0cm ht. 3.2cm

64 ZUR/K2H/25 K2H
Nile B2 Diam. 28.0cm ht. 4.5cm

65 ZUR/K2H/35 K2H
Nile B2 Diam. 30.0cm ht. 4.5cm

66 ZUR/KX/4 KX
Nile B2 Diam. 32.0cm ht. 4.5cm

67 ZUR/K/108d K0,7
Nile D Diam. 26.0cm ht. 3.2cm

68 ZUR/K/119a K1,4
ZUR B Diam. 27.0cm ht. 4.5cm

69 ZUR/KE/27 KE
ZUR B Diam. 22.0cm ht. 3.4cm

I.1.2b Plates with modelled rim and round base

Plates with modelled rim and round bases (see also Martin, 2008: 249 for a discussion of the prevalence of plates, dishes and bowls with round bases over flat bases during the Ramesside period) have been found at Qantir (Aston, 1998: no. 368) and at most New Kingdom sites in Egypt – such as Gurob (Petrie, 1890: pl xx.4, Brunton and Engelbach, 1927: Pl. xxxiii.2), Deir el-Medina (Nagel, 1938: Pl.VII, 1176.14, 1922.94 and 1176.12), Memphis (Bourriau, 2010: Fig. 60, 1.8.5) and Saqqara (Aston, 1991: Pl. 47.3–6).

70 ZUR/K/294f K0,6
Nile D Diam. 38.0cm ht. 4.6cm

71 ZUR/KZ/16a KZ
ZUR B Diam. 38.0cm ht. 5.5cm

I.2 Dishes

I.2.1 Dishes with direct rims

Along with plates and bowls, dishes of various designs are a main-stay of all Ramesside sites. Various forms of dishes were found both broken and complete during the excavations of Area K. The type falls easily into the predetermined typology for plates and bowls although with a minor addendum, I.2.3 ledge-rim dishes.

72 ZUR/K/339b K1,4
Nile B2 Diam. 22.0cm

73 ZUR/K/345e K5,6
Nile B2 Diam. 26.0cm

74 ZUR/K2H/36 K2H
Nile B2 Diam. 20.0cm

75 ZUR/K/336h K1,2
Nile B2 Diam. 26.0cm

76 ZUR/K/61b K0,7
Nile B2 Diam. 16.0cm ht. 5.0cm

77 ZUR/K/345f K5,6
Nile B2 Diam. 25.0cm ht. 6.6cm

78 ZUR/K/346o K5,7
Nile B2 Diam. 26.0cm ht. 7.6cm

79 ZUR/K/364a K4,6
Nile B2 Diam. 26.0cm ht. 7.5cm

80 ZUR/K/16f K1,8
Nile B2 Diam. 35.0cm ht. 7.0cm

81 ZUR/K/16ac K1,8
Nile B2 Diam. 28.0cm ht.7.5cm

82 ZUR/K/336q K1,2
Nile D Diam. 36.0cm

83 ZUR/K/16u K1,8
Nile D Diam. 39.0cm

84 ZUR/K/108i K0,7
Nile D Diam. 20.0cm

85 ZUR/K/261b K1,5
Nile D Diam. 42.0cm

86 ZUR/K/336f K1,2
Nile D Diam. 28.0cm

87 ZUR/K/278b K1,8
Nile D Diam. 22.0cm

88 ZUR/K/278e K1,8
Nile D Diam. 24.0cm

89 ZUR/K/289b K0,8
Nile D Diam. 26.0cm

90 ZUR/K/336n K1,2
Nile D Diam. 26.0cm

91 ZUR/K/16r K1,8
Nile D Diam. 24.0cm

92 ZUR/K/16aa K1,8
Nile D Diam. 28.0cm

93 ZUR/K/16ae K1,8
Nile D Diam. 19.0cm

94 ZUR/K/140d K1,4
Nile D Diam. 12.0cm

95 ZUR/K/140u K1,5
Nile D Diam. 22.0cm

96 ZUR/K/346a K5,7
Nile D Diam. 23.0cm

97 ZUR/K/320c K4,0
ZUR A Diam. 21.0cm

98 ZUR/KV/10 KV
ZUR A Diam. 28.0cm ht. 5.6cm

99 ZUR/KZ/25 KZ
ZUR A Diam. 26.0cm ht. 9.0cm

100 ZUR/K/16m K1,8
ZUR A Diam. 25.0cm ht. 5.1cm

101 ZUR/K2H/20 K2H
ZUR A Diam. 24.0cm ht. 7.8cm

102 ZUR/K/111c K0,7
ZUR B Diam. 16.0cm

103 ZUR/K/140o K1,4
ZUR B Diam. 20.0cm

104 ZUR/K/183a K2,8
ZUR B Diam. 28.0cm

105 ZUR/K/194e K1,4
ZUR B Diam. 42.0cm

106 ZUR/K/215h K0,4
ZUR B Diam. 20.0cm

107 ZUR/K/215j K0,4
ZUR B Diam. 26.0cm

108 ZUR/K/215k K0,4
ZUR B Diam. 29.0cm

109 ZUR/K/336y K1,2
ZUR B Diam. 30.0cm

110 ZUR/K/346s K5,7
ZUR B Diam. 26.0cm

111 ZUR/K/320h K4,0
ZUR B Diam. 23.0cm

112 ZUR/K/320f K4,0
ZUR B Diam. 25.0cm

113 ZUR/K/215e K0,4
ZUR B Diam. 30.0cm

114 ZUR/K/140q K1,4
ZUR B Diam. 20.0cm

115 ZUR/K/320e K4,0
ZUR B Diam. 29.0cm

116 ZUR/K/320l K4,0
ZUR B Diam. 19.0cm

117 ZUR/K/335g K1,2
ZUR B Diam. 36.0cm

118 ZUR/K/16x K1,8
ZUR B Diam. 22.0cm ht. 5.8cm

119 ZUR/K/168c K3,4
ZUR B Diam. 16.0cm ht. 4.6cm

120 ZUR/K/111a K0,7
ZUR B Diam. 16.0cm ht. 4.4cm

121 ZUR/K2H/38 K2H
ZUR B Diam. 24.0cm ht. 6.8cm

122 ZUR/K/289e K0,8
ZUR C Diam. 20.0cm

124 ZUR/K/336l K1,2
ZUR C Diam. 20.0cm

123 ZUR/K/346q K5,7
ZUR C Diam. 24.0cm

I.2.1a Dishes with direct rims and flat bases

Type I.2.1a, dishes with direct rims and flat bases are widely attested in the published corpus from Ramesside settlement sites (Qantir, Aston, 1998: nos. 421–6 and 783–90, Memphis, Bourriau, 2010: Fig. 60, 3.2.1 and Deir el-Medina: Nagel, 1938: Pl. IX, 1927.86) as well as cemeteries (Saqqara, Bourriau et al., 2005: 35–6 as well as Aston, 2012: Fig. VII.13, no. 69–70 and Thebes, Dziobek, 1992: Pl. 67, 11/10) in Egypt and also from foreign territory under Egyptian influence, such as Nubia (Holthoer, 1977: Pl. 25, Type IR/0/f-g and Williams, 1993: Fig. 116e).

125 ZUR/KB/66 KB
Nile B2 Diam. 20.0cm ht. 5.4cm

128 ZUR/KI/3 KI
ZUR B Diam. 32.0cm ht. 6.8cm

126 ZUR/KI/16 KI
Nile B2 Diam. 22.5cm ht. 5.8cm

129 ZUR/K/134d K3,6
Nile B2 Diam. 28.0cm ht. 5.8cm

127 ZUR/K/194h K1,4
Nile B2 Diam. 46.0cm ht. 9.5cm

I.2.1b Dishes with direct rims and round bases

Type I.2.1b is even more commonly associated with Ramesside remains at sites such as Qantir (Aston, 1998: nos. 334-342), Memphis (Bourriau, 2010: Fig. 60, 3.1.8), Deir el-Medina (Nagel, 1938: Pl. I, type II), Gurob (Brunton and Engelbach, 1927: Pl. xxxiii.7), Saqqara (Bourriau and Aston, 1985: Pl. 35.1–2, Bourriau et al., 2005: Fig. 21:10b and Aston, 2011: Fig. VI.23, no. 182) and various locations in Nubia (Holthoer, 1977: Pl. 25, type IR/0/d-e and Williams, 1993: fig. 105f) and Canaan (cf. Deir el-Balah, Gould, 2010: Fig. 2.1.1).

144 *Subsistence Strategies at Zawiyet Umm el-Rakham*

130 ZUR/KE/16 KE
Nile B2 Diam. 16.0cm ht. 5.4cm

131 ZUR/KAB/43 KAB
Nile D Diam. 24.0cm ht. 6.8cm

132 ZUR/KZ/38 KZ
Nile D Diam. 16.0cm ht. 4.8cm

133 ZUR/K/108l K0,7
ZUR A Diam. 24.0cm ht. 7.1cm

134 ZUR/K/119b K1,4
ZUR A Diam. 37.0cm ht. 9.6cm

135 ZUR/K/108e K0,7
ZUR A Diam. 22.0cm ht. 6.2cm

136 ZUR/K2H/24 K2H
ZUR B Diam. 26.0cm ht. 9.1cm

137 ZUR/K2H/32 K2H
ZUR B Diam. 14.0cm ht. 3.8cm

138 ZUR/KZ/15 KZ
ZUR B Diam. 74.0cm ht. 15.0cm

139 ZUR/K/108n K0,7
ZUR B Diam. 24.0cm ht. 8.0cm

140 ZUR/K/116g K0,7
ZUR B Diam. 13.0cm ht. 4.0cm

141 ZUR/KZ/38 KZ
ZUR B Diam. 16.0cm ht. 4.8cm

142 ZUR/K2H/22 K2H
ZUR B Diam. 16.0cm ht. 3.5cm

143 ZUR/K2H/29 K2H
ZUR B Diam. 16.0cm ht. 5.2cm

144 ZUR/K/294e K0,6
ZUR B Diam. 26.0cm ht. 7.6cm

I.2.2 Dishes with modelled rims

145 ZUR/K/289a K0,8
Nile B2 Diam. 34.0cm

146 ZUR/K/322d K1,2
Nile D Diam. 44.0cm

147 ZUR/K/108f K0,7
Nile D Diam. 30.0cm

148 ZUR/K/346p K5,7
Nile D Diam. 38.0cm

149 ZUR/K2H/18 K2H
Nile D Diam. 30.0cm

150 ZUR/KE/13 KE
ZUR B Diam. 28.0cm

151 ZUR/K/183c K3,5
Nile B2 Diam. 26.0cm ht. 7.0cm

152 ZUR/K/16ab K0,7
Nile B2 Diam. 47.0cm ht. 13.0cm

I.2.2a Dishes with modelled rims and flat bases

Only a single example of this kind of vessel – similar to those found at Qantir (Aston,1998: 408–15) and Deir el-Medina (Nagel, 1938: Pl. X, 1169.129) – was found within Area K.

153 ZUR/K2A/19 K2A
ZUR B Diam. 34.0cm ht. 9.4cm

I.2.2b Dishes with modelled rims and round bases

Type I.2.2b, dishes with modelled rims and round bases were common at the site, the modelled rim found in two distinct incarnations: the more traditional out-turned modelling achieved when the potter pulls the rim of the vessel downwards before removing it from the wheel (paralleled both at Qantier, Aston, 1998: nos. 367–84, Deir el-Medina, Nagel, 1938: Pl. viii, type X, Saqqara, Aston, 2012: Fig. VII.15) and Deir el-Balah, Gould, 2010: Fig. 2.1.4) and the more atypical 'flanged' modelling achieved by pressing the rim into a more angular shape (defined by Aston, 1998: nos. 416–19, but also found at Tell el-Amarna, Peet and Woolley, 1923: Pl. xlvi, IV/7, and Deir el-Medina, Nagel, Pl. viii, type XI).

154 ZUR/K/339c K1,4
Nile B2 Diam. 29.0cm ht. 8.0cm

155 ZUR/KM/2 KM
Nile B2 Diam. 17.5cm ht. 6.0cm

I.2.3 Ledge-rim dishes

The final type of dish-shape is the ledge-rim dish, so named for the characteristic ledge which has been added underneath the vessel's lip, and which most likely served a pragmatic purpose, easing the lifting of the vessel. This particular type of vessel is commonly found at Qantir in a number of incarnations, especially the angle of the lip above the ledge is prone to variety (Aston, 1998: nos. 832–6) but it is also attested at other contemporary sites, such as Memphis (Bourriau, 2010: Figs 68, 3.10.8).

156 ZUR/K/168a K3,4
Nile B Diam. 38.0cm

159 ZUR/K/345g K5,7
ZUR A Diam. 49.0cm

157 ZUR/KV/6 KV
Nile B2 Diam. 58.0cm

160 ZUR/K/134a K0,5
Zur A Diam. 62.0cm

158 ZUR/K2H/17 K2H
Nile D Diam. 32.0cm

I.3 Bowls

I.3.1 Bowls with direct rim

Bowls represent the most varied sub-type of the open forms in the Area K corpus, even though they are less numerically prevalent than dishes. The most commonly identified type of diagnostic within this category were bowls with direct rims which could not, because of their state of preservation, be further subdivided into either type I.1.3.1a or type I.1.3.1b.

161 ZUR/K/140c K1,4
Nile B1 Diam. 20.0cm

163 ZUR/K2H/28 K2H
Nile B2 Diam. 24.0cm

162 ZUR/KZ/28 KZ
Nile B1 Diam. 12.0cm ht. 5.0cm

164 ZUR/K/61a K0,7
Nile B2 Diam. 20.0cm

165 ZUR/K/140x K1,4
Nile B2 Diam. 30.0cm

166 ZUR/K/289h K0,8
Nile B2 Diam. 30.0cm

167 ZUR/K/116h K1,4
Nile B2 Diam. 26.0cm

168 ZUR/K/346u K5,7
Nile B2 Diam. 24.0cm

169 ZUR/K/16n K1,8
Nile B2 Diam. 22.0cm

170 ZUR/K/108g K0,7
Nile B2 Diam. 22.0cm

171 ZUR/K/140p K1,4
Nile B2 Diam. 24.0cm

172 ZUR/K/261c K1,5
Nile B2 Diam. 28.0cm

173 ZUR/K/289g K0,8
Nile B2 Diam. 24.0cm

174 ZUR/K/336e K1,2
Nile B2 Diam. 14.0cm

175 ZUR/K/346t K5,7
Nile B2 Diam. 28.0cm

176 ZUR/K/108k K0,7
Nile B2 Diam. 28.0cm ht. 9.2cm

177 ZUR/K/140i K1,4
Nile B2 Diam. 22.0cm ht. 6.0cm

178 ZUR/K/320k K4,0
Nile B2 Diam. 22.0cm ht. 6.5cm

179 ZUR/KE/15 KE
Nile B2 Diam. 20.0cm ht. 8.2cm

180 ZUR/K/336c K1,2
Nile B2 Diam. 26.0cm ht. 11.0cm

181 ZUR/KE/34 KE
Nile D Diam. 20.0cm ht. 9.5cm

182 ZUR/K/346v K5,7
Nile D Diam. 22.0cm ht. 8.1cm

183 ZUR/K/345(1)f K5,6
Nile D Diam. 18.0cm

184 ZUR/K/346f K5,7
Nile D Diam. 20.0cm

185 ZUR/K/346r K5,7
Nile D Diam. 22.0cm

186 ZUR/K/140ag K1,4
Nile D Diam. 20.0cm

187 ZUR/K/289n K0,8
Nile D Diam. 26.0cm

188 ZUR/KAB/42 KAB
ZUR A Diam. 16.0cm

189 ZUR/K/344g K4,5
ZUR A Diam. 20.0cm

190 ZUR/K/140a K1,4
ZUR A Diam. 34.0cm

191 ZUR/K/140f K1,4
ZUR A Diam. 32.0cm

192 ZUR/K/140ae K1,4
ZUR A Diam. 18.0cm ht. 7.9cm

193 ZUR/K/16i K1,8
ZUR B Diam. 14.0cm

194 ZUR/K/116c K1,4
ZUR B Diam. 20.0cm

195 ZUR/K/278f K1,8
ZUR B Diam. 20.0cm

196 ZUR/K/108h K0,7
ZUR B Diam. 20.0cm

197 ZUR/K/344h K4,5
ZUR B Diam. 9.0cm

198 ZUR/K/346x K5,7
ZUR B Diam. 14.0cm

199 ZUR/K/108o K0,7
ZUR B Diam. 32.0cm

200 ZUR/K/ 320g K4,0
ZUR B Diam. 20.0cm

201 ZUR/K/346c K5,7
ZUR B Diam. 30.0cm

202 ZUR/K/140g K1,4
ZUR C Diam. 20.0cm

203 ZUR/K/140j K1,4
ZUR C Diam. 16.0cm

204 ZUR/K/289j K0,8
ZUR C Diam. 22.0cm

205 ZUR/KE/30 KE
ZUR C Diam. 22.0cm

206 ZUR/K/346c K5,7
ZUR C Diam. 30.0cm ht. 10.0cm

I.3.1a Bowls with direct rims and flat bases

While represented by only a single mostly preserved vessels with the corpus of pottery from Area K, bowls and dishes with direct rims and flat bases are nevertheless known from several New Kingdom contexts, including Nubian contexts from the early eighteenth Dynasty (Holthoer, 1977: Pl. 25) as well as examples from Qantir-Piramesses (Aston, 1998: no. 268) and Saqqara (Bourriau et al., 2005: Fig. 16).

207 ZUR/KAB/63 KAB
Nile D Diam. 26.0cm

I.3.1b Bowls with direct rims and round bases

This type encompasses smaller bowls with direct rims and round bases. These vessels, described as drinking cups or goblets by Holthoer (1977: Pl. 26, type GO1 – IR/0/c-d), are represented across a wide array of contemporary Ramesside sites, such as Qantir (Aston, 1998: nos. 448–51), Saqqara (Bourriau and Aston, 1985: Pl. 35.17), Deir el-Medina (Nagel, 1938: Pl. ii, Type IV), Deir el-Balah (Gould, 2010: Fig. 2.1.2) and Memphis (Bourriau, 2010: Fig. 62, 4.1.5).

208 ZUR/K2A/23 K2A
ZUR B Diam. 12.0cm ht. 5.2cm

210 ZUR/KKI/4 KKI
ZUR C Diam . 14.0cm ht. 5.2cm

209 ZUR/K/61c K0,7
ZUR B Diam. 14.0cm ht. 6.0cm

I.3.2 Bowl with modelled rims

No bowls with modelled rims (I.3.2) were found in a sufficient state of completeness to reconstruct their bases, so these have not been subdivided further. The closest parallels to similar bowls with modelled rims come from the contemporary settlement site of Kom Firin (no. C714, Smoláriková, 2014: 125).

211 ZUR/K/215i K0,4
Nile B2 Diam. 42.0cm

213 ZUR/K2A/27 K2A
Nile B2 Diam. 52.0cm

212 ZUR/K/344e K4,6
Nile B2 Diam. 47.0cm

214 ZUR/KE/33 KE
Nile D Diam. 24.0cm

215 ZUR/KB/76 KB
ZUR B Diam. 26.0cm

217 ZUR/K/336d K1,2
ZUR B Diam. 24.0cm hat. 9.0cm

216 ZUR/K/289x K0,8
ZUR B Diam. 32.0cm

I.3.3 Bowls with rolled rims

Type I.3.3, bowls with the characteristic 'rolled' rims, created by the potter outwardly rolling the edge of the vessel prior to firing is also found in the Area K corpus in significant quantities (seventeen diagnostics of this type), although the particular shape is poorly represented in the published corpus, possibly due to the lack of section-drawings of vessels in earlier publications making it difficult to distinguish between vessels with modelled and rolled rims. However, parallels for the Area K vessels of this form have been found at Kom Firin (no. C801, Smoláriková, 2014: 126).

218 ZUR/KAB/46 KAB
Nile B2 Diam. 22.0cm

223 ZUR/K/346y K5,7
Nile B2 Diam. 44.0cm

219 ZUR/KAB/53 KAB
Nile B2 Diam. 58.0cm

224 ZUR/K/262 K1,2
Nile B2 Diam. 54.0cm

220 ZUR/KZ/19 KZ
Nile B2 Diam. 26.0cm

225 ZUR/K2A/17 K2A
Nile D Diam. 28.0cm

221 ZUR/KZ/31 KZ
Nile B2 Diam. 26.0cm

226 ZUR/K/344a K4,5
Nile D Diam. 35.0cm

222 ZUR/K/346d K5,7
Nile B2 Diam. 28.0cm

227 ZUR/K/346d K5,7
Nile D Diam. 28.0cm

228 ZUR/KAB/46 KAB
ZUR B Diam. 22.0cm

229 ZUR/KB/44 KB
ZUR B Diam. 24.0cm

230 ZUR/KE/35 KE
ZUR B Diam. 30.0cm

231 ZUR/KAB/45 KAB
ZUR C Diam. 20.0cm

232 ZUR/K2H/14 K2H
Nile C Diam. 62.0cm

233 ZUR/K/140z K1,4
Nile C Diam. 65.0cm

I.3.4a Carinated bowls

Type I.3.4a carinated bowls with direct rims are also commonly found at New Kingdom contexts, such as Qantir (Aston, 1998: nos. 457 and 851–2), Tell el-Borg (Hummel, 2014: Pl. 7.4), Saqqara (Aston, 2012: Fig. VII.24, nos. 150–2) and Memphis (Bourriau, 2010: Fig. 62, 4.5.2).

234 ZUR/K2A/20 K2A
Nile B2 Diam. 24.0cm

235 ZUR/K2A/2 K2A
ZUR B Diam 15.5cm ht. 8.5cm

236 ZUR/KZ/24 KZ
ZUR C Diam. 20.0cm ht. 7.5cm

I.3.4b Carinated basins with modelled rims

While relatively rare, type I.3.4b carinated basins with modelled rims are paralleled by contemporary material from Gurob (GU07/F18A/142/P, Valentina Gasperini, pers. comm).

237 ZUR/K/345b K5,6
Nile C Diam. 45.0cm

I.3.4c Carinated basins with decorative lugs

Type I.3.4c, a carinated basin with a series of decorative lugs around the rim, were only evidenced by two diagnostic sherds from Area K. Possible parallel vessels were also found at Qantir (Aston, 1998: no. 2144) and Memphis (Bourriau, 2010: Pl. 68/4.11.18).

238 ZUR/KD/15 KD
Nile D Diam. 52.0cm

239 ZUR/KD/19 KD
Nile D Diam. 60.0cm

I.4 Spinning bowls

Ceramic spinning bowls are well-represented at Area K (see Section 4.4). A 'spinning bowl' – a somewhat broad term in common usage – has been defined as any open vessel which has a series of loops attached to the interior floor of the vessel regardless of whether the vessel is mathematically to be considered a plate, dish or bowl. The six ceramic examples found are made respectively of Nile B2 (3), Nile D (1) and ZUR B (2). All examples – both the single complete example (ZUR/K(2014)/1) and the various fragments of vessel bases showing either complete loops or evidence of broken loops in the form of scars in the ceramics – were double-looped (similar to those found at Tell el-Amarna, Kemp and Vogelsang-Eastwood, 2001: 291–306, see also Rose, 2007: Figs 148–9). Aside from Tell el-Amarna, this particular type of vessel is found at other contemporary settlement sites both in Egypt (such as Deir el-Medina, Nagel, 1938: Pl. XI: Type XVI and Kom Firin, no. C815, Smoláriková, 2014: 133) as well as Canaan (Gould, 2010: 42–5, Figs 2.1–10), an understandable spread considering the prevalence of linen manufacture and the value of linen garments during the Ramesside period (Pap. Cairo 65739, see Gardiner, 1935).

240 ZUR/KAB/57 KAB
Nile B2 Diam. 14.0cm (est.)

242 ZUR/K2H/15 K2H
Nile B2 Diam. 17.0cm (est.)

241 ZUR/K2A/29 K2A
Nile B2 Diam. 40.0cm

243 ZUR/K/232 K5,7
Nile D Diam. 12.0cm (est.)

244 ZUR/K/107 K0,7
ZUR B Diam. 10.0cm (est.)

245 ZUR/2014(K)/1 None given
ZUR B Diam. 27.8cm ht. 8.5cm

I.5 Snake-head bowls

Crudely manufactured ceramic cobra figurines are commonly found at New Kingdom settlement sites, such as Kom Rabi'a (Giddy, 1999: 13–28), Tell el-Amarna (Peet and Woolley, 1923: Pl. xxiii), Beth Shan (James and McGovern, 1993: Pl. 83–5), Kom Firin (Spencer, 2014: 145) and Qantir (Aston, 1998: nos. 1423–8). Commonly associated with bowls or household shrines, the purpose of these figurines were most likely protection of the owner and/or household by 'sympathetic magic' (Giddy, 1999: 18–19) and their crude manufacture also testifies to their place within the magico-mythical beliefs of the populace as a whole. Although no such cobra heads were found in Area K, the complete profile of a snake-head bowl (ZUR/KKI/10) made from local fabric (ZUR B) was recovered. The shape of the vessel is identical to an example found at the New Kingdom site of Kamid el-Loz in Canaan (Echt, 1982: 37, Pl. 12.2).

246 ZUR/KKI/10 KKI
ZUR B Diam. 14.0cm ht. 6.9cm

I.6 Beakers

I.6.1 Beakers

Two types of vessels most likely to be considered as beakers have been identified in the Area K corpus. The first, I.6.1 is a typical round-based cup-like vessel with a restricted incurving direct rim defined as a 'wine goblet' by Holthoer (1977: Pl. 68.2) with parallels also found at Tell el-Amarna (Rose, 2007: Fig. 306). A similar vessel though with a slightly modelled rim was also found at the contemporary site of Qantir (Aston, 1998: no. 275).

247 ZUR/K/140m K1,4
Nile D Diam. 12.0cm

249 ZUR/K/2 Surface
ZUR C Diam. 5.0cm ht. 8.0cm

248 ZUR/K/147 K3,6
ZUR A Diam. 6.0cm ht. 9.8cm

I.6.2 Beaker with notched rim

The second type of beaker (I.6.2) is distinguishable primarily by the internal grove or 'notch' along the rim which facilitates the securing of a lid, with parallels from Qantir (Aston, 1998: nos. 160–3), Tell el-Amarna (Hope, 1991: Fig. 3c) and Gurob (Brunton and Engelbach, 1927: Pl. xxxvii.67E). As with type I.3.3 the vessel may be underrepresented in much of the early literature due to the lack of section drawings in many of these publications.

250 ZUR/K2H/26 K2H
Nile D Diam. 28.0cm

I.7 Bread-plates

The colloquial term for this vessel type – which designates a flat hand-moulded 'platter' with a distinctive carination under the rim – was coined due to the similarity between this vessel type and modern *dokkas*, a type of platter commonly used in Egypt in the baking of 'eish shams (Aston, 1998: no. 134, see also a recent discussion of this vessel type by Marchand, 2017 as well as examples from Sai Island, Budka, 2019: Fig. 7). The vessel – unlike the majority of the Ramesside ceramic corpus – is entirely hand-moulded by the pressing of a lump of clay into a rough circle on a flat surface and the addition of rims by coiling (Aston, 1998: no. 134). Commonly found across Ramesside settlement sites such as Qantir (Aston, 1998: nos. 279–82), Memphis (Bourriau, 2010: Fig. 68, 17.1.9), Tell el-Amarna (Peet and Woolley, 1923, Pl. xlvi) and Deir el-Medina (Nagel, 1938: Pl. I, Type I), the very small amount of such vessels found at Zawiyet Umm el-Rakham (only a single diagnostic sherd of this type) is peculiar and may suggest that other types of vessels, such as dishes or plates were utilised in the baking process in lieu of the bread plates. The only example of this vessel was manufactured from Nile silt (Nile B2) and is therefore not locally produced.

251 ZUR/KN/53 KN
Nile B2 Diam. 18.0cm ht. 5.5cm

II.1 Globular jars

II.1.1 Globular jars with modelled rim

Jars with globular bodies and modelled rims (II.1.1) are among the most prevalent closed vessels found in in Area K and are also common at contemporary sites in Egypt (Bourriau, 2010: Pl. 67/11.15.13; Holthoer, 1977: Pl. 35 Type VP/0/f–g; Laemmel, 2008: Pl. 2:2 and 2:3 and Nagel, 1938: Pl. 81.4). They bear some resemblance to the colloquially named 'meat jars' fabricated in Marl D (Aston, 1998: no. 478 and Laemmel, 2008: Pl. 2:4). 66.13 per cent of the globular jars from Area K are made from Nile silt imported from Egypt (predominately Nile D at 33.87 per cent), with the remainder being locally produced, most commonly (25.81 per cent) with ZUR B fabric.

252 ZUR/K/108a K0,7
Nile B2 Diam. 28.0cm

253 ZUR/K/116a K1,4
Nile B2 Diam. 20.0cm

254 ZUR/K/289c K0,8
Nile B2 Diam. 26.0cm

255 ZUR/K/289l K0,8
Nile B2 Diam. 27.0cm

256 ZUR/K2H/33 K2H
Nile B2 Diam. 12.0cm

257 ZUR/K2H/34 K2H
Nile B2 Diam. 18.0cm

258 ZUR/K/263a K1,2
Nile B2 Diam. 30.0cm

259 ZUR/KAB/38 KAB
Nile B2 Diam. 18.0cm

260 ZUR/K2H/39 K2H
Nile B2 Diam. 28.0cm

261 ZUR/K/140b K1,4
Nile B2 Diam. 30.0cm

262 ZUR/K/140af K1,4
Nile B2 Diam. 24.0cm

263 ZUR/K/278g K1,8
Nile B2 Diam. 22.0cm

264 ZUR/K/336s K1,2
Nile B2 Diam. 20.0cm

265 ZUR/K/345(1)b K5,6
Nile B2 Diam. 18.0cm

266 ZUR/K/364b K4,6
Nile B2 Diam. 20.0cm

267 ZUR/KB/36 KB
Nile B2 Diam. 24.0cm

268 ZUR/KE/6 KE
Nile B2 Diam. 20.0cm

269 ZUR/KZ/17 KZ
Nile B2 Diam. 26.0cm

270 ZUR/K2A/9 K2A
Nile B2 Diam. 12.0cm

271 ZUR/K2A/28 K2A
Nile B2 Diam. 12.0cm

272 ZUR/K/345h K5,6
Nile D Diam. 18.0cm

273 ZUR/K/116b K1,4
Nile D Diam. 22.0cm

274 ZUR/K/294b K0,6
Nile D Diam. 11.0cm

275 ZUR/K/294d K0,6
Nile D Diam. 20.0cm

276 ZUR/KE/20 KE
Nile D Diam. 24.0cm

277 ZUR/KZ/18 KZ
Nile D Diam. 13.0cm

278 ZUR/KZ/26 KZ
Nile D Diam. 18.0cm

279 ZUR/KZ/37 KZ
Nile D Diam. 18.0cm

280 ZUR/K2A/22 K2A
Nile D Diam. 30.0cm

281 ZUR/KZ/34 KZ
Nile D Diam. 12.0cm

282 ZUR/K2H/30 K2H
Nile D Diam. 14.0cm

283 ZUR/K/140ab K1,4
Nile D Diam. 24.0cm

284 ZUR/K/203 K1,4
Nile D Diam. 17.0cm

285 ZUR/K/322a K1,2
Nile D Diam. 28.0cm

286 ZUR/K/346a K5,7
Nile D Diam. 20.0cm

287 ZUR/KAB/38 KAB
Nile D Diam. 18.0cm

288 ZUR/KB/19 KB
Nile D Diam. 26.0cm

289 ZUR/KI/14 KI
Nile D Diam. 24.0cm

290 ZUR/KS/2 KS
Nile D Diam. 12.0cm

291 ZUR/KZ/22 KZ
Nile D Diam. 20.0cm

292 ZUR/K/345(1)c K5,6
ZUR A Diam. 32.0cm

293 ZUR/KB/22 KB
ZUR A Diam. 28.0cm

294 ZUR/KB/25 KB
ZUR Diam. 16.0cm

295 ZUR/KB/27 KB
ZUR A Diam. 32.0cm

296 ZUR/KB/78 KB
ZUR A Diam. 20.0cm

297 ZUR/KE/32 KE
ZUR B Diam. 16.0cm

298 ZUR/KS/2 KS
ZUR B Diam. 14.0cm

299 ZUR/K2A/18 K2A
ZUR B Diam. 10.0cm

300 ZUR/K/16e K1,8
ZUR B Diam. 45.0cm

301 ZUR/K/117 K1,4
ZUR B Diam. 18.0cm

302 ZUR/K/183b K3,5
ZUR B Diam. 17.0cm

303 ZUR/K//320a K4,0
ZUR B Diam. 22.0cm

304 ZUR/K/320d K4,0
ZUR B Diam. 23.0cm

305 ZUR/K/344j K4,5
ZUR B Diam. 16.0cm

306 ZUR/K/345(1)d K5,6
ZUR B Diam. 20.0cm

307 ZUR/2014(K)/7 None given
ZUR B Diam. 26.0cm

308 ZUR/KB/16 KB
ZUR B Diam. 40.0cm

309 ZUR/KB/73 KB
ZUR B Diam. 24.0cm

310 ZUR/KE/19 KE
ZUR B Diam. 28.0cm

311 ZUR/K2A/26 K2A
ZUR B Diam. 22.0cm

II.1.2 Globular jar with vertical handles

The less common types of globular jars are: Type II.1.2, a globular jar with two vertical handles, and similar to examples found at Tell el-Amarna (Rose, 2007: Fig. 495).

312 ZUR/KAB/41 KAB
ZUR A Diam. 14.0cm

313 ZUR/K2A/4 K2A
Nile D Diam. 16.0cm

II.1.3 Globular jar with round base and horizontal handles

Type II.1.3 is a globular jar with a round base and two horizontal handles, similar to a type found at Qantir (Aston, 1998: no. 512) and Tell el-Amarna (Rose, 2007: Figs 620–1).

314 ZUR/K/88 K0,7
Nile D Diam. 10.0cm ht. 25.0cm

315 ZUR/2014(K)/3 None given
Marl D Diam. 13.0cm ht. 15.0cm

II.1.4 Globular jar with flaring mouth and pointed base

Type II.1.4 has a flaring mouth and pointed base and is similarly attested at Tell el-Amarna (Rose, 2007: Fig. 484), Saqqara (Aston, 2012: Fig. VII.38) and Qantir (Laemmel, 2008: Fig. 4:5).

316 ZUR/K/140ac K1,4
ZUR Diam. 10.0cm

317 ZUR/K/165 K1,4
ZUR B Diam. 6.0cm ht. 10.7cm

II.1.5 Globular jar with flat base

Type II.1.5, a small globular jar with a flat base, is rarely found at Zawiyet Umm el-Rakham and only a single mostly preserved vessel is recorded from Area K. It is paralleled at the contemporary site of Qantir (Aston, 1998: no. 1971).

318 ZUR/K/6 K1,8
Marl D Diam. 8.0cm

II.2 Funnel-neck jars

Funnel-neck jars are also among the most common closed vessel types found in Area K and at Zawiyet Umm el-Rakham as a whole, representing 14.63 per cent of all diagnostic sherds and whole vessels recorded from Area K. As discussed by Aston (1998: 188), this storage jar with an ovoid body, round base and flaring or divergent neck is exceedingly common across all eighteenth- and nineteenth-Dynasty sites (after which the vessel shape becomes less prevalent, Aston, 1998: 188) both in Egypt at sites such as Qantir (Aston, 1998: nos. 549–76), Saqqara (Bourriau and Aston, 1985: Pl. 36.61–2 and Bourriau et al., 2005: Fig. 7.44, see also recent discoveries published by Aston, 2020: 256 of funnel-necked jars from the tombs of Ptahemwia and Sethnakht and associated with ritual breaking as well as Aston, 2011: Figs VI.21–VI.22 and Aston, 2012: Fig. VII.33), Gurob (Petrie, 1890: Pl. xx.II), Deir el-Medina (Nagel, 1938: 82.10) and Memphis (Bourriau, 2010: Fig. 65, 10.4.16) as well as sites in Canaan, such as Deir el-Balah (Gould, 2010: Figs 2.4.4–8) and Nubia (Holthoer, 1977: Pl. 33, Type FU1). The vessel is made in several parts; the diverging neck is separately thrown and then attached to the ovoid body and in some cases the base also shows the distinctive thickness by comparison to the walls of the main body of the vessel, which indicates separate manufacture. This tripartite manufacturing process is also seen on comparable material from the contemporary site of Qantir (Aston, 1998: 188). As with the majority of the closed and restricted vessels, the funnel-neck jars from Area K were more commonly manufactured in Egypt and transported to Zawiyet Umm el-Rakham, with 55.71 per cent of the funnel-neck jars being made from the two major Nile silts represented in the corpus, Nile B2 and Nile D. However, as with Type II.1.1, a significant minority in the form of 22.86 per cent of all funnel-neck jars are nonetheless made from the local ZUR B fabric.

319 ZUR/K/140v K1,4
Nile B2 Diam. 12.0cm

320 ZUR/KS/4 KS
Nile B2 Diam. 18.0cm

321 ZUR/K2A/25 K2A
Nile B2 Diam. 14.0cm

322 ZUR/K/226 K0,4
Nile B2 Diam. 24.0cm

323 ZUR/KN/44 KN
Nile B2 Diam. 12.0cm

324 ZUR/KN/45+46 KN
Nile B2 Diam. 12.0cm

325 ZUR/KAB/67 KAB
Nile D Diam. 12.0cm

326 ZUR/KZ/33 KZ
Nile B2 Diam. 16.0cm

327 ZUR/K2A/16 K2A
Nile B2 Diam. 12.0cm

328 ZUR/K/345(1)g K5,6
Nile B2 Diam. 14.0cm

329 ZUR/KE/21 KE
Nile B2 Diam. 12.0cm

330 ZUR/KZ/32 KZ
Nile B2 Diam. 11.0cm

331 ZUR/K/259 K0,9
Nile D Diam. 24.0cm

332 ZUR/KE/18 KE
Nile D Diam. 16.0cm

333 ZUR/KZ/20 KZ
Nile D Diam. 16.0cm

334 ZUR/K/16p K1,8
Nile D Diam. 14.0cm

335 ZUR/KE/24 KE
Nile D Diam. 16.0cm

336 ZUR/KG/6 KG
Nile D Diam. 24.0cm

337 ZUR/KG/7 KG
Nile D Diam. 14.0cm

338 ZUR/KN/25 KN
Nile D Diam. 14.0cm

Appendix: Catalogue of Area K Ceramic Vessels

339 ZUR/KG/3a KG
Nile D Diam. 11.0cm

340 ZUR/KG/3b KG
Nile D Diam. 12.0cm

341 ZUR/KN/29 KN
Nile D Diam. 8.0cm

342 ZUR/K/1 Surface find
Nile D Diam. 14.5 ht. 36.0cm

343 ZUR/K/345i K5,6
Nile D Diam. 14.0cm

344 ZUR/K/140t K1,5
Nile D Diam. 14.0cm

345 ZUR/K/16z K1,8
Nile D Diam. 20.0cm

346 ZUR/K/89 K0,7
Nile D Diam. 12.2cm

347 ZUR/K/336k K1,2
Nile D Diam. 14.0cm

348 ZUR/K/346i K5,7
Niel D Diam. 15.0cm

349 ZUR/K/346k K5,7
Nile D Diam. 22.0cm

350 ZUR/2014(K)/8 None given
Nile D Diam. 12.0cm

351 ZUR/K/289o K0,8
ZUR A Diam. 14.0cm

352 ZUR/K/16v K1,8
ZUR A Diam. 15.0cm

353 ZUR/K/194c K1,4
ZUR A Diam. 22.0cm

354 ZUR/KE/25 KE
ZUR A Diam. 12.0cm

355 ZUR/KAB/40 KAB
ZUR A Diam. 12.0cm

356 ZUR/2014(K)/5 None given
ZUR A Diam. 14.0cm

357 ZUR/K/140y K1,4
ZUR A Diam. 22.0cm

358 ZUR/K/215a+b K0,4
ZUR A Diam. 12.0cm

359 ZUR/K/231a K1,4
ZUR A Diam. 12.0cm

360 ZUR/K/278d K1,8
ZUR A Diam. 14.0cm

361 ZUR/KZ/23 KZ
ZUR A Diam. 16.0cm

362 ZUR/K/345j K5,6
ZUR B Diam. 13.0cm

363 ZUR/KA/9 KA
ZUR B Diam. 16.0cm

364 ZUR/KY/6 KY
ZUR B Diam. 13.0cm

365 ZUR/K2H/19 K2H
ZUR B Diam. 18.0cm

366 ZUR/K2H/37 K2H
ZUR B Diam. 16.0cm

367 ZUR/K/194d K1,4
ZUR B Diam. 14.0cm

368 ZUR/K/320m K4,0
ZUR B Diam. 14.0cm

369 ZUR/K/108m K0,7
ZUR B Diam. 18.0cm

370 ZUR/K/116l K1,4
ZUR N Diam. 14.0cm

371 ZUR/K2H/23 K2H
ZUR B Diam. 22.0cm

372 ZUR/KB/4 KB
ZUR B Diam. 12.0cm

373 ZUR/K2A/24 K2A
ZUR B Diam. 18.0cm

374 ZUR/K2H/6 K2H
ZUR B Diam. 10.0cm

375 ZUR/K/140l K1,4
ZUR C Diam. 12.0cm

376 ZUR/K/336t K5,7
ZUR C Diam. 14.0cm

377 ZUR/KV/9 KV
ZUR C Diam. 12.0cm

II.3 Beer jars

As with Types II.1 and II.2, the crudely manufactured beer jars are characteristic of all New Kingdom sites across Egypt and at sites with a strong Egyptian influence in Canaan and Nubia (Aston, 1998: nos. 523–48; Bourriau, 2010: Fig. 65, 10.8.32; Gould, 2010: 31–8, Figs 2.5.4–10; Holthoer, 1977: Pl. 18, type BB4; Nagel, 1938: 20.19; Petrie, 1890: Pl. xx.21, Rose, 2007: Fig. 410 and Ruffieux, 2016: Fig. 5, see also Hummel, 2019b: 257 for an assemblage of beer (or offering) jars found at Tell el-Borg as well as Aston, 2020: 270 for examples from the chapel of Ptahemwia at Saqqara as well as Aston, 2011: Fig. VI.11 and Aston, 2012: Fig. VII.28). The vessels were usually wheel-made but with a hand-moulded base often preserving the finger prints of the potters who made them. The versatility of this vessel type – despite its somewhat limiting colloquial name – is remarked upon by Gould (2010: 31–8) and this versatility is also manifested at Zawiyet Umm el-Rakham where one example (ZUR/G4E/10) found in Area G was filled with ceramic net sinkers (see Section 4.3 above). The use of this vessel type for temporary storage of a wide variety of materials can also be seen in Area QV at Qantir where a complete beer jar (2000/0342A) in locus PQ b/9 was found to contain broken calcite-alabaster inlays and other industrial waste evidently destined to be reduced to a powder and used to insulate crucibles for glass production (Pusch and Rehren, 2007: 45–6).

Unlike the majority of closed vessels from Area K, the beer jars found at the site were primarily locally produced (62.5 per cent). Even though some examples were imported from Egypt, the choice to primarily produce this vessel type locally is readily explainable; beer jars are generally undecorated without any surface treatment; taken together with their rough manufacture they are unsuitable for long-term storage of liquids, and rather than being designated as storage vessels for a specific type of objects or foodstuffs, they seem to have been multi-functional. Considering the low level of expertise and time required to manufacture these vessels, it was certainly more beneficial to simply manufacture them locally when needed as opposed to wait for shipments of goods transported in this vessel type to arrive from the Nile Valley. A notable aspect of the corpus of beer jars as a whole are two examples found with perforated bases, similar to examples uncovered at Ashkelon (Martin, 2008: 252–5) where they may have been used in the fermentation process of beer (Homan, 2004: 89), a function they most likely fulfilled at Zawiyet Umm el-Rakham as well.

378 ZUR/K/16a K1,8
Nile B2 Diam. 10.0cm

379 ZUR/K/345c K5,6
Nile B2 Diam. 7.5cm

380 ZUR/KH/10 KH
Nile B2 Diam. 9.0cm ht. 25.5cm

381 ZUR/K/289r K0,8
Nile D Diam. 10.0cm

382 ZUR/K/336j K1,2
Nile D Diam. 12.0cm

383 ZUR/K/346m K5,7
Nile D Diam. 12.0cm

384 ZUR/KE/11 KE
Nile D Diam. 10.0cm

385 ZUR/KI/15 KI
Nile D Diam. 9.5 ht. 24.4cm

386 ZUR/K/15 K0,7
ZUR A Diam. 9.0cm ht. 23.5cm

387 ZUR/K/140h K1,4
ZUR A Diam. 8.0cm

388 ZUR/K/194a K1,4
ZUR A Diam. 10.0cm

389 ZUR/K/322b K1,2
ZUR A Diam. 12.0cm

390 ZUR/K/322c K1,2
ZUR A Diam. 10.0cm

391 ZUR/KE/7 KE
ZUR A Diam. 9.0cm ht. 24.5cm

392 ZUR/KE/28 KE
ZUR A Diam. 10.0cm

393 ZUR/KE/29 KE
ZUR A Diam. 9.0cm

394 ZUR/KI/4 KI
ZUR A Diam. 10.0cm

395 ZUR/KY/4 KY
ZUR A Diam. 10.0cm ht. 25.0cm

396 ZUR/K2H/31 K2H
ZUR A Diam. 10.0cm

397 ZUR/K/344d K4,5
ZUR B Diam. 10.0cm

398 ZUR/2014(K)/4 None given
ZUR B Diam. 9.5cm ht. 23.0cm

399 ZUR/KAB/68 KAB
ZUR B Diam. 9.0cm

400 ZUR/KZ/30 KZ
ZUR B Diam. 11.0cm

401 ZUR/K/16g K1,8
ZUR A Diam. 9.0cm

II.4.1 Egyptian amphorae

The classical Ramesside Egyptian amphora with two vertical handles and a straight modelled neck is poorly represented in Area K, with only eleven diagnostic sherds. Commonly (although not exclusively) made from Marl D, and usually covered with a thick cream-white slip, the vessel type is commonly found in across New Kingdom Egyptian sites (see Aston, 2004 for a full discussion of New Kingdom amphora types), such as Qantir (Aston, 1998: nos. 1763–98), Tell el-Amarna (Hope, 1989: Figs 2–3), Deir el-Medina (Nagel, 1938: 83.11–12) and Deir el-Balah (Gould, 2010: Fig. 2.6.1). Clear parallels were also found at Memphis and in the Tomb of Horemheb (see Bourriau, 2010: Pl. 58.e-f for comparative illustrations). The most complete example, **412** is made from Marl D and of a type labelled by Aston (2004: Fig. 8) as B2 with a distinctly squatter body and carinated base. This type appears during the reign of Ramesses II in addition to the more slender Marl D Type B1 which continues in use (Aston, 2004: 189–93).

402 ZUR/K/13a K1,7
Marl D Diam. 12.0cm

403 ZUR/K/116j K1,4
Marl D Diam. 12.0cm

404 ZUR/K/116o K1,4
Marl D Diam. 28.0cm

405 ZUR/K/280 K1,8
Marl D Diam. 14.0cm

406 ZUR/K2A/21 K2A
Marl D Diam. 22.0cm

407 ZUR/K2H/16 K2H
Marl D Diam. 12.0cm

408 ZUR/K/336b K1,2
Marl D Diam. 8.0cm

409 ZUR/K2H/27 K2H
Marl D Diam. 4.8cm

II.4.2 Large storage jars

Two sherds in the Area K corpus are comparable to a vessel type described as a large storage jar by Aston (1998: no. 579). It is possible that these are much larger versions of funnel-necked jars with modelled rims, but the two examples from Area K are too incomplete to make a certain identification.

410 ZUR/KZ/36 KZ
Nile B2 Diam. 22.0cm

411 ZUR/K/13b K1,7
Nile B2 Diam. 26.0cm

II.5 Bottles and flasks

Bottles and flasks (II.5) have been categorised into three sub-types within the Area K corpus.

II.5.1. Ovoid bottle with moulded neck

Type II.5.1 was most likely an ovoid bottle with a neck protrusion caused by the application of force to the top of the vessel prior to firing and which may have helped secure a string around the neck for carrying (Nielsen, 2014) and only a single diagnostic sherd of this type has so far been recorded.

412 ZUR/K/294a K0,6
Nile B2 Diam. 6.0cm

II.5.2. Squat globular bottle with modelled neck

Type II.5.2 is a squat globular bottle with a short modelled neck, and is comparable to examples found at Qantir (Aston, 1998: 962) although – as Aston states – they do not appear elsewhere in the corpuses of Ramesside pottery.

413 ZUR/K/157 K0,7
ZUR B Diam. 4.4cm ht. 13.8cm

II.5.3. Cosmetic flask

Type II.5.3 is a small hand-moulded 'cosmetic' flask made from Marl D, which is similar to a recently published example from Kom Firin (Smoláriková, 2014: 128) though the example from Area K is distinctly narrower and the base more rounded.

414 ZUR/KN/49 KN
Marl D Diam. 1.6cm ht. 8.0cm

II.6. Tall ovoid jars

Tall ovoid jars, usually thrown in two pieces (base and body) with the joint clearly discernible by a thickening in the wall towards the base are fairly common during the eighteenth and nineteenth Dynasty, although as Aston has noted (1998: 344) they are primarily found with a blue-painted surface decoration. This is not always the case and indeed the majority of these vessel types from Area K are undecorated and their basic shape and the lack of decoration is paralleled at a variety of contemporary sites such as Qantir (Aston, 1998: nos. 1185–6), Gurob (Petrie, 1890: Pl. xxi.46) and across Nubia (Holthoer, 1977: Pl. 38, type IR/0/e–h). The decorated variety of this vessel type – usually painted with bands of Egyptian blue and/or lines of red dots – is also widely evidenced from funerary sites such as Saqqara (Bourriau and Aston, 1985: Pl. 35.41–44 and Takamiya, 2007: 1761) as well as settlement sites (Aston, 1998: nos. 1312–20; Bourriau, 2010: Pl. 64, 9.6.5 and Hope, 1991: 31–46). In Area K the tall ovoid vessels are primarily made in the two predominant Nile silt clays, Nile B2 and Nile D, which combined account for eleven out of the fifteen whole vessels and diagnostic sherds of this type recorded. Five of the ten imported vessels are decorated with blue and red paint (see Section 6.5.5), whereas the four examples of this vessel type made from local silt ware (ZUR A) are all undecorated.

415 ZUR/KY/2 KY
Nile B2 Diam. 11.0cm

416 ZUR/KZ/27 KZ
Nile B2 Diam. 16.0cm

417 ZUR/KN/19+20 KN
Nile D Diam. 12.0cm

418 ZUR/KN/24 KN
Nile D Diam. 10.0cm

419 ZUR/KN/31 KN
Nile D Diam. 12.0cm

420 ZUR/KN/41 KN
Nile D Diam. 8.0cm

421 ZUR/K/260 K4,6
Nile D Diam. 13.0cm

422 ZUR/K/263b K1,2
Nile D Diam. 13.0cm

423 ZUR/K/289m K0,8
Nile D Diam. 18.0cm

424 ZUR/KE/14 KE
Nile D Diam. 14.0cm

425 ZUR/2014(K)/2 None given
ZUR A Diam. 12.0cm ht. 27.8cm

426 ZUR/KZ/27 KZ
ZUR A Diam. 16.0cm

427 ZUR/K/215l K0,4
ZUR A Diam. 14.0cm

428 ZUR/K/289k K0,8
ZUR A Diam. 10.0cm

II.7. Imitation pilgrim flasks

The colloquial term 'pilgrim flask' has been accepted within the Egyptian ceramic corpus to describe a lentoid vessel with a single spout and two loop handles due to its similarity in appearance to the Medieval 'costrel' flask used by Pilgrims as water carriers during the European Middle Ages (Aston, 1998: 44). Unknown in Egypt before the eighteenth Dynasty, the vessel type may have originated on Crete during the Middle Minoan II/IIIA periods and on the Mycenaean mainland during Mycenaean IIIA (Killebrew, 2010: 96) before finally arriving in Canaan (Killebrew, 2010: 96) and Egypt, most likely due to increased contacts within the Eastern Mediterranean (Aston, 1998: 44, for an overview of early examples of this flask in Egypt and its general history of usage see both Holthoer, 1977: 99–100 and Gould, 2010: 49–52). Egyptian imitation vessels of this type were commonly manufactured from Marl D and usually covered in a thick cream-white slip (Aston, 1998: nos. 1691–5 and 1944–6, Brunton and Engelbach, 1927: Pl. xxxix.93b, Frankfort and Pendlebury, 1933: Pl. liii.XVII.8 and Nagel, 1938: fig. 35.6). Out of the ten examples of Egyptian-made pilgrim flasks, nine are made from Marl D with a thick cream slip, while a single example is made from Marl F and left uncoated. Though rarer, this is not a unique occurrence (see for instance Aston, 1998: nos. 2046–8).

429 ZUR/K/285 K1,2
Marl D Diam. 5.2cm

430 ZUR/K/343 K5,6
Marl D Diam. 6.0cm

431 ZUR/KAB/19 KAB
Marl D Diam. 3.2cm

432 ZUR/KH/11 KH
Marl D Diam. 5.0cm

433 ZUR/KI/5 KI
Marl D Diam. 6.0cm

434 ZUR/KKI/14 KKI
Marl D Diam. 5.5cm

435 ZUR/KN/42 KN
Marl D Diam. 3.0cm

436 ZUR/KN/43 KN
Marl D Diam. 4.0cm

437 ZUR/KN/47 KN
Marl D Diam. 4.0cm

438 ZUR/KKII/15 KKII
Marl F Diam. 5.0cm

III.1 Ceramic ring stands

The ceramic ring stands, can be defined as open-ended 'vessels' with a mouth both at their rim and base. Two types of ring stands were found in Area K.

III.1.1 Ring stand

Type III.1.1 is a narrow, squat ring stand which has been commonly found throughout contemporary Egyptian sites (Aston, 1998: nos. 511–12 and Peet and Woolley, 1923: Pl. xlvi I/43) and also at Egyptian sites in Canaan such as Deir el-Balah (Gould, 2010: Fig. 2.8.4).

439 ZUR/K/16h K1,8
Nile B2 Diam. 10.0cm

440 ZUR/KAB/61 KAB
Nile B2 Diam. 26.0cm

441 ZUR/KZ/35 KZ
Nile B2 Diam. 32.0cm

442 ZUR/K/130 K3,6
Nile D Diam. 20.5 ht. 19.0cm

443 ZUR/KM/19 KM
ZUR A Diam. 12.2cm ht. 3.8cm

444 ZUR/KM/20 KM
ZUR A Diam. 13.5 ht. 4.6cm

445 ZUR/K/16o K1,8
ZUR B Diam. 20.0cm

446 ZUR/KR/1 KR
ZUR B Diam. 9.0cm

III.1.2 Ring stand with buttress

Type III.1.2 constitutes a much larger ring stand with added 'buttresses', which Aston (1998: 180) has speculated may have added additional support to the entire object, but also a series of holes cut through the walls of the vessel during its leather-hard stage (Aston, 1998: nos. 900–1). This particular type of ring stand has been found both at Qantir (Aston, 1998: no. 513) and Tell el-Amarna (Peet and Woolley, 1923: Pl. xlvi I/1019) although only with added buttresses; examples with both buttresses and perforated holes have so far not been published from contemporary sites.

447 ZUR/KJ/14 KJ
Nile B2 Diam. 38.0cm

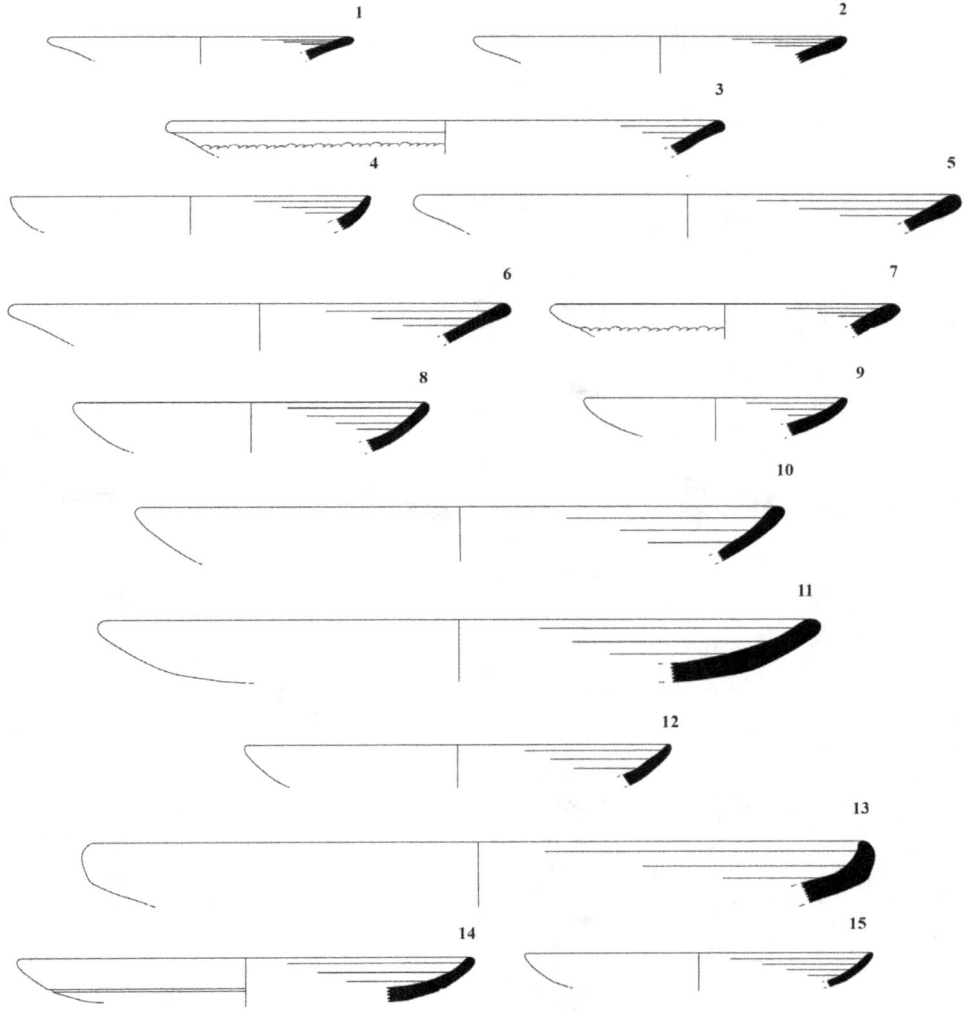

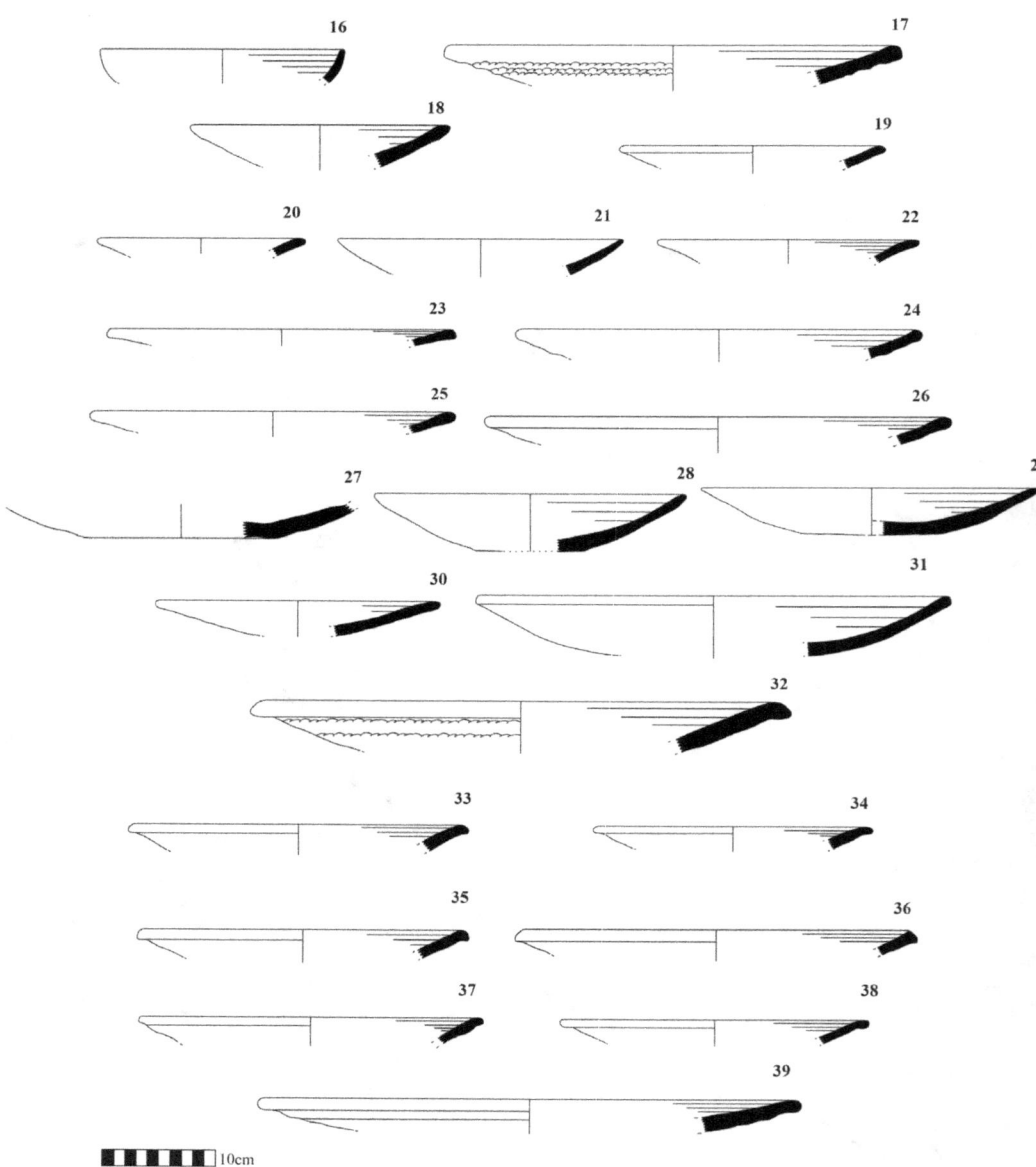

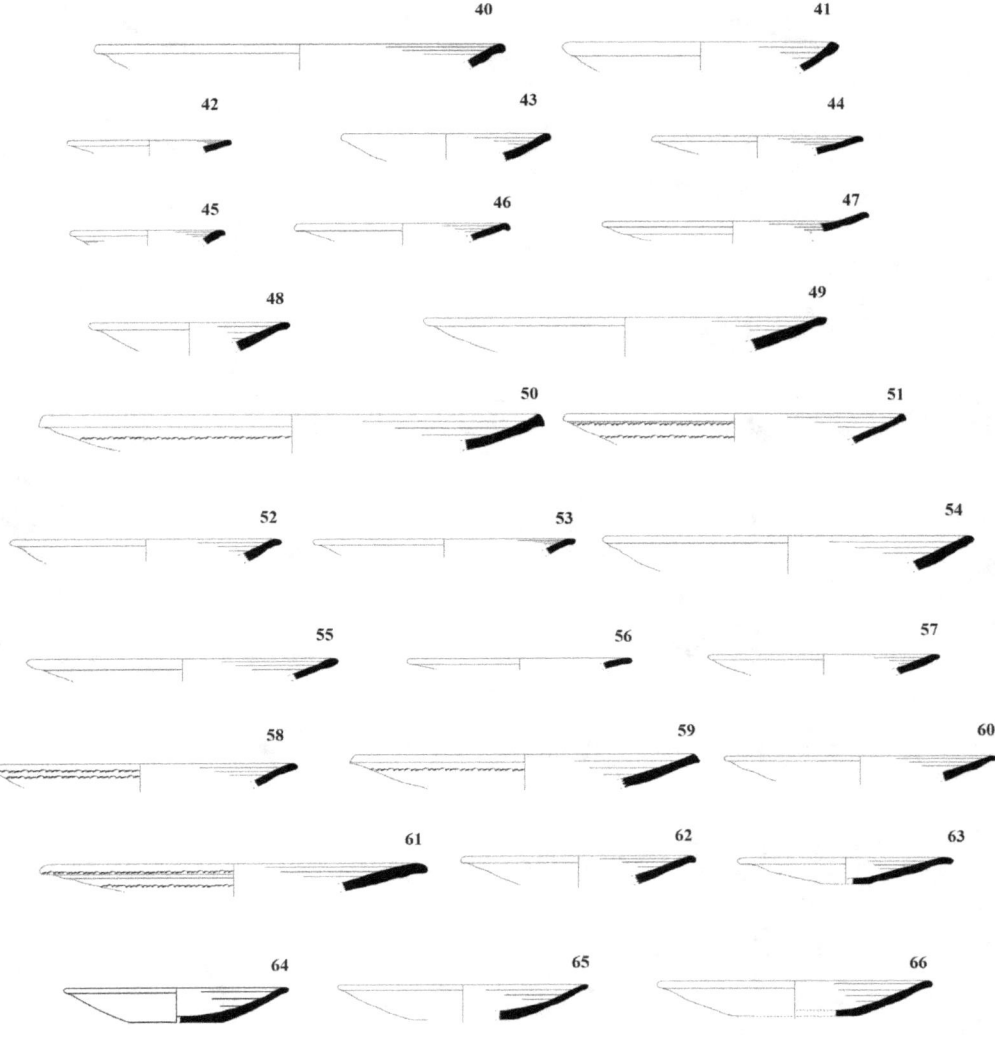

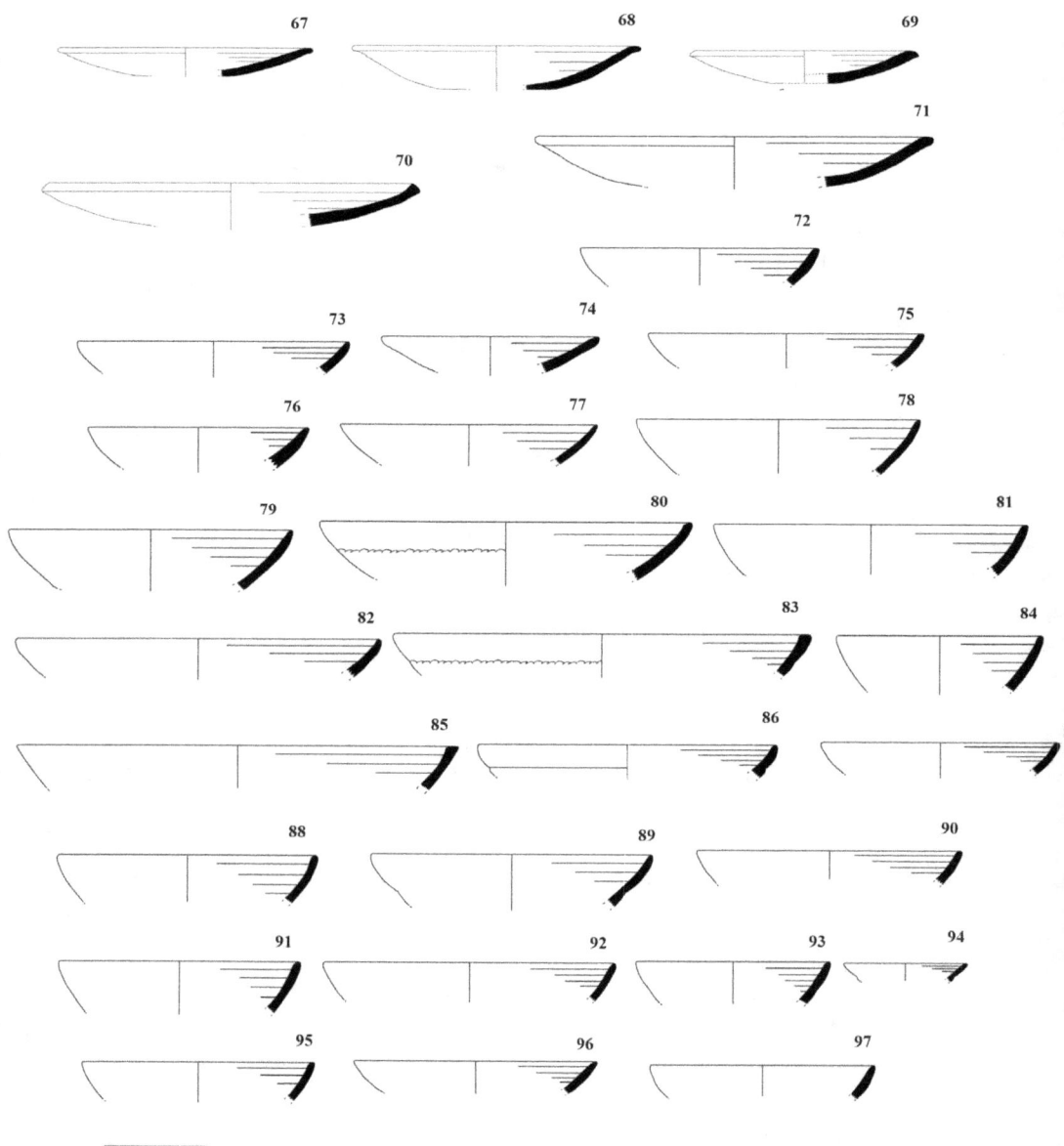

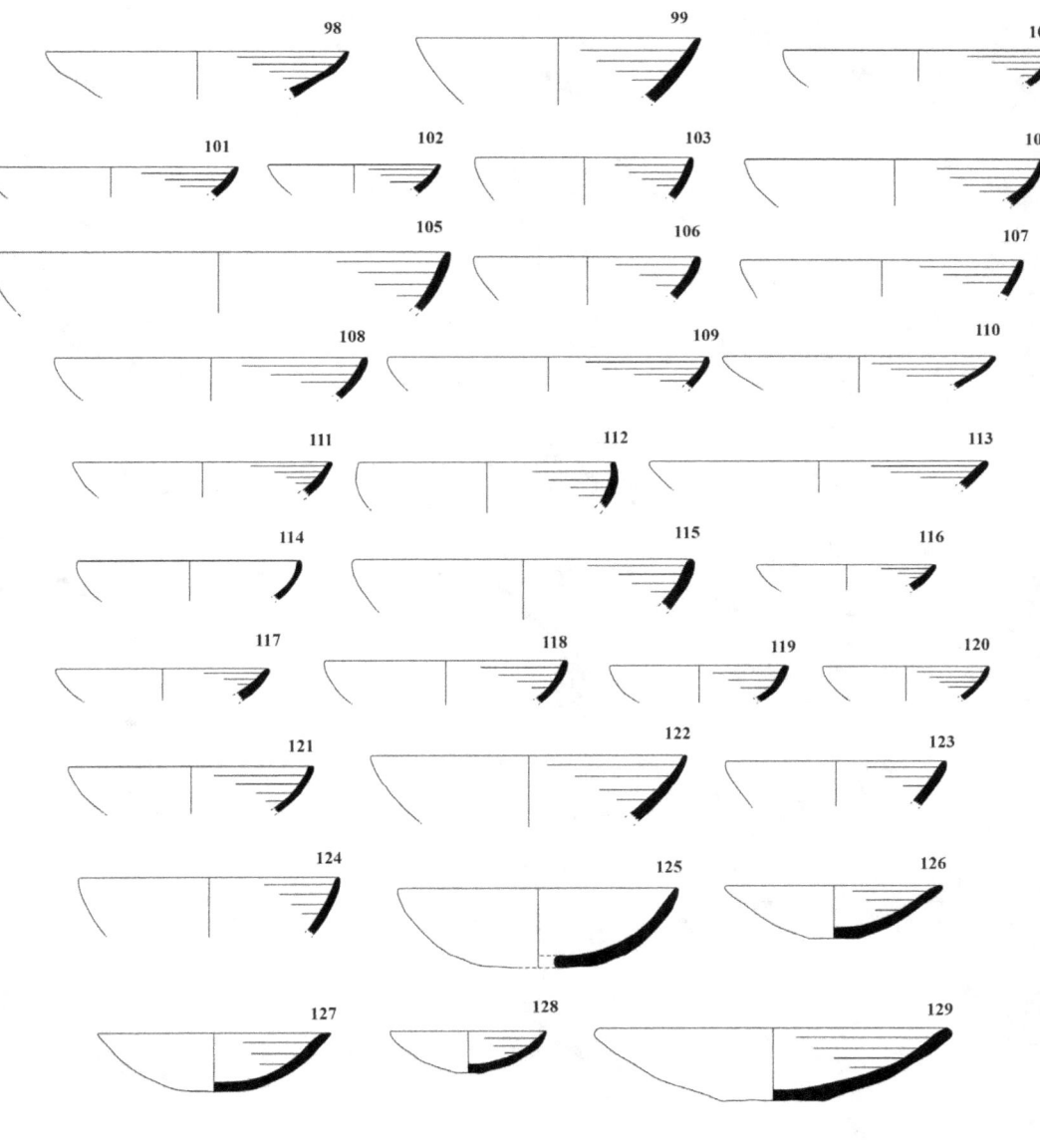

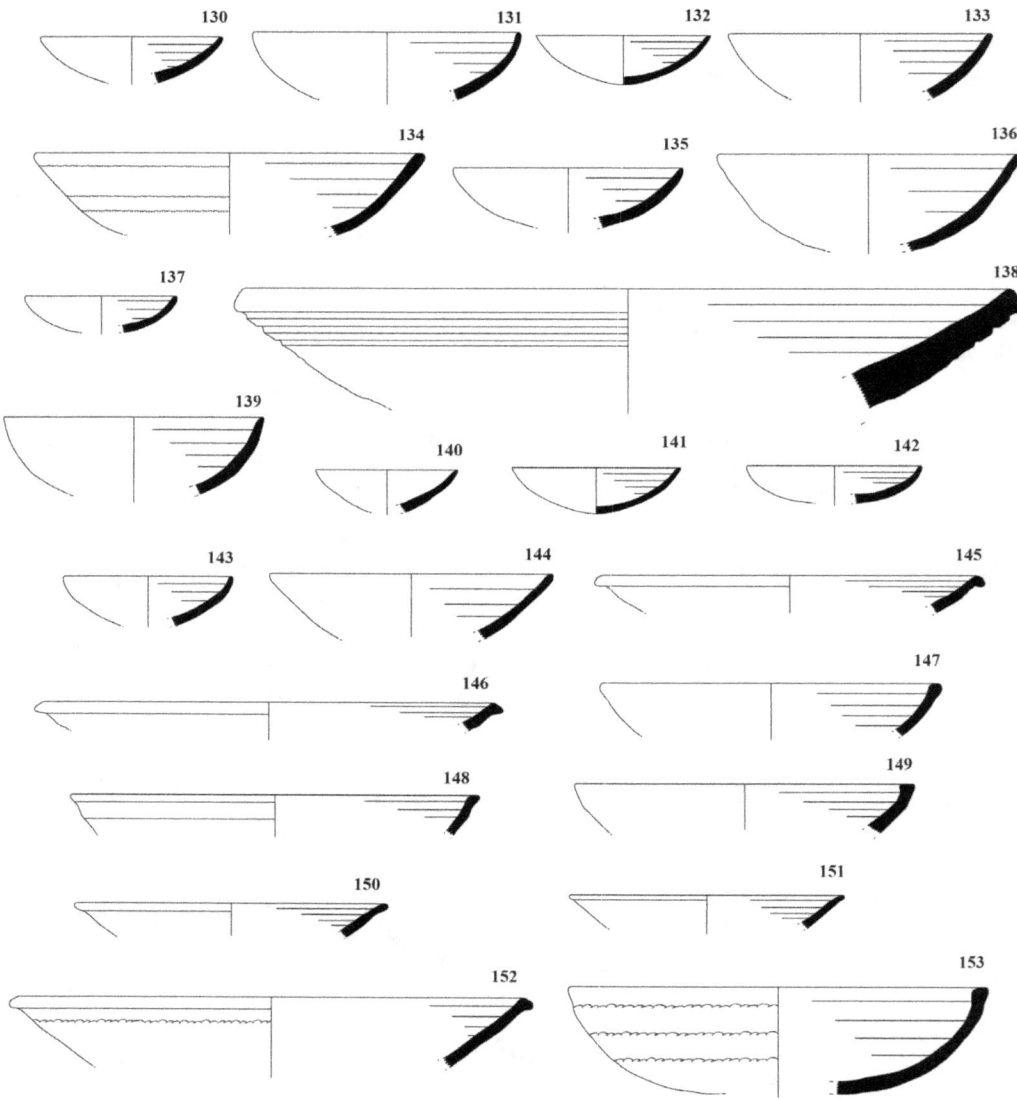

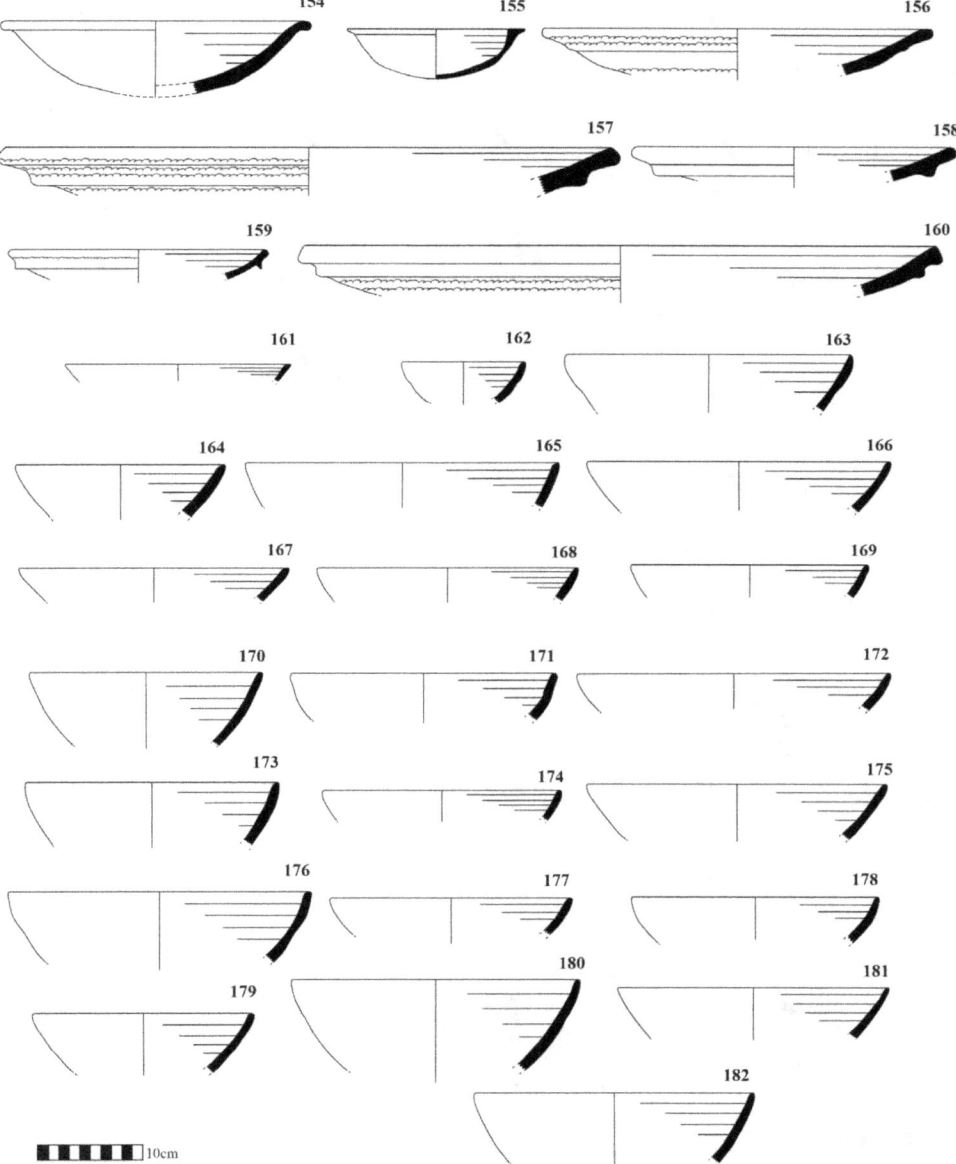

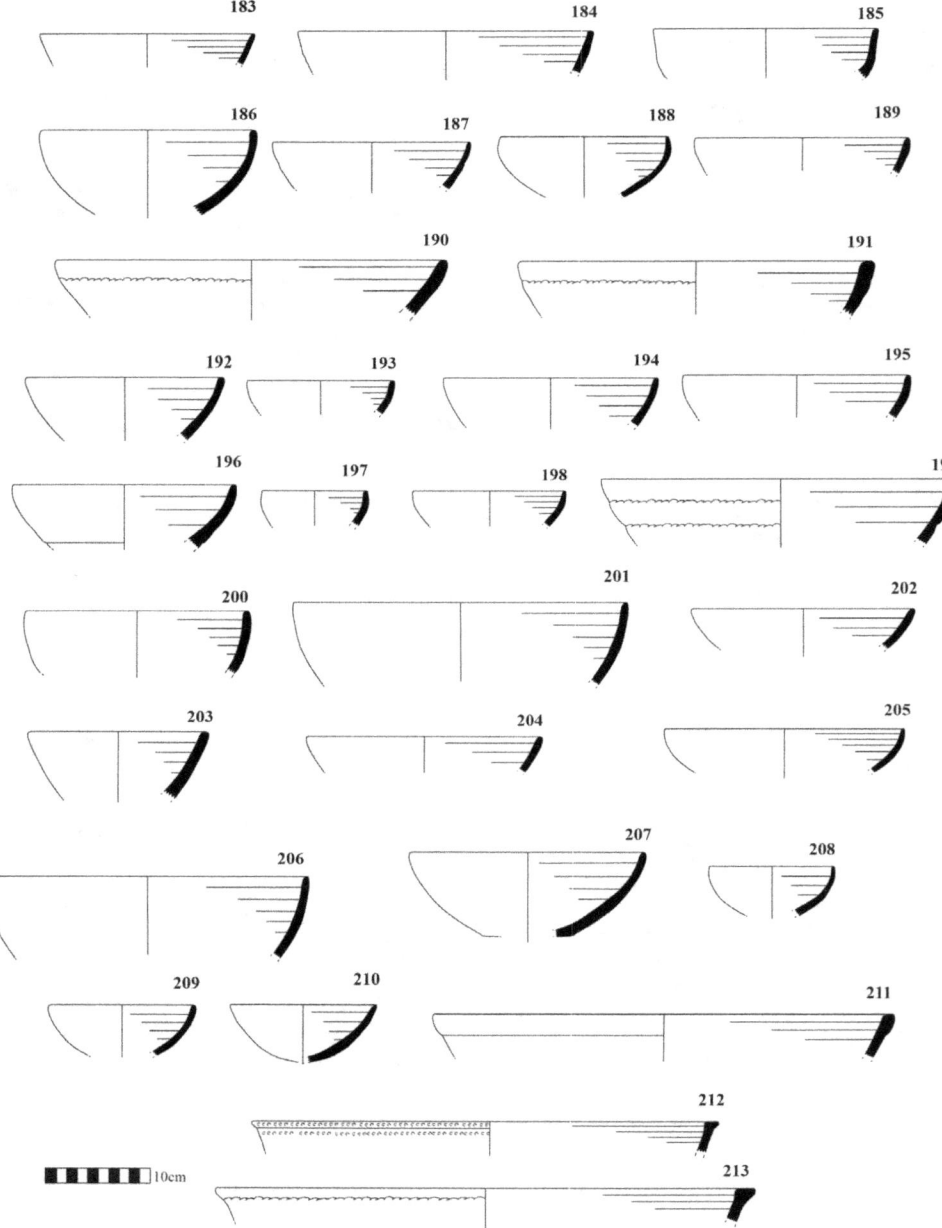

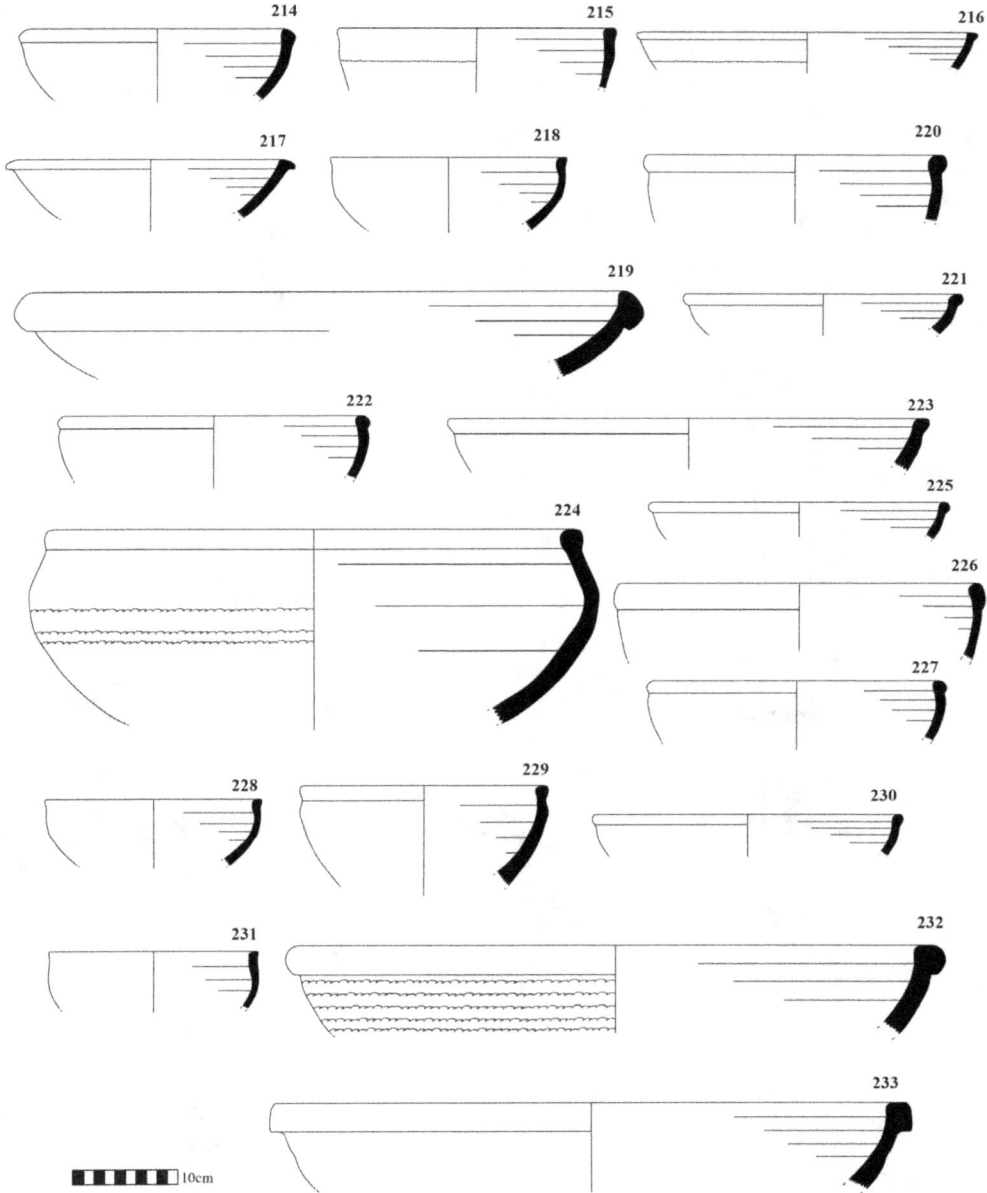

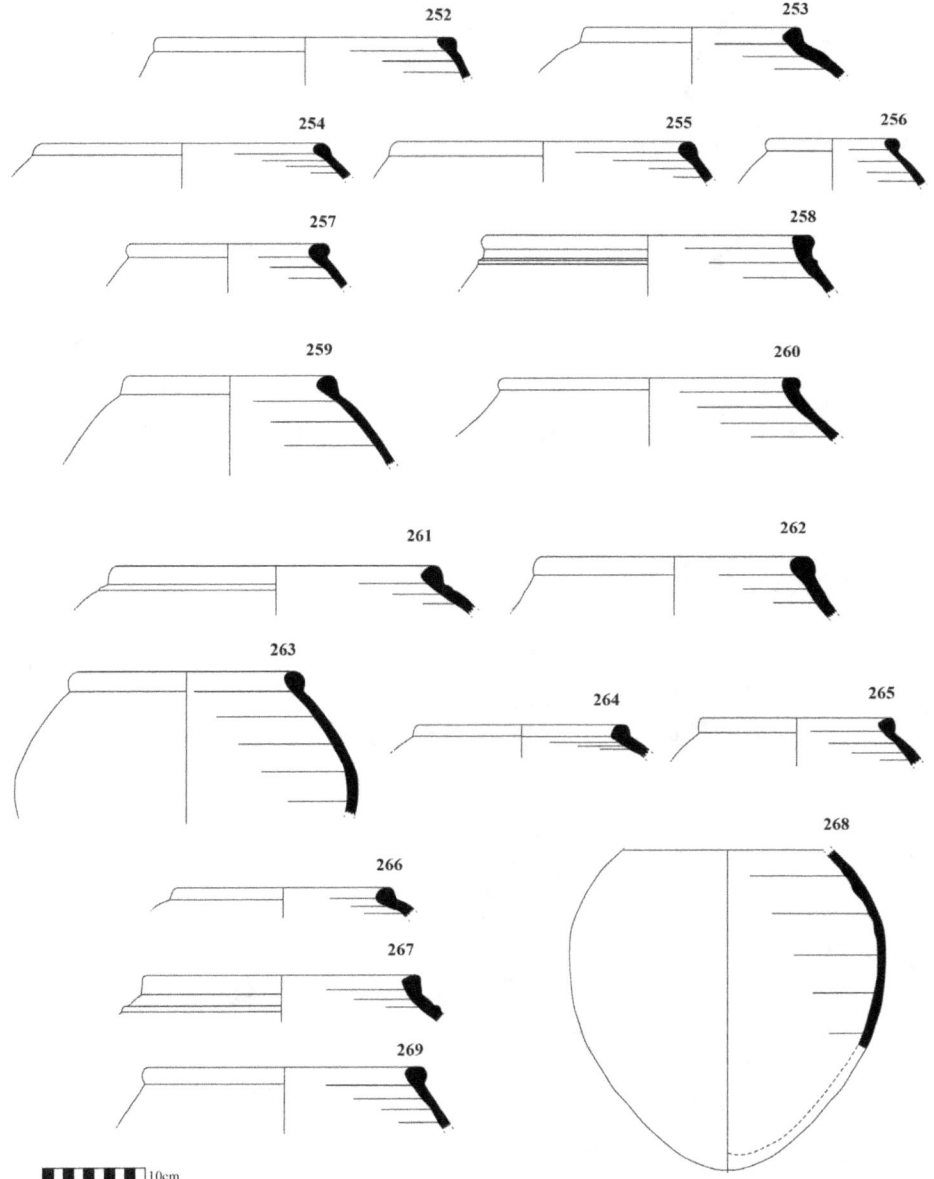

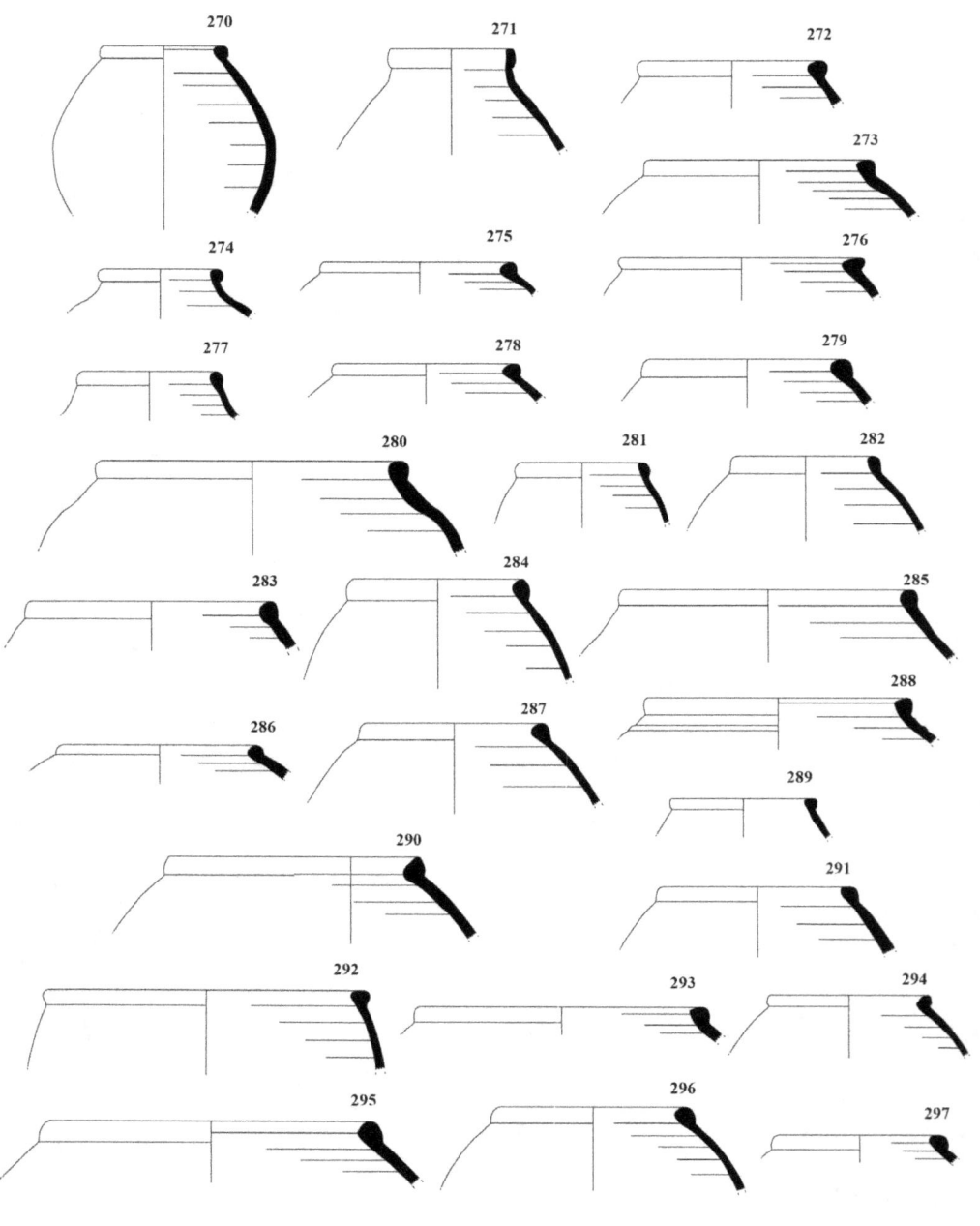

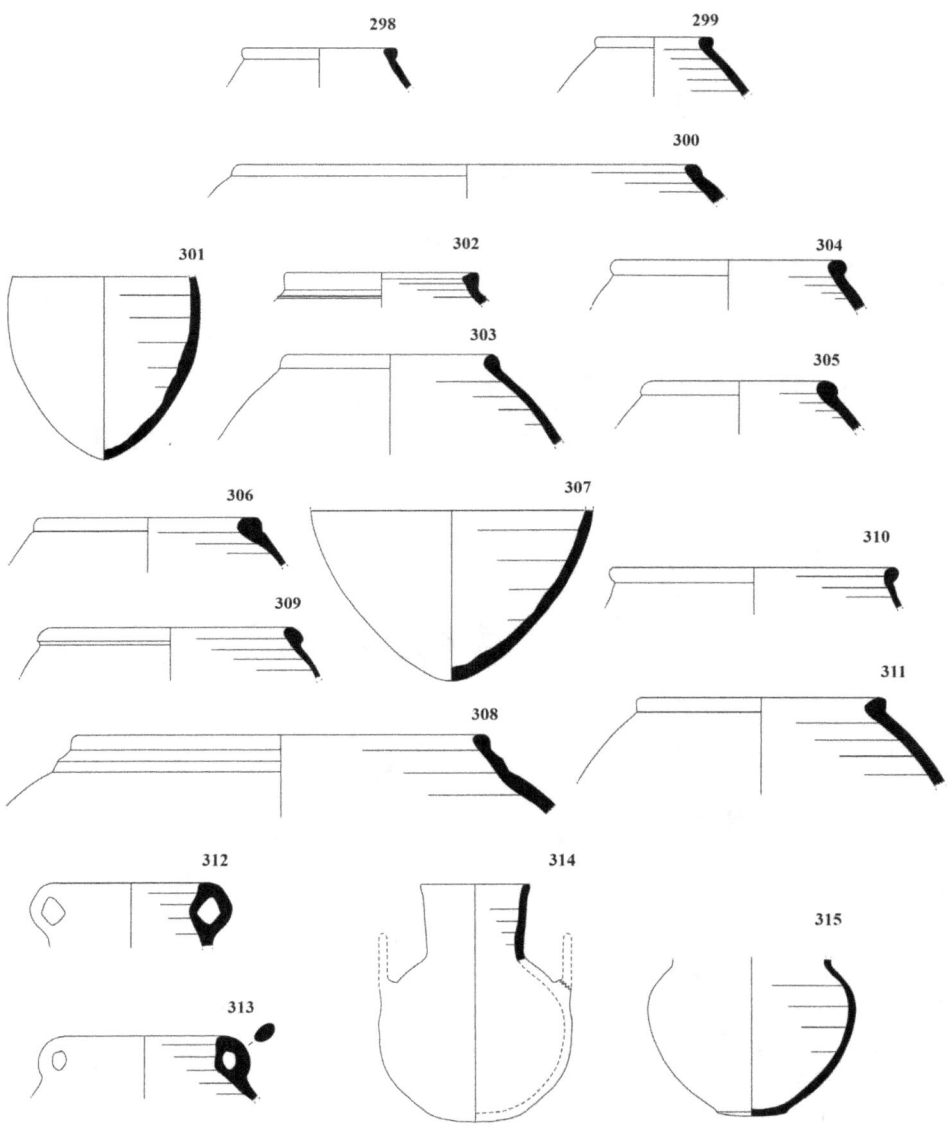

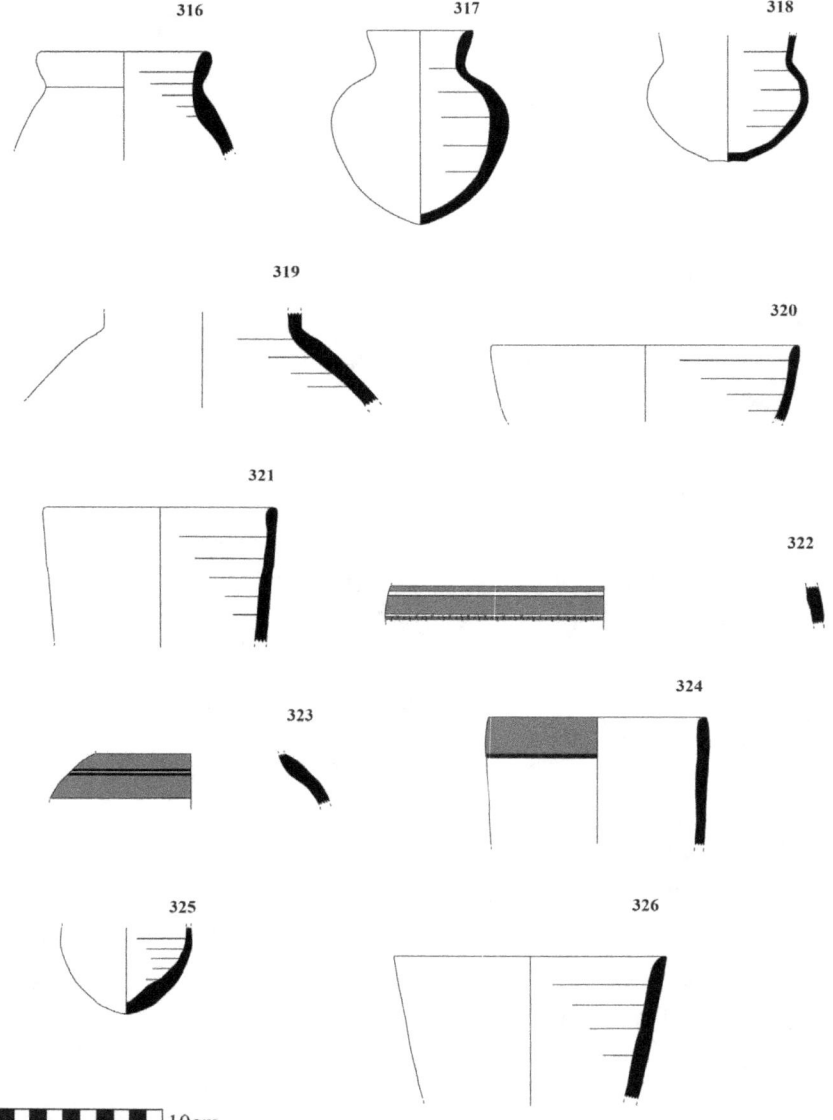

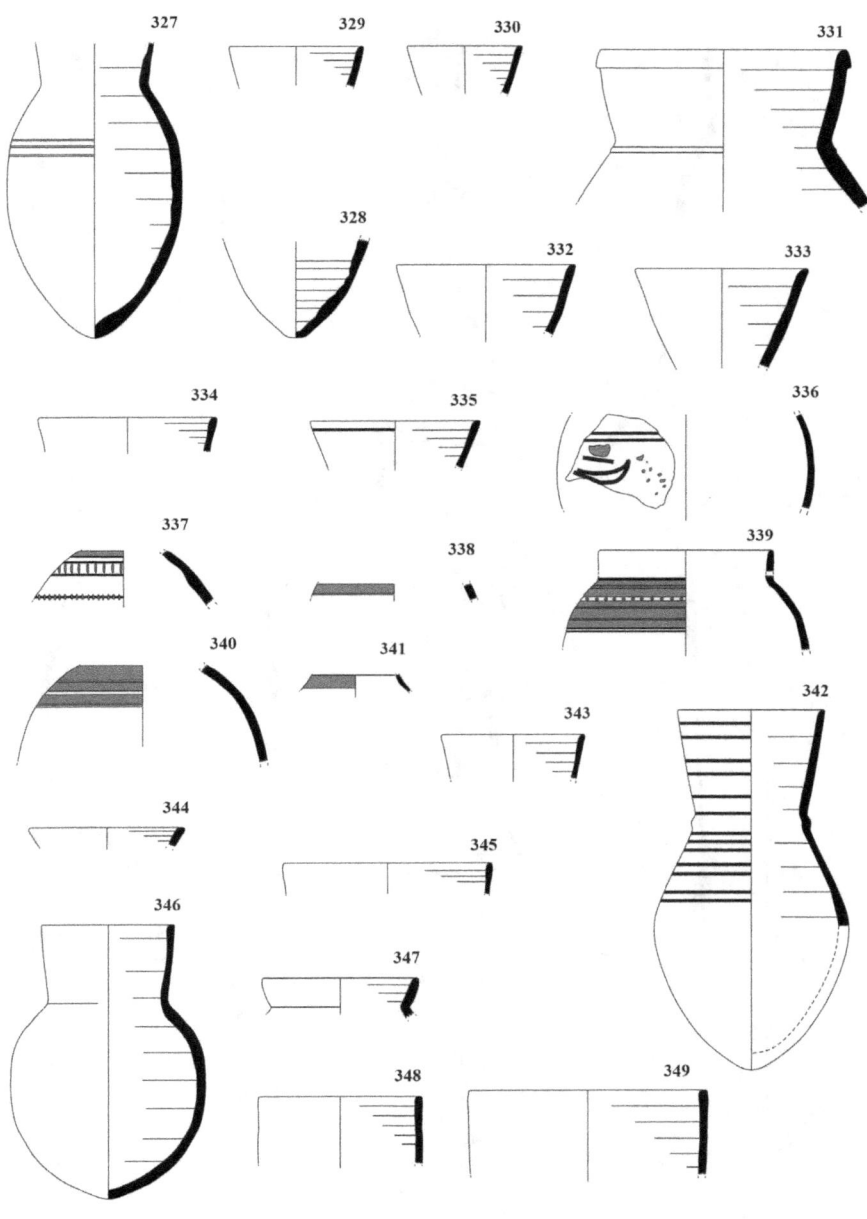

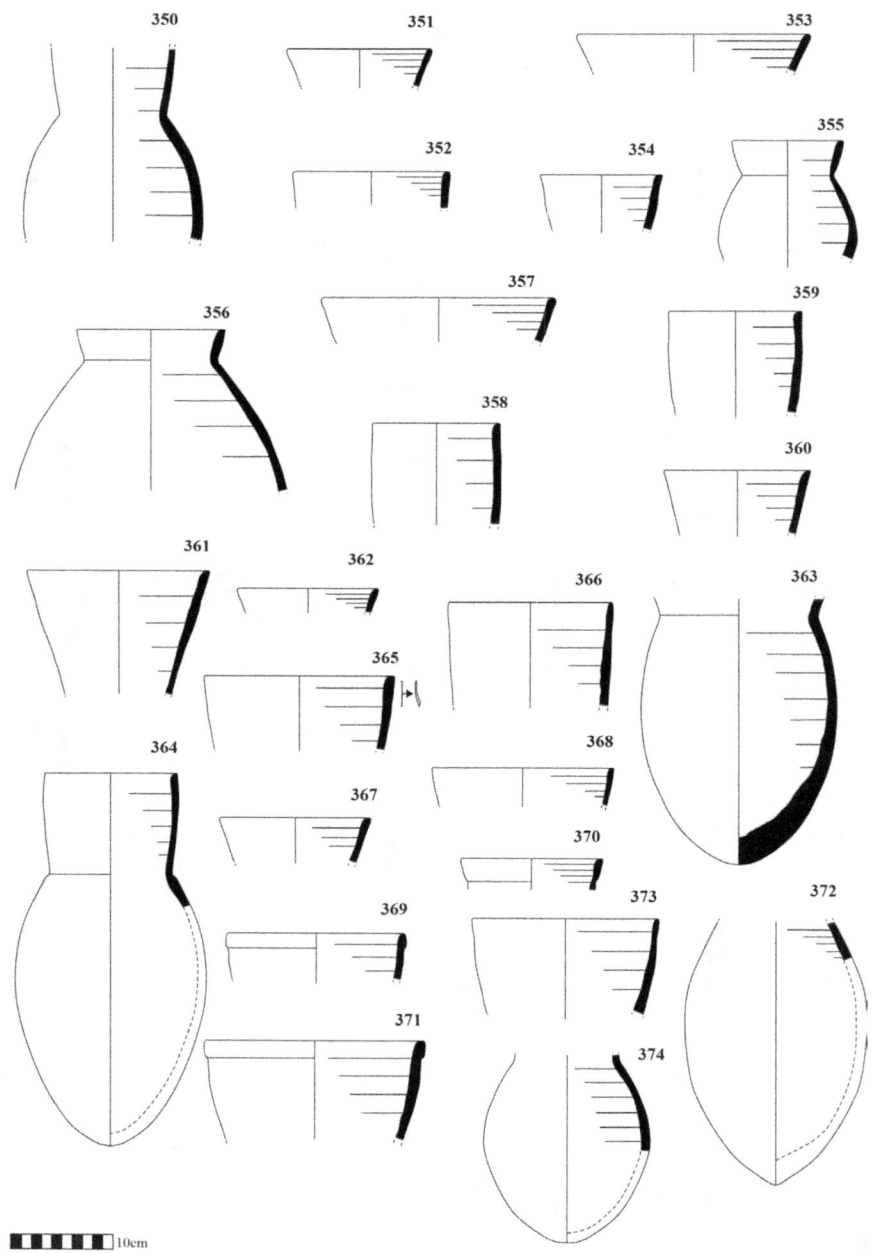

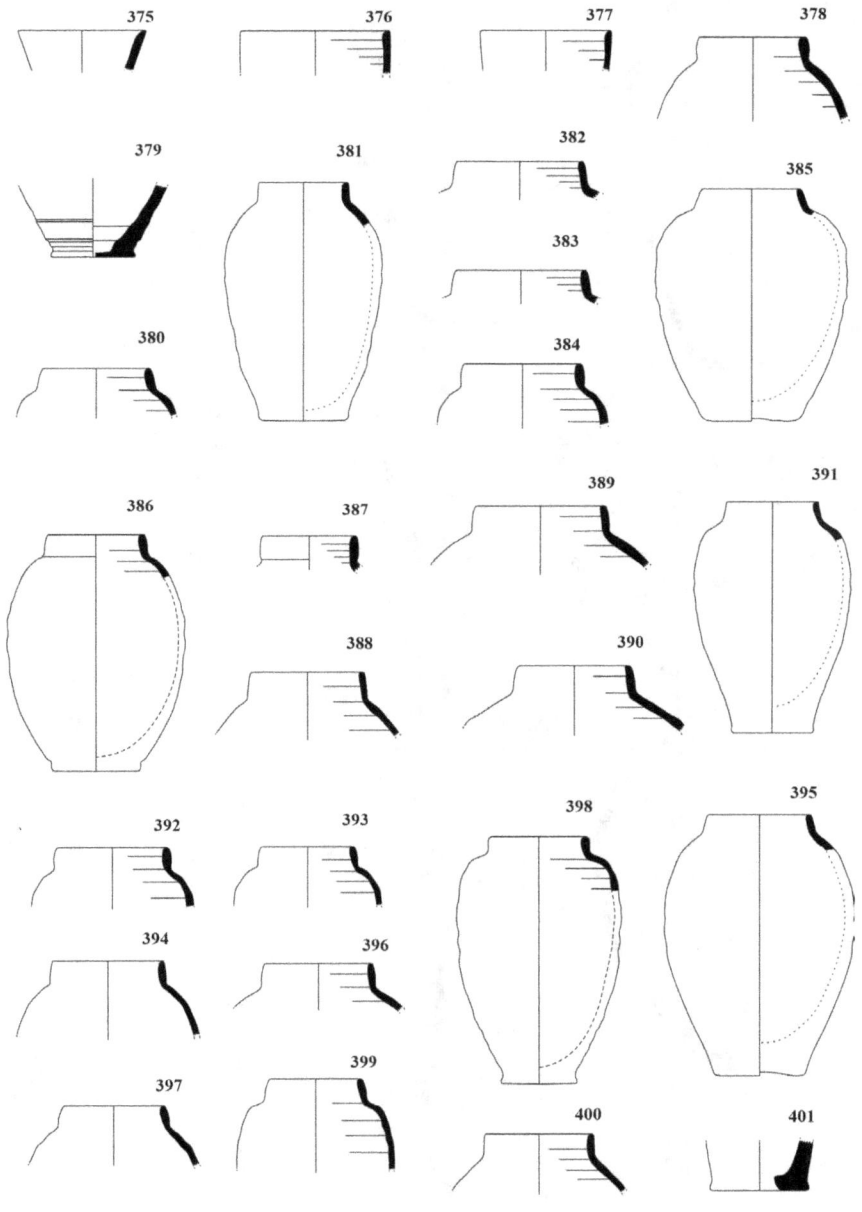

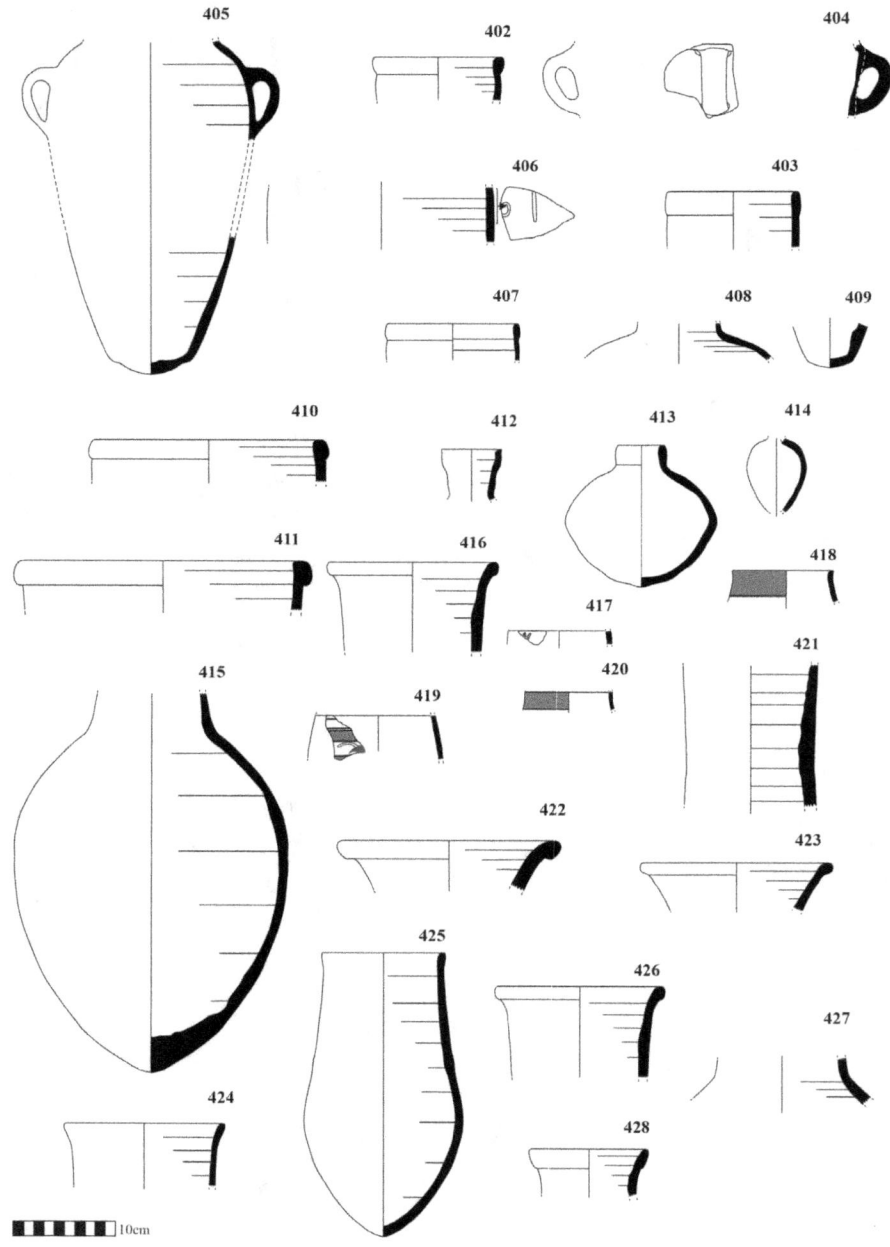

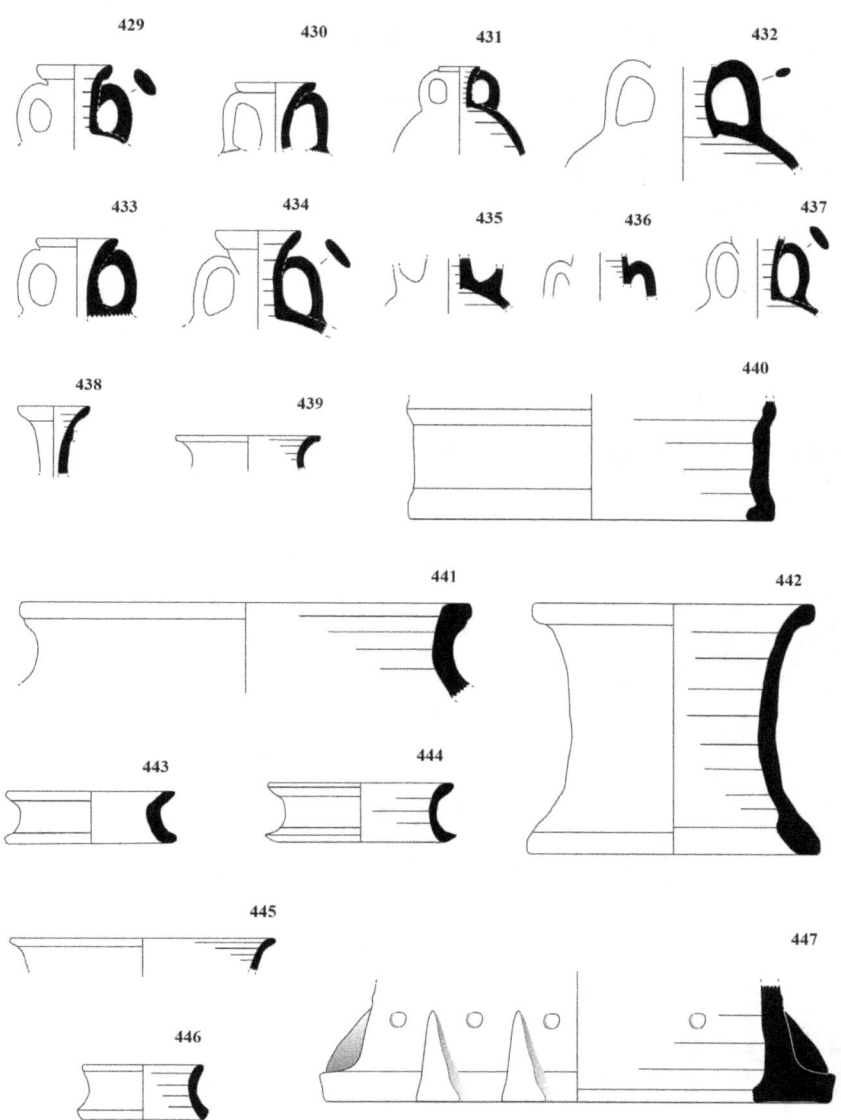

Bibliography

Abdallah, A. M. 1965. 'Observations on the Qattara-Moghra region, Western Desert' *Abstracts of the 3rd Annual Meeting. Geological Society of Egypt*, Cairo.

Abdallah, A. M., 1966. 'Geology of some gypsum deposits in the northern Western Desert of Egypt' in *Geological Survey of Egypt* 41, 1–11.

Allen, J. P. 2002. *The Heqanakht Papyri*. Metropolitan Museum of Art, New York.

Applebaum, S. 1979. *Jews and Greeks in Ancient Cyrene*. E. J. Brill, Leiden.

Aref, M. A. M., el-Khoriby, E. and Hamdan, M. A. 2002. 'The role of salt weathering in the origin of the Qattara Depression, Western Desert, Egypt' in *Geomorphology* 45, 181–95.

Arnold, D. and Bourriau, J. D. (eds) 1993. *An Introduction to Ancient Egyptian Pottery*. Phillipp von Zabern, Mainz.

Artzy, M. and Asaro, F. 1977. *Origin of Tell el-Yahidiyah Ware*. Lawrence Berkeley Laboratory Report LBL-4399, Berkeley.

Aston, B. G. 2011. 'The pottery' in M. J. Raven, V. Verschoor, M. Vugts and R. van Walsem (eds) *The Memphite Tomb of Horemheb Commander in Chief of Tutankhamun V: The Forecourt and the Area South of the Tomb with some notes on the Tomb of Tia*. Brepols, Leiden, 191–303.

Aston, B. G. 2012. 'The pottery' in H. D. Schneider (ed.) *The Tomb of Iniuia in the New Kingdom Necropolis of Menphis at Saqqara*. Brepols, Leiden, 139–217.

Aston, B. G. 2020. 'The pottery' in M. J. Raven (ed.) *The Tombs of Ptahemwia and Sethnakht at Saqqara*. Sidestone Press, Leiden, 239–321.

Aston, B. G., Harrell, J. A. and Shaw, I. 2000. 'Stone' in P. T. Nicholson and I. Shaw (eds) *Ancient Egyptian Materials and Technology*. Cambridge University Press, Cambridge, 5–77.

Aston, D. A. 1998. *Die Keramik des Grabungsplatzes Q1*. Verlag Philipp von Zabern: Mainz.

Aston, D. A. 2004. 'Amphorae in New Kingdom Egypt' in *Ä&L* 14, 175–213.

Aston, D. A. 2011. 'Blue painted pottery of the late eighteenth Dynasty: The material from the tomb of Maya and Merit at Saqqara' in *CCE* 9, 1–35.

Badawy, A. 1954. *A History of Egyptian Architecture: From the Earliest Times to the End of the Old Kingdom*. Studio Misr, Giza.

Baer, K. 1963. 'An Eleventh Dynasty farmer's letters to his family' in *JAOS* 83(1), 1–19.

Bates, O. 1914. *The Eastern Libyans*. MacMillan and Co. Limited, London.

Bates, O. 1917. 'Ancient Egyptian fishing' in *Harvard African Studies* 1, 199–271.

Bats, A. 2019. 'Les céréales et les produits céréaliers au Moyen Empire. Histoire technique et économique'. Doctoral dissertation: Sorbonne University.

Bats, A. 2020. 'The production of bread in conical moulds at the beginning of the Egyptian Middle Kingdom: The contribution of experimental archaeology' in *Journal of Archaeological Science: Reports* 34, 102631.

Behnke, R. H. 1980. *The Herders of Cyrenaica*. University of Illinois Press, Illinois.

Bertini, L. 2007. 'Correlating tooth eruption/wear and long bone fusion rates: a test sample using Zawiyet Umm el-Rakham and Tell el-Amarna faunal remains'. Master's Thesis, University of Liverpool.

Bertini, L. 2019. 'Chapter 13: The faunal remains from the 2004–2007 excavations at Tell el-Borg' in J. K. Hoffmeier (ed.) *Excavations in North Sinai: Tell el-Borg II*. Penn State University Press, Philadelphia, 404–13.

Bertini, L. 2014. 'Faunal remains at Kom Firin' in S. Neal, *Kom Firin II: The Urban Fabric and Landscape*, British Museum Press, London, 306–11.

Bertini, L. and Linseele, V. 2011. 'Faunal remains' in P. Wilson, *Sais I The Ramesside-Third Intermediate Period at Kom Rebwa*. Egypt Exploration Society, London, 277–85

Binder, M., Spencer, N. and Millet, M. 2011. 'Cemetery D at Amara West: The Ramesside period and its aftermath' in *British Museum Studies in Ancient Egypt and the Sudan* 16, 47–99.

Borchardt, L. 1907. *Das Grabdenkmal des Königs Ne-User-Re*. J.C. Hinrichs'sche Buchhandlung, Leipzig.

Borchardt, L. 1913. *Das Grabdenkmal des Königs Sa-Hu-Re*, v. II. J.C. Hinrichs'sche Buchhandlung, Leipzig.

Borojevic, K. and Terry Childs, S. 2018. 'Bread baking experiments' in K. A. Bard and R. Fattovich (eds) *Seafaring Expeditions to Punt in the Middle Kingdom: Excavations at Mersa/Wadi Gawasis, Egypt*. Brill: Leiden, 117–25.

Bourriau, J. D. 2006. 'Egyptian pottery fabrics: a comparison between NAA groupings and the "Vienna System"' in E. Czerny, I. Hein, H. Hunger, D. Melman, and A. Schwab (eds) *Timelines: Studies in Honour of Manfred Bietak*, v. 3. Peeters, Leuven, 261–92.

Bourriau, J. D. 2010. *The Survey of Memphis IV: Kom Rabia: The New Kingdom Pottery*. Egypt Exploration Society, London.

Bourriau, J. 2016. 'Observations on the New Kingdom ceramics at Saqqara and Memphis with partiuclar refereence to the reign of Ramesses II' in J. van Dijk (ed.) *Another Mouthful of Dust: Egyptological Studies in Honour of Geoffrey Thorndike Martin*. Peeters, Leiden, 63–75.

Bourriau, J. D. and Aston, D. A. 1985. 'The pottery' in G.T. Martin et al., *The Tomb Chapels of Paser and Ra'ia at Saqqara*. Egypt Exploration Society, London, 32–55.

Bourriau, J. D., D. A. Aston, M. J. Raven, and R. van Walsem. 2005. *The Memphite Tomb of Horemheb, Commander-in-chief of Tut'ankhamun III: The New Kingdom Pottery*. Egypt Exploration Society, London.

Bourriau, J., Bellido, A., Bryan, N. and Robinson, V. 2006. 'Egyptian pottery fabrics: a comparison between NAA groupings and the "Vienna System"' in E. Czerny, I. Hein, H. Hunger, D. Melman, and A. Schwab (eds) *Timelines: Studies in Honour of Manfred Bietak*, vol. 3. Peeters, Leuven, 261–92.

Bourriau, J. D., Nicholson, P. T. and Rose, P. 2000. 'Pottery' in P. T. Nicholson and I. Shaw (eds) *Ancient Egyptian Materials and Technology*. Cambridge University Press, Cambridge, 121–47.

Boyce, A. 1995. 'House P46.33: the finds' in B. J. Kemp (ed.) *Amarna Reports VI*. Egypt Exploration Society, London, 44–136.

Braekmans, D., V. Boschloos, H. Hameeuw and A. Van der Perre. 2019. 'Tracing the provenance of unfired ancient Egyptian clay figurines from Saqqara through non-destructive X-ray fluorescence spectrometry' in *Microchemical Journal* 145, 1207–17.

Braulinska, K. 2012. 'Implement, accessory or weapon? Selected worked bone finds from Tell el-Retaba' in *GM* 232, 7–28.

Breccia, E. 1913. *Rapport sur la marche du service du Musée en 1912*. Société des publications égyptiennes, Alexandria.

Brewer, D. J. and Friedman, R. F. 1989. *Fish and Fishing in Ancient Egypt*. Aris and Phillips, Warminster.

Brinton, J. 1942. 'Some recent discoveries at el-Alamein' in *Bulletin de la Société royale d'archéologie-Alexandrie* 11(35): 78–81.

Brunton, G. 1947. 'The dating of the cemetery at Kom el-Hisn' in *ASAE* 46, 143–5.

Brunton, G. and Caton-Thompson, G. 1928. *The Badarian Civilisation and Predynastic Remains near Badari*. British School of Archaeology in Egypt, London.

Brunton, G. and Engelbach, R. 1927. *Gurob*. British School of Archaeology in Egypt, London.

Bruyère, B. 1937–39. *Rapport sur les Fouilles de Deir el Medineh, 1933–34, 1934–35*. Imprimerie de l'Institut Francais d'Archeologie Orientale, Cairo.

Budka, J. 2001. *Der König an der Haustür: die Rolle des Ägyptischen Herrschers an Dekorierten Türgewänden von Beamten im Neuen Reich*. Afro-Pub, Vienna.

Budka, J. 2015. 'Pot marks on New Kingdom amphorae from the oases: The case of Umm el-Qaab' in J. Budka, F. Kammerzell and S. Rzepka (eds) *Non-textual Marking Systems in Ancient Egypt (and Elsewhere)*. Widmaier, Hamburg, 299–305

Budka, J. 2017. *AcrossBorders I: The New Kingdom Town of Sai Island, Sector SAV1 North*. Austrian Academy of Sciences, Vienna.

Budka, J. 2019. 'Pottery of the Middle and the New Kingdom from Lower and Upper Nubia' in G. Emberling and B. B. Williams (eds) *The Oxford Handbook of Ancient Nubia*, Oxford University Press, Oxford, 465–89.

Budka, J. 2020. *Across Borders 2: Living in New Kingdom Sai Island*. OAV, Vienna.

Caneva, I. 1992. 'Instruments lithiques de Héboua (Nord-Sinaï)' in *CRIPEL* 14, 39–44.

Carter, T. H. 1963. 'Reconnaissance in Cyrenaica' in *Expedition* 5(4), 18–27.

Caton Thompson, G. 1952. *Kharga Oasis in Prehistory*. The Athlone Press, University of London.

Černý, J. 1954. 'Prices and wages in Egypt in the Ramesside period' in *JWH* 1(4), 903–21.

Coulson, W. D. and A. Leonard 1979. 'A preliminary Survey of the Naukratis Region in the Western Nile Delta' in *JFA* 6, 151–68.

Crowfoot, G. M. 1931. *Methods of Hand Spinning in Egypt and the Sudan*. Bankfield Museum Notes Second Series no. 12, Halifax.

Dalton, M. and P. Ryan. 2020. 'Variable ovicaprid diet and faecal spherulite production at Amara West, Sudan' in *Environmental Archaeology*, 25(2), 178–97.

Davies, B. G. 1997. *Egyptian Historical Inscriptions of the Nineteenth Dynasty*. Paul Astroms Forlag, Jonsered.

Davies, N. de G. 1929. 'The Town House in Ancient Egypt' in *MMS* 1(2), 233–55.

de Cosson, A. D. 1935. *Mareotis: being a short account of the history and ancient monuments of the north-western desert of Egypt and of Lake Mareotis*. Country Life, London.

Desroches Noblecourt, Ch., Donadoni, S. and Edel, E. 1971. *Grand temple d'Abou Simbel II: la Bataille de Qadech. Description et Inscriptions, Dessins et Photographies*. Centre de Documentation et d'études sur l'ancienne Égypte, Cairo.

Dhennin, S. and C. Somaglino. 2022. 'Un temple de Ramsès II au Kôm el-Nogous (Plinthine): nouvelles données sur l'implication ramesside en Maréotide بيانات جديدة عن انخراط الرعامسة في منطقة بحيرة مريوطة معبد رمسيس الثاني في كوم النجوس (پلانتين):' in *BIFAO* 122, 209–43.

Ditze, B. 2007. 'Gedrückt – geritzt – gekratzt: die Gefäße mit Topfmarken' in E. B. Pusch (ed.) *Die Keramik des Grabungsplatzes Q I. Teil 2: Schaber – Marken – Scherben*. Gerstenber, Hildesheim, 269–507.

Dothan, T. and Brandl, B. 2010. *Deir el-Balah: Excavations in 1977–1982 in the Cemetery and Settlement: Stratigraphy and Architecture*. Institute of Archaeology, Hebrew University of Jerusalem, Jerusalem.

Dunham, D. 1967. *Second Cataract Forts, Volume 2: Uronarti, Shalfak and Mirgissa*. Museum of Fine Arts, Boston.

Dziobek, E. 1992. *Das Grab des Ineni: Theben Nr. 81*. Philipp von Zabern, Mainz.

Eisenlohr, A. 1897. 'The Rollin papyri and their baking calculations' in *Proceedings of the Society of Biblical Archaeology* 19, 91–104, 115–20, 147–55 and 252–65.

el-Ayedi, A. el-R. 2006. 'The dwelling of the lion' in *ASAE* 80, 35–43.

el-Barasi, Y. M. M. and Saaed, M. W. B. 2013. 'Threats to plant diversity in the north eastern part of Libya (El-Jabal, El-Akahdar and Marmarica Plateau)' in *Journal of Environmental Science and Engineering* A:2, 41–58.

el-Maksoud, M. A. 1998. *Tell Heboua (1981–1991): Enquête archéologique sur la deuxième période intermédiaire et le Nouvel Empire à l'extrémité Orientale du Delta*. Ministère des Affaires Etrangères, Editions Recherche sur les Civilisations, Paris.

el-Maksoud, M. A. and Valbelle, D. 2005. 'Tell Heboua-Tjarou: L'apport de L'Epigraphie' in *RdE* 56, 1–43.

el-Shahat, A. 1993. 'Middle Miocene carbonates from the Northern Plateau of the Western Desert (Egypt): Petrography and geochemistry' in *Facies* 28(1), 67–76.

Enmarch, R. 2008. *A World Upturned: Commentary on and Analysis of* The Dialogue of Ipuwer and the Lord of All. Oxford University Press, London.

Epigraphic Survey, 1934. *Medinet Habu, V. III: The Calendar, 'The Slaughter House' and Minor Records of Ramesses III*. University of Chicago, Chicago.

Erman, A. 1894. *Life in Ancient Egypt*. Macmillan and Co., London and New York.

Exell, K. 2009. *Soldiers, Sailors and Sandalmakers: A Social Reading of Ramesside Period Votive Stelae*. Golden House Publications, London.

Faulkner, R. O. 1953. 'Egyptian military organization' in *JEA* 39, 32–47.

Fitton, L., Hughes, M. and Quirke, S. 1998. 'Northerners at Lahun: neutron activation analysis of Minoan and related pottery in the British Museum' in S. Quirke (ed.) *Lahun Studies*. SIA, Reigate, 112–40

Foaden, G. and Fletcher, F. 1908. *Textbook of Egyptian Agriculture*, I. National Printing Department, Cairo.

Folk, R. L. 1965. *Petrology of Sedimentary Rocks*. Hemphill Publishing Company, Texas.

Forster, N., Grave, P., Vickery, N. and Kealhofer, L. 2011. 'Non-destructive analysis using PXRF: Methodology and application to archaeological ceramics' in *X-Ray Spectrometry* 40(5), 389–98.

Frances, W. J. and P. McGovern. 1993. *The Late Bronze Age Egyptian Garrison at Beth Shan: A Study of Levels VII and VIII*. The University Museum, Philadelphia.

Frankel, D. and Webb, J. M. 2012. 'Pottery production and distribution in Prehistoric Bronze Age Cyprus: An Application of pXRF Analysis' in *JAS* 39(5), 1380–7.

Frankfort, H. and Pendlebury, J. D. S. 1933. *The City of Akhenaten. Part II: The North Suburb and the Desert Altars*. Egypt Exploration Society, London.

Fuscaldo, P. 1992. 'Aksha (Serra West): la Datación del Sitio' in *REE* 3, 5–34.

Fuscaldo, P. 1994. 'Some more on Aksha' in *REE* 5, 9–24.

Gabolde, L. and Fahid, A. 2003. 'Door jamb with a proscynema to Amun-Rê-Horakhty and Montu (95 CL 381)' in *GM* 196, 19–23.

Gallorini, C. n.d. 'Innovation through Interactions: A Tale of Three Pilgrim Flasks' available at: https://www.researchgate.net/publication/260495223_Innovation_Through_Interactions_A_Tale_of_Three_%27Pilgrim_Flasks%27 (accessed 14 July 2023).

Garcia, J. C. M. 2014. 'Invaders or just herders? Libyans in Egypt in the 3rd and 2nd millennia BCE' in *World Archaeology* 46(4), 610–23

Gardner, E. A. 1888. *Naukratis II*. Egypt Exploration Fund, London.

Gasperini, V. 2016. 'Goods from the wine-dark sea: typology of imports excavated at Zawiyet Umm el-Rakham', in H. Franzmeier, Th. Rehren and R. Schulz (eds) *Mit archäologischen Schichten Geschichte schreiben Festschrift für Edgar B. Pusch zum 70. Geburtstag*. Forschungen in der Ramses-Stadt 10, Gerstenberg-Verlag, Hildesheim, 121–35

Giddy, L. 1999. *The Survey of Memphis II: Kom Rabi'a: The New Kingdom and Post-New Kingdom Objects*. Egypt Exploration Society, London.

Goren, Y., Mommsen, H. and Klinger, J. 2011. 'Non-destructive provenance study of Cuneiform tablets using portable x-ray fluorescence (pXRF)' in *JAS* 38, 684–96.

Goren, Y., Oren, E. D. and Feinstein, R. 1995. 'The archaeological and ethnoarchaeological interpretation of a ceramological enigma: pottery production in Sinai (Egypt) during the New Kingdom Period' in *KVHAA Konferenser* 34, 101–20.

Gorka, K. and Rzepka, S. 2011. 'Infant burials or infant sacrifices? New discoveries from Tell el-Retaba' in *MDAIK* 67, 99–106.

Gould, B. 2010. 'Egyptian pottery' in T. Dothan and B. Brandl (eds) *Deir el-Balaḥ: Excavations in 1977–1982 in the Cemetery and Settlement: The Finds*. Institute of Archaeology, Hebrew University of Jerusalem, Jerusalem, 7–56.

Grayson, D. K. 1984. *Quantitative Zooarchaeology*. Academic Press, New York.

Grezak, A. 2020. 'Animal economy at the settlement of Tell el-Retaba in the third Intermediate Period reconstructed on the basis of faunal remains excavated in seasons 2014–2019' in *Ä&L* 30, 157–77.

Habachi, L. 1955. 'Decouverte d'un temple-forteresse de Ramses II' in *La Revue du Caire* 33, 62–5.

Habachi, L. 1963. 'King Benhepetre Mentuhotep: his monuments, place in history, deification and unusual representations in the form of gods' in *MDAIK* 19, 16–52.

Habachi, L. 1980. 'The military posts of Ramesses II on the coastal road and the western part of the Delta' in *BIFAO* 80, 13–30

Halstead, P. and Jones, G. 1997. 'Agrarian ecology in the Greek Islands: time stress, scale and risk' in P. N. Kadulias and M. T. Shutes (eds) *Aegean Strategies: Studies of Culture and Environment on the European Fringe*. Rowman and Littlefield, Lanham, 271–94.

Hamada, A. and el-Amir, M. 1946. 'Excavations at Kom el-Hisn, season 1943' in *ASAE* 46, 101–41.

Hamada, A. and Farid, S. 1947. 'Excavations at Kom el-Hisn, season 1945' in *ASAE* 46, 195–235.

Hamada, A. and Farid, S. 1949. 'Excavations at Kom el-Hisn 3rd season 1946' in *ASAE* 48, 299–325.

Hamada, A. and Farid, S. 1950. 'Excavations at Kom el-Hisn 4th sSeason 1947' in *ASAE* 50, 367–78.

Hayward, H. E. and Spurr, W. B. 1944. 'The tolerance of flax to saline conditions: Effect of sodium chloride, calcium chloride, and sodium sulfate' in *JASA* 36, 287–300.

Heagren, B. 2007. 'Logistics of the Egyptian Army in Asia' in P. Kousoulis and K. Magliveras (eds) *Moving Across Borders: Foreign Relations, Religion and Cultural Interactions in the Ancient Mediterranean*. Peeters, Leuven, Paris, Dudley, 139–56.

Helck, W. 1970. *Die Prophezeieung des Nfr-tj*. Harrassowitz, Wiesbaden.

Helck, W. 1971. *Das Bier im Alten Agypten*. Gesellschaft fur die Geschichte und Bibliographie des Brauwesens, Berlin.

Hikade, T. 1999. 'An early dynastic flint workshop at Helwan' in *BACE* 10, 47–57.

Hikade, T. 2001. 'Silex-Pfeilspitzen in Ägypten' in *MDAIK* 57, 109–25

Hillman, G. C. 1984. 'Interpretation of archaeological plant remains: application of ethnographic models from Turkey' in W. Casparie and W. van Zeist (eds) *Plants and Ancient Man*. Balkema: Rotterdam, 1–41.

Hodel-Hoenes, S. 2000. *Life and Death in Ancient Egypt: Scenes from Private Tombs in New Kingdom Thebes*. Cornell University Press, Ithaca.

Hoffmeier, J. K. 2004. 'Tell el-Borg on Egypt's eastern frontier: a preliminary report on the 2002 and 2004 seasons' in *JARCE* 41, 85–111.

Hoffmeier, J. K. and el-Maksoud, M. A. 2003. 'A new military site on "the ways of Horus": Tell el-Borg 1999–2001: a preliminary report' in *JEA* 89, 16997.

Hoffmeier, J. K., Knudstad, J. E., Frey, R. A. Mumford, G. and Kitchen, K. A. 2014b. 'The Ramesside Period fort' in J. K. Hoffmeier (ed.) *Tell el-Borg, Volume I: Excavations in North Sinai*. Eisenbrauns, Winona Lake, 207–345.

Holscher, W. 1955. *Libyer und Agypter: Beitrage zur Ethnologie und Geschichte Libyscher Volkerschaften nach den Altagyptischen Quellen*. J.J. Augustin, Gluckstadt, Hamburg and New York.

Holthoer, R. 1977. *New Kingdom Pharaonic Sites – The Pottery*. SJE 5:1. Scandinavian University Books, Copenhagen, Oslo and Stockholm.

Homan, M. 2004. 'Beer and its drinkers: an Ancient Near Eastern love story' in *Near Eastern Archaeology* 67(2), 84–95.

Hope, C. A. 1987. 'Innovations in the decoration of ceramics in the mid-18th dynasty' in *CCE* 1, 97–122.

Hope, C. A. 1991. 'Blue painted and polychrome decorated pottery from Amarna: a preliminary corpus' in *CCE* 2, 17–92.

Hope, C. A. 1997. 'Some memphite blue painted pottery of the mid-18th dynasty' in J. Phillips (ed.) *Ancient Egypt, the Aegean and the Near East: Studies in Honor of Martha Rhodes Bell*. Van Siclen Book, San Antonio, 249–86.

Hope, C. A. 2016. *Survey of Memphis X: Kom Rabia: The Blue Painted Pottery*. Egypt Exploration Fund, London.

Hounsell, D. D. U. 2002. 'The occupation of Marmarica in the Late Bronze Age: an archaeological and ethnographical study'. PhD Thesis, University of Liverpool.

Hulin, L. 2001. 'Marmaric wares: New Kingdom and later examples' in *LibStud* 32, 67–78.

Hulin, L. 2009. 'Pragmatic technology and the Libyan Bronze Age' in *JAEI* 1(1), 18–21.

Hulin, L. 2018. 'Marsa Matruh revisited: modelling interaction at a Late Bronze Age harbour on the Egyptian coast' in A. Manzo, C. Zazzaro and D. J. De Falco (eds) *Stories of Globalisation: The Red Sea and the Persian Gulf from Late Prehistory to Early Modernity*. Brill, Leiden, 53–64.

Hummel, R. 2014. 'A report on the ceramics recovered from Tell El-Borg' in J. K. Hoffmeier (ed.) *Tell el-Borg, Volume I: Excavations in North Sinai*. Eisenbrauns, Winona Lake, 364–435.

Hummel, R. 2019a. 'Excursus I: ceramic report from field II at Tell el-Borg' in J. K. Hoffmeier (ed.) *Excavations in North Sinai: Tell el-Borg II*. Penn State University Press, Philadelphia, 136–64.

Hummel, R. 2019b. 'Excursus: a deposit of restorable pottery from a cemetery pit' in J. K. Hoffmeier (ed.) *Excavations in North Sinai: Tell el-Borg II*. Penn State University Press, Philadelphia, 236–58.

Hummel, R. 2019c. 'Excursus: pottery from Field VI.1 AA' in J. K. Hoffmeier (ed.) *Excavations in North Sinai: Tell el-Borg II*. Penn State University Press, Philadelphia, 299–303.

Hummel, R. 2019d. 'Pottery from Field VI Area III Fosse' in J. K. Hoffmeier (ed.) *Excavations in North Sinai: Tell el-Borg II*. Penn State University Press, Philadelphia, 342–6.

Huret, T. 1990. 'Les pointes de flèches métalliques en Égypte ancienne: essai de typologie' in *CRIPEL* 12, 57–66.

Ibrahim, M. M. and Mohamed, H. M. 2019. 'Analytical methods of archaeological pottery sarcophagus excavated from Saqqara, Egypt' in *Scientific Culture* 5(1), 49–59.

Ikram, S. 1995. *Choice Cuts: 𓃀𓄿𓋴𓏛 Meat Production in Ancient Egypt.* Peeters, Leuven.

James, F. W. and McGovern, P. E. 1993b. *The Late Bronze Egyptian Garrison at Beth Shan: a Study of Levels VII and VIII*, vol. II. University of Pennsylvania, University Museum, Philadelphia.

Janssen, J. J. 1975. *Commodity Prices from the Ramesside Period: An Economic Study of the Village Necropolis Workmen at Thebes*. E. J. Brill, Leiden.

Janssen, J. J. 1997. *Village Varia: Ten Studies on the History and Administration of Deir el-Medina*. Nederlands Instituut voor het Nabije Oosten, Leiden.

Janssen, J. J. 2004. *Grain Transport in the Ramesside Period: Papyrus Baldwin (BM EA 10061) and Papyrus Amiens*. British Museum Press, London.

Jeffreys, D., Malek, J. and Smith, H. S. 1986. 'Memphis 1984' in *JEA* 72, 1–14.

Johnson, A. C. 1959. *Roman Egypt: To the Reign of Diocletian*. Pageant Books, Paterson

Kaplan, M. F. 1980. *The Origin and Distribution of Tell el Yahudiyeh Ware*. Paul Astroms Forlag, Goteborg.

Kemp, B. J. 1986. 'Large Middle Kingdom granary buildings and the archaeology of administration' in *ZÄS* 113, 120–36.

Kemp, B. J. 1989. *Ancient Egypt: Anatomy of a Civilization*. Routledge, New York and London.

Kemp, B. J. 1995. 'Outlying temples at Amarna' in B. J. Kemp (ed.) *Amarna Reports VI*. Egypt Exploration Society, London, 411–62, 433–8.

Kemp, B. J. and Stevens, A. 2010a. *Busy Lives at Amarna: Excavations in the Main City (Grid 12 and the House of Ranefer, N49.18), Vol. 1: The Excavations, Architecture and Environmental Remains*. Egypt Exploration Society, London.

Kemp, B. J. and Stevens, A. 2010b. *Busy Lives at Amarna: Excavations in the Main City (Grid 12 and the House of Ranefer, N49.18), Vol. 2: The Objects*. Egypt Exploration Society, London.

Kemp, B. J. and Vogelsang-Eastwood, G. 2001. *The Ancient Textile Industry at Amarna*. Egypt Exploration Society, London.

Kemp, B. J., Samuel, D. and Luff, R. 1994. 'Food for an Egyptian city: Tell el-Amarna' in R. Luff and P. Rowley-Conwy (eds) *Whither Environmental Archaeology?* Oxbow, Oxford, 133–70.

Killebrew, A. E. 2010. 'Canaanite pottery' in T. Dothan and B. Brandl (eds) *Deir el-Balaḥ: Excavations in 1977–1982 in the Cemetery and Settlement: The Finds*. Institute of Archaeology, Hebrew University of Jerusalem, Jerusalem, 75–110.

Kirby, C. J., Orel, S. E. and Smith, S. T. 1998. 'Preliminary report on the survey of Kom El-Hisn, 1996' in *JEA* 84(1), 23–43.

Kitchen, K. A. 1990. 'The arrival of the Libyans in Late New Kingdom Egypt' in A. Leahy (ed.) *Libya and Egypt: 1300–750 BC*. University of London, London, 15–27.

Kitchen, K. A. 1993a. *Ramesside Inscriptions, Translated & Annotated: Translations, Volume I. Ramesses I, Sethos I and Contemporaries*. Blackwell, Oxford.

Kitchen, K. A. 1993b. 'A "fan bearer on the King's Right Hand" from Ashdod' in *Atiqot* 23, 109–10.

Kitchen, K. A. 1996. *Ramesside Inscriptions, Translated & Annotated: Translations, Volume II. Ramesses II, Royal Inscriptions*. Blackwell, Oxford.

Kitchen, K. A. 2001. *Ramesside Inscriptions, Translated & Annotated: Translations, Volume III. Ramesses II, His Contemporaries*. Blackwell, Oxford.

Kitchen, K. A. 2003. *Ramesside Inscriptions, Translated & Annotated: Translations, Volume IV. Merenptah and the Late Nineteenth Dynasty*. Blackwell, Oxford.

Kitchen, K. A. 2008. *Ramesside Inscriptions, Translated & Annotated: Translations, Volume V. Setnakht, Ramesses III & Contemporaries*. Blackwell, Oxford.

Klein, A. 2010. 'Stone Implements and Related Objects' in T. Dothan and B. Brandl (eds) *Deir el-Balaḥ: Excavations in 1977–1982 in the Cemetery and Settlement: The Finds*. Institute of Archaeology, Hebrew University of Jerusalem, Jerusalem, 279–302.

Knudsen, J. 2003. 'Manufacturing methods of pilgrim flasks and related vessels from Cemetery 500 at el-Ahaiwah' in C. A. Redmount and C. A. Keller (eds) *Egyptian Pottery: Proceedings of the 1990 Pottery Symposium at the University of California, Berkeley*. University of California Publications in Egyptian Archaeology, Berkeley, 87–94.

Korobkova, G. F. 1981. 'Ancient reaping tools and their productivity in light of experimental traceware analysis' in P. L. Kohl (ed.) *The Bronze Age Civilization of Central Asia: Recent Soviet Discoveries*. M. E. Sharpe, New York, 325–49.

Kuentz, C. 1928. *La bataille de Qadech: les Textes ('Poème de Pentaour' et 'Bulletin de Qadech') et les Bas-reliefs*. Imprimerie de l'Institut français d'archéologie orientale, Cairo.

Laemmel, S. 2008. 'Preliminary report on the pottery from area QIV at Qantir/Pi-Ramesse: excavations of the Roemer-Pelizaeus Museum, Hildesheim' in *Ä&L* 18, 173–202.

Leclant, J. 1954. 'Fouilles et travaux en Égypte 1952–1953' in *Orientalia* 23, 64–79.

Leclant, J. 1955. 'Fouilles et travaux en Égypte 1953–1954' in *Orientalia* 24, 296–317.

Leclant, J. 1956. 'Fouilles et travaux en Égypte 1954–1955' in *Orientalia* 25, 251–68.

Legge, A. J. 2008. 'The mammal bones from grid 12' in B. J. Kemp and A. Stevens (eds) *Busy Lives at Amarna: Excavations in the Main City (grid 12 and the House of*

Ranefer, N49.18), Vol. 1: The Excavations, Architecture and Environmental Remains. Egypt Exploration Society, London, 445–52.

Legge, A. J. 2012. 'Animal remains at the Stone Village' in A. Stevens (ed.) *Akhenaten's Workers: the Amarna Stone Village Survey, 2005–2009, Vol. 2: The Faunal and Botanical Remains, and Objects*. Egypt Exploration Society, London, 9–13.

Lernau, H. 1988. 'Fish remains' in B. Rothenberg (ed.) *The Egyptian Mining Temple at Timna*. The University of London, London, 241–6.

Lewis, O. 1951. *Life in a Mexican Village: Tepozlan Restudied*. University of Illinois Press, Urbana.

Linseele, V. and Van Neer, W. 2010. 'Exploitation of desert and other wild game in ancient Egypt: the archaeozoological evidence from the Nile Valley' in H. Riemer, F. Förster, M. Herb and N. Pöllath (eds) *Desert Animals in the Eastern Sahara*. Heinrich Barth Institute, Köln, 47–78.

Loredana, S. 1988. 'Food production' in A. M. D. Roveri (ed.) *Egyptian Civilization*, vol. I. Electa Editrice, Milan, 46–75.

Lorton, D. 1990. 'The Aswan/Philae inscription of Thutmosis II' in S. Israelite-Groll (ed.) *Studies in Egyptology Presented to Miriam Lichtheim*, Vol. 2. Magnes Press, Jerusalem, 668–79.

Luff, R. M. 1994. 'Butchery at the workmen's village, Tell el-Amarna, Egypt' in R. M. Luff and P. Rowley-Conwy (eds) *Whither Environmental Archaeology?* Oxbow, Oxford, 158–70.

Lyon, G. F. 1821. *A Narrative of Travels in Northern Africa in the Years 1818–1819 and 1820*. John Murray, London.

Malleson, C. 2022. 'Archaeological approaches to the logistics of feeding Ancient Egyptian workforces: the value of traditional techniques and consistent methods' in A. Quiles and B. Gehad (eds) *Proceedings of the First International Conference on the Science of Ancient Egyptian Materials and Technologies*. IFAO, 133–42.

Manassa, C. 2003. *The Great Karnak Inscription of Merneptah: Grand Strategy in the 13th Century BC*. Oxbow, Oxford.

Mansour, K. M. 1995. 'Underutilized fruit crops in Egypt' in *Cahier Options Méditerranéennes* 13, 13–19.

Marchand, S. 2017. 'Remarques sur les moules à pain dans L'Égypte ancienne' in *BCEg* 27, 223–50.

Martin, G. T. 1989. *The Memphite Tomb of Horemheb Commander-in-Chief of Tutankhamun I: The Reliefs, Inscriptions, and Commentary*. Egypt Exploration Society, London.

Martin, M. A. S. 2004. 'Egyptian and Egyptianized pottery in Late Bronze Age Canaan: typology, chronology, ware fabrics and manufacture techniques. Pots and people?' in *Ä&L* 14, 265–84.

Martin, M. A. S. 2007. 'A collection of Egyptian and Egyptian-style pottery at Beth Shean' in M. Bietak and E. Czerny (eds) *The Synchronisation of Civilisations in the Eastern Mediterranean in the Second Millennium BC: Proceedings of the SCIEM 2000–2nd EuroConference, Vienna, 28th of May – 1st of June 2003*. Osterreichische Akademie der Wissenschaften, Vienna, 375–88.

Martin, M. A. S. 2008. 'Egyptians at Ashkelon? An assemblage of Egyptian and Egyptian-style pottery' in *Ä&L* 18, 245–74.

Martin, M. A. S. and Ben-Dov, R. 2008. 'Egyptian and Egyptian-style pottery at Tel Dan' in *Ä&L* 17, 191–204.

Meigs, P. 1966. *Geography of Coastal Deserts*. UNESCO, Paris.

Midant-Reynes, B. 1998. *Les Silex de Ayn Asil Oasis de Dakhle-Balat*. IFAO, Cairo.

Miller, R. 1987. 'Appendix: ash as an insecticide' in B. J. Kemp (ed.) *Amarna Reports IV*. Egypt Exploration Society, London, 14–16.

Moeller, N. 2010. 'Tell Edfu: preliminary report on season 2005–2009' in *JARCE* 46, 81–111.

Moeller, N. 2015. 'Multifunctionality and hybrid households: the case of Ancient Egypt' in M. Müller (ed.) *Household Studies in Complex Societies: (Micro) Archaeological and Textual Approaches*. The Oriental Institute, Chicago, 437–46.

Moens, M. and Wetterstrom, W. 1988. 'The agricultural economy of an Old Kingdom town in Egypt's West Delta: insights from the plant remains' in *JNES* 47(3), 159–73.

Morgenstein, M. and Redmount, C. A. 2005. 'Using portable energy dispersive x-ray fluorescence (EDXRF): analysis for on-site study of ceramic sherds at El Hibeh, Egypt' in *JAS* 32(11), 1613–23.

Morris, E. F. 2005. *The Architecture of Imperialism: Military Bases and the Evolution of Foreign Policy in Egypt's New Kingdom*. Brill, Leiden.

Moshier, S. O. 2014. 'The geological setting of Tell el-Borg with implications for ancient geography of Northwest Sinai' in J. K. Hoffmeier (ed.) *Tell el-Borg, Volume I: Excavations in North Sinai*. Eisenbrauns, Winona Lake, 62–84.

Mueller, K. 2006. *Settlements of the Ptolemies: City Foundations and New Settlement in the Hellenistic World*. Peeters, Leuven.

Mueller, K. and Lee, W. 2005. 'From mess to matrix and beyond: estimating the size of settlements in the Ptolemaic Fayum/Egypt' in *JAS* 32, 59–67.

Murnane, W. J. *The Road to Kadesh: A Historical Interpretation of the Battle Reliefs of King Sety I at Karnak*. The University of Chicago, Chicago.

Murray, M. A. 2000. 'Cereal production and processing' in P. T. Nicholson and I. Shaw (eds) *Ancient Egyptian Materials and Technology*. Cambridge University Press, Cambridge, 5–77.

Nagel, G. 1938. *La ceramique du Nouvelle Empire*. DFIFAO, Cairo.

Nielsen, N. 2014. 'Some notes on a New Kingdom ovoid bottle in the Liverpool World Museum' in *JEA* 100, 485–9.

Nielsen, N. 2015. 'Subsistence strategies and craft production at the Ramesside fort of Zawiyet Umm el-Rakham'. Doctoral dissertation, University of Liverpool.

Nielsen, N. 2016. 'A corpus of Nineteenth Dynasty Egyptian pottery from Zawiyet Umm el-Rakham' in *JAEI* 9, 59–71.

Nielsen, N. 2017. 'Cereal cultivation and nomad-sedentary interactions at the Late Bronze Age settlement of Zawiyet Umm el-Rakham' in *Antiquity* 91(360), 1561–73.

Nielsen, N. 2018. *Pharaoh Seti I: Father of Egyptian Greatness*. Pen & Sword: Barnsley.

O'Connor, D. 1990. 'The nature of Tjemhu (Libyan) society in the later New Kingdom' in A. Leahy (ed.) *Libya and Egypt: 1300–750 BC*. University of London, London, 29–114.

Oren, E. D. 1987. 'The "Ways of Horus" in North Sinai' in A. F. Rainey (ed.) *Egypt, Israel, Sinai: Archaeological and Historical Relationships in the Biblical Period*. Tel Aviv University, Tel Aviv, 69–119.

Oriental Institute Epigraphic Survey. 1986. *The Battle Reliefs of King Sety I*. University of Chicago, Chicago.

Osing, J. 1980. 'Libyen, Libyer' in W. Helck and W. Westendorf (eds) *Lexicon der Ägyptologie*, V. III, Harrassowitz, Wiesbaden, cols 1015–33.

Ownby, M. F. 2006. 'Non-destructive x-ray fluorescence spectrometry of marl C sherds from Kahun, Egypt'. Unpublished MSc Thesis, Institute of Archaeology, University College London, London.

Ownby, M. F. 2010. 'Canaanite jars from Memphis as evidence for trade and political relationships in the Middle Bronze Age'. PhD Thesis, University of Cambridge.

Ownby, M. F. 2012. 'The importance of imports: petrographic analysis of Levantine jars in Egypt' in *JAEI* 4(3), 23–9.

Ownby, M. F. 2016a. 'Petrographic analysis of Egyptian ceramic fabrics in the Vienna system' in B. Bader, C. M. Knoblauch and E. C. Köhler (eds) *Vienna 2: Ancient Egyptian Ceramics in the 21st Century*. Peeters, Leuven, 459–70.

Ownby, M. F. 2016b. 'Provenance study of Middle Bronze Age Cananaite Jars' in J. Bourriau and C. Gallorini (eds) *The Survey of Mephis VIII, Kom Rabia: The Middle Kingdom and Second Intermediate Period Pottery*. Egypt Exploration Society, London, 257–70.

Ownby, M. F. and Bourriau, J. 2009. 'The movement of Middle Bronze age transport jars: a porvenance study based on petrographic and chemical analysis of Canaanite jars from Memphis, Egypt' in P. Quinn (ed.) *Interpreting Silent Artefacts: Petrographic Approaches to Archaeological Ceramics*. Archaeopress, Oxford, 173–88.

Ownby, M. F. and Brand, M. 2019. 'Advances in Egyptian ceramic petrography' in *BCEg* 29, 371–91.

Ownby, M. F. and Griffiths, D. 2009. 'Issues of scum: technical analyses of Egyptian Marl C to answer technological questions' in *Ä&L* 19, 229–39.

Ownby, M. F. and Smith, L. M. V. 2011. 'The impact of changing political situations on trade between Egypt and the Near East: a provenance study of Canaanite jars from Memphis, Egypt' in K. Duistermaat and I. Regulski (eds) *Intercultural Contacts in the Ancient Mediterranean: Proceedings of the International Conference at the Netherlands Flemish Institute in Cairo, 25th to 29th October 2008*. Peeters, Leuven, 267–84.

Ownby, M. F., Franzmeier, H., Laemmel, S. and Pusch, E. 2014. 'Late Bronze Age imports at Qantir: petrographic and contextual analysis of fabric groups' in *JAEI* 6(3), 11–21.

Padgham, K. 2014. *The Scale and Nature of the Late Bronze Age Economies of Egypt and Cyprus*. Archaeopress, Oxford.

Parkinson, R. and Schofield, L. 1995. 'Images of Mycenaeans: a recently acquired painted papyrus from El-Amarna' in W. Vivian Davies and L. Schofield (eds) *Egypt, the Aegean and the Levant: Interconnections in the Second Millenium BC*. British Museum Press, London.

Peet, T. E. and Woolley, C. L. 1923. *The City of Akhenaten*, Vol. 1. Egypt Exploration Society, London.

Peters-Desteract, M. 2005. *Pain, bière et toutes bonnes choses . . . L'alimentation dans l'Égypte ancienne*. Champollion, Monaco.

Petrie, W. M. F. 1886. *Naukratis I*. Egypt Exploration Fund, London.

Petrie, W. M. F. 1917. *Tools and Weapons: Illustrated by the Egyptian Collection in University College, London, and 2000 Outlines from Other Sources*. Bernard Quaritch, London.

Petrie, W. M. F. 1927. *Objects of Daily Use*. Bernard Quaritch, London.

Petrie, W. M. F. and Duncan, J. G. 1906. *Hyksos and Israelite Cities*. Bernard Quaritch, London.

Posener, G. 1940. *Princes et pays d'Asie et de la Nubia: Textes hieratiques sur des figurines d'envoutement du Moyen Empire*. Fondation Égyptologique Reine Élisabeth, Bruxelles.

Potvin, M. and Pierrat-Bonnefois, G. 2002. *Les conventions plastiques de l'art égyptien au temps des pharaons*. Musée du Louvre, Paris.

Prell, S. 2011. *Einblicke in die Werkstätten der Residenz – Die Stein – und Metallwerkzeuge des Grabungsplatzes QI*. FoRa 8, Hildesheim.

Pusch, E. B. 1990. 'Metallverarbeitende Werkstatten der frühen Ramessidenzeit in Qantir-Piramesse/Nord – Ein Zwischenbericht' in *Ä&L* 1, 75–113.

Pusch, E. B. 1994. 'Divergierende Verfahren der Metallverarbeitung in Theben und Qantir? Bemerkungen zur Konstruktion und Technik' in Ä&L 4, 145–70.

Pusch, E. B. and T. Rehren. 2007. *Hochtemperatur-Technologie in der Ramses-Stadt Rubinglass fur den Pharao – Teil 1 Text.* Gerstenberg, Hildesheim.

Raedler, C. 2003. 'Zur Repräsentation und Verwirklichung pharaonischer Macht in Nubien: Der Vizekönig Setau' in R. Gundlach und U. Rössler-Köhler (eds) *Das Königtum der Ramessidenzeit: Voraussetzungen, Verwirklichung, Vermächtnis.* Harrassowitz, Wiesbaden, 129–73.

Riefstahl, E. 1956. 'Two hairdressers of the Eleventh Dynasty' in *JNES* 15(1), 10–17.

Rieger, A., Vetter, T. and Möller, H. 2012. 'The desert dwellers of Marmarica, Western Desert: second millennium BCE to first millennium CE' in H. Barnard and K. Duistermaat (eds) *The History of the Peoples of the Eastern Desert.* University of California, Los Angeles, 157–73.

Rizk, Z. S. and Davis, A. D. 1991. 'Impact of the proposed Qattara Reservoir on the Moghra aquifer of Northwestern Egypt' in *Ground Water* 29(2), 232–8.

Robins, G. 1993. *Women in Ancient Egypt.* British Museum Press, London.

Roller, G. 1992. 'Archaeobotanical remains from Tell Ibrahim Awad' in E. C. M. Brink (ed.) *The Nile Delta in Transition: 4th –3rd Millennium BC: Proceedings of the Seminar Held in Cairo, 21–24 October 1990, at the Netherlands Institute of Archaeology and Arabic Studies.* E. C. M. van den Brink, Tel Aviv, 111–15.

Rose, P. J. 2007. *The Eighteenth Dynasty Pottery Corpus from Amarna.* Egypt Exploration Society, London.

Rosen, S. A. 1997. *Lithics after the Stone Age: A Handbook of Stone Tools from the Levant.* AltaMira Press, Walnut Creek.

Rosen, S. A. and Goring-Morris, A. N. 2010. 'The Lithic assemblage' in T. Dothan and B. Brandl (eds) *Deir el-Balaḥ: Excavations in 1977–1982 in the Cemetery and Settlement: The Finds.* Institute of Archaeology, Hebrew University of Jerusalem, Jerusalem, 273–8.

Rowe, A. 1948. *New Light on Ægypto-Cyrenæan Relations: Two Ptolemaic Statues Found in Tolmeita.* Imprimerie de l'Institut Francais d'Archeologie Orientale, Cairo.

Rowe, A. 1953. 'A contribution to the Archaeology of the Western Desert 1' in *Bulletin of the John Rylands Library* 36, 128–45.

Rowe, A. 1954. 'A contribution to the Archaeology of the Western Desert 2' in *Bulletin of the John Rylands Library* 37, 484–500.

Royal Geographical Society. 1916. 'The north-west frontier of Egypt' in *Geographical Journal* 47(2), 130–4.

Ruffieux, P. 2016. 'Pottery of the 18th Dynasty at Dukki Gel (Kerma): classical repertoire and local style' in B. Bader, C. M. Knoblauch and E. C. Köhler (eds) *Vienna 2: Ancient Egyptian Ceramics in the 21st Century*, Peeters, Leuven, 507–25.

Ryan, P. 2017. 'From raw resources to food processing: archaeobotanical and ethnographic insights from Amara West and present day Ernetta Island in North Sudan' in L. Steel and K. Zinn (eds) *Exploring the Materiality of Food 'Stuffs': Archaeological and Anthropological Perspectives*. Routledge, London, 15–38.

Ryan, P., Cartwright, C. and Spencer, N. 2012. 'Archaeobotanical research in a pharaonic town in ancient Nubia' in *British Museum Technical Research Bulletin* 6, 97–106.

Rzepka, S., Hudec, J. and Jarmuzek, L. 2013. 'Tell el-Retaba: season 2010' in *Polish Archaeology in the Mediterranean* 22, 79–95.

Rzepka, S., el-Din, M. N., Wodzińska, A. and Jarmuzek, L. 2012–13. 'Egyptian mission rescue excavations in Tell el-Retaba. Part 1: New Kingdom remains' in *Ä&L* 22–23, 253–87.

Rzepka, S., Wodzińska, A., Hudec, J. and Herbich, T. 2009. 'Tell el-Retaba 2007–2008' in *Ä&L* 19, 241–80.

Rzepka, S., Wodzińska, A., Malleson, C., Hudec, J., Jarmuzek, L., Misiewicz, K., Malkowski, W. and Bogacki, M. 2011. 'New Kingdom and the third intermediate period in Tell el-Retaba: results of the Polish-Slovak archaeological mission, seasons 2009–2010' in *Ä&L* 21, 129–84.

Sagrillo, T. 2012. 'Šîšaq's army: 2 chronicles 12:2–3 from an Egyptological perspective', in G. Galil, A. Gilboa, A. M. Maeir and D. Kahn (eds) *The Ancient Near East in the 12th–10th Centuries BCE: Culture and History. Proceedings of the International Conference Held at the University of Haifa, 2–5 May, 2010*. Ugarit-Verlag, Münster, 425–50.

Samuel, D. 1989. 'Their staff of life: initial investigations on Ancient Egyptian bread baking' in B. J. Kemp (ed.) *Amarna Reports V*. Egypt Exploration Society, London, 253–90.

Samuel, D. 1992. 'Ancient Egyptian baking and brewing' in S. Curto and A.-M. Donadoni-Roveri (eds) *Sesto Congresso Internazionale di Egittologia*. Vol. 1. Società Italiana per il Gas, Turin, 120–34.

Samuel, D. 1996. 'Investigation of ancient Egyptian baking and brewing methods by correlative microscopy' in *Science* 273(5274), 488–90.

Samuel, D. 1999. 'Bread making and social interactions at the Amarna Workmen's Village, Egypt' in *World Archaeology* 31, 121–44.

Samuel, D. 2000. 'Brewing and baking' in P. T. Nicholson and I. Shaw (eds), *Ancient Egyptian Materials and Technology*. Cambridge University Press, Cambridge, 537–76

Samuel, D. 2009. 'Experimental grinding and Ancient Egyptian flour production' in S. Ikram and A. Dodson (eds) *Beyond the Horizon: Studies in Egyptian Art,*

Archaeology and History in Honour of Barry J. Kemp, vol. 2. Supreme Council of Antiquities, Cairo, 456–77.

Schneider, H. D. 1996. *The Memphite Tomb of Horemheb, Commander-In-Chief of Tutankhamun II: A Catalogue of the Finds*. Egypt Exploration Society, London.

Schulman, A. R. 1964. 'Military organization in pharaonic Egypt' in *JARCE* 3, 51–69.

Schwartzer, C. L. 1990. 'House E' in P. Lacovara (ed.) *Deir el-Ballas: Preliminary Report on the Deir el-Ballas Expedition, 1980–1986*. American Research Centre in Egypt, Winona Lake, 6–8.

Sethe, K. 1929. *Ägyptische Texte zum Gebrauch im akademischen Unterricht: Texte der mittleren Reiches*. Georg Olms, Hildesheim.

Sethe, K. 1933. *Urkunden des Alten Reichs*. Hinrichs, Leipzig.

Sethe, K. 1961. *Urkunden der 18. Dynastie: Vierter Band*. Akademie-Verlag, Berlin.

Shaw, I. 1992. 'Ideal homes in Ancient Egypt: the archaeology of social aspiration' in *CAJ* 2(2), 147–66.

Simpson, F. 2002. 'Evidence for a Late Bronze Age Libyan presence in the Egyptian fortress at Zawiyet Umm el-Rakham'. PhD Thesis, University of Liverpool.

Smith, S. T. 2003. *Wretched Kush: Ethnic Identifies and Boundaries in Egypt's Nubian Empire*. Routledge, London.

Smoláriková, K. 2014. 'Ceramics from the Ramesside enclosure' in N. Spencer (ed.) *Kom Firin II: The Urban Fabric and Landscape*. British Museum Press, London, 47–52.

Snape, S. 1995. 'Egypt's North-Western defenses in the Late New Kingdom' in C. J. Eyre (ed.) *Seventh International Congress of Egyptologists, Cambridge, 3–9 September 1995: Abstract of Papers*. Oxbow, Oxford, 170–2.

Snape, S. 1998. 'Walls, wells and wandering merchants: Egyptian control of Marmarica in the Late Bronze Age' in C. J. Eyre (ed.) *Proceedings of the Seventh International Congress of Egyptologists, Cambridge, 3–9 September 1995*. Peeters, Leuven, 1081–4.

Snape, S. 2001. 'Neb-Re and the heart of darkness: the latest discoveries from Zawiyet Umm el-Rakham (Egypt)' in *Antiquity* 75, 19–20.

Snape, S. 2003. 'The emergence of Libya on the horizon of Egypt' in D. B. O'Connor and S. Quirke (eds) *Mysterious Lands*. UCL Press, London, 93–106.

Snape, S. 2004. 'The excavations of the Liverpool University mission to Zawiyet Umm el-Rakham 1994–2001' in *ASAE* 78, 149–60.

Snape, S. 2010. 'Vor der Kaserne: external supply and self-sufficiency at Zawiyet Umm el-Rakham' in M. Bietak, E. Czerny and I. Forstner-Müller (eds) *Cities and Urbanism in Ancient Egypt: Papers from a Workshop in November 2006 at the Austrian Academy of Sciences*. Verlag der Österreichischen Akademie der Wissenschaften, Wien, 271–88.

Snape, S. 2013. 'A stroll along the corniche: coastal routes between the Nile Delta and Cyrenaica in the Late Bronze Age' in F. Förster and H. Riemer (eds) *Desert Road Archaeology in Ancient Egypt and Beyond*. Heinrich-Barth-Institut, Cologne, 439–54.

Snape, S. and Godenho, G. In press. *Zawiyet Umm el-Rakham II: The Monuments of Nebre*. Rutherford Press, Bolton.

Snape, S. and Wilson, P. 2007. *Zawiyet Umm el-Rakham I: The Temple and Chapels*. Rutherford Press, Bolton.

Spalinger, A. J. 1979a. 'The Northern Wars of Seti I: an integrative study' in *JARCE* 16, 29–47.

Spalinger, A. J. 1979b. 'Some notes on the Libyans of the Old Kingdom and the later historical reflexes' in *JSSEA* 9(3), 125–60.

Spalinger, A. J. 1986. 'Baking during the reign of Seti I' in *BIFAO* 86, 307–52.

Spalinger, A. J. 1987. 'The grain system of dynasty 18' *SAK* 14, 283–311.

Spalinger, A. J. 2005. *War in Ancient Egypt: The New Kingdom*. Blackwell, Oxford.

Sparks, R. T. 2007. *Stone Vessels in the Levant*. Maney Publishing, London.

Spataro, M., Millet, M. and Spencer, N. 2014. 'The New Kingdom settlement of Amara West (Nubia, Sudan): mineralogical and chemical investigation of the ceramics' in *Archaeological and Anthropological Sciences* 7, 399–421.

Spence, K. 2015. 'Ancient Egyptian houses and households: architecture, artefacts, conceptualisation and interpretation' in M. Müller (ed.) *Household Studies in Complex Societies: (Micro) Archaeological and Textual Approaches*. The Oriental Institute, Chicago, 83–100.

Spence, K., Rose, P. J., Bradshaw, R., Collet, P., Hassan, A., MacGinnis, J., et al. 2011. 'Sesebi 2011' in *Sudan & Nubia* 15, 34–8.

Spencer, N. 2008. *Kom Firin I: the Ramesside Temple and the Site Survey*. British Museum, London.

Spencer, N. 2012. 'Insights into life in occupied Kush during the New Kingdom: new research at Amara West' in *Der Antike Sudan. Mitteilungen der Sudanarchäologischen Gesellschaft zu Berlin* 23, 21–8.

Spencer, N. 2014. *Kom Firin II: The Urban Fabric and Landscape*. British Museum Press, London.

Spencer, N. 2015. 'Creating a neighbourhood within a changing town: household and other agencies at Amara West, Nubia' in M. Müller (ed.) *Household Studies in Complex Societies: (Micro) Archaeological and Textual Approaches*. The Oriental Institute, Chicago, 169–210

Steensberg, A. 1943. *Ancient Harvesting Implements: A Study in Archaeology and Human Geography*. Nordisk Forlag, Copenhagen.

Stevens, A. 2006. *Private Religion at Amarna: The Material Evidence*. Archaeopress, Oxford.

Strassler, R. B., ed. 2009. *The Landmark Herodotus: The Histories*. Anchor, New York.
Takahashi, K. 2014. 'Blue painted pottery from North Saqqara' in J. Kondo (ed.) *Quest for the Dream of the Pharaoh: Studies in Honour fo Sakuji Yoshimura*. Cairo, 115–33.
Takahashi, K. 2017. 'Blue painted pottery from the mid-18th Dynasty royal mud brick structure in North West Saqqara' in G. Rosati and M. C. Guidotti (eds) *Proceedings of the XIth International Congress of Egyptologists*. Archaeopress, Oxford, 613–18.
Takahashi, K. 2019. 'Blue Painted pottery with intentional holes and/or breakings after firing in Northwest Saqqara' in *BCEg* 29, 85–99.
Takahashi, K. 2020. 'Simplification in pottery technology of blue painted pottery in New Kingdom Egypt' in *BCEg* 30, 5–33.
Takamiya, I. H. 2007. 'Blue-painted pottery from a New Kingdom Site at North Saqqara: a preliminary report of the Waseda University expedition' in J. Goyon and C. Cardin (eds) *Proceedings of the Ninth International Congress of Egyptologists: Grenoble, 6–12 septembre 2004*, Vol. 2. Leuven, Peeters, 1757–68.
Tassie, G. J. 2008. 'The social and ritual contextualisation of Ancient Egyptian hair and hairstyles from the Protodynastic to the end of the Old Kingdom: Volume 1 (Text)'. PhD Thesis, University College London.
Thomas, A. P. 1981. *Gurob: a New Kingdom town*, V. I. Aris & Phillips Ltd, Warminster.
Thomas, S. 2000. 'Aspects of technology and trade in Egypt and the Eastern Mediterranean during the Late Bronze Age'. PhD Thesis, The University of Liverpool, Liverpool.
Thomas, S. 2003. 'Imports at Zawiyet Umm el-Rakham' in Z. Hawass and L. Pinch Brock (eds) *Egyptology at the Dawn of the Twenty-First Century: Proceedings of the Eight International Congress of Egyptologists, Cairo, 2000*, Vol. 1. American University in Cairo Press, Cairo, 530–5.
Thomas, S. 2011. 'Chariots, cobras and Canaanites: a Ramesside miscellany from Tell Abqa'in' in M. Collier and S. Snape (eds) *Ramesside Studies in Honour of K. A. Kitchen*. Rutherford, Bolton, 519–31.
Tietze, C. 1985. 'Amarna: Analyse des Wohnhäuser und Soziale Struktur der Stadtbewohner' in *ZÄS* 112, 48–84.
Trampier, J. R. 2014. *Landscape Archaeology of the Western Nile Delta*. Wilbour Studies in Egypt and Ancient Western Asia 2. Lockwood, Atlanta.
Traunecker, C. 1981. 'Code analytique de profits de céramique de l'ancienne Égypte' in D. Arnold (ed.) *Studien zur Altägyptischen Keramik*. Philipp von Zabern, Mainz, 49–77.
Trudgill, S. T. 1985. *Limestone Geomorphology*. Longmans, London
Tylor, J. and Griffith, F. 1894. *The Tomb of Paheri at El Kab*. EEF, London.
Vandier, J. 1972. *Catalogue des objets de Toilette Egyptien*. Éditions des Musées Nationaux, Paris.

Verhoeven, U. 1984. *Grillen, Kochen, Backen im Alltag und im Ritual Altägyptens: ein Lexikographischer Beitrag*. Fondation Égyptologique Reine Élisabeth, Bruxelles.

Vetter, T., Rieger, A. and Möller, H. 2013. 'Water, routes and rangelands: ancient traffic and grazing infrastructure in the eastern Marmarica (northwestern Egypt)' in F. Förster and H. Riemer (eds) *Desert Road Archaeology in Ancient Egypt and Beyond*. Heinrich-Barth-Institut, Cologne, 455–84.

Vetter, T., Rieger, A. and Nicolay, A. 2009. 'Ancient rainwater harvesting systems in the north-eastern Marmarica (northwestern Egypt)' in *LibStud* 40, 9–23.

Vetter, T., Rieger, A. and Nicolay, A. 2014. 'Disconnected runoff contributing areas: evidence provided by ancient watershed management systems in arid north-eastern Marmarica (NW-Egypt)' in *Geomorphology* 212, 41–57.

Vutiropulos, N. 1991. 'The sling in the Aegean Bronze Age' in *Antiquity* 65, 279–86.

Vogelsang-Eastwood, G. 1992. *The Production of Linen in Pharaonic Egypt*. Leiderdorp, Leiden.

Vogelsang-Eastwood, G. 2000. 'Textiles' in P. T. Nicholson and I. Shaw (eds) *Ancient Egyptian Materials and Technology*. Cambridge University Press, Cambridge, 268–98.

Webley, D. 1972. 'Soils and site location in prehistoric Palestine' in E. S. Higgs (ed.) *Papers in Economic Prehistory*. Cambridge University Press, Cambridge.

Wegner, J. 1998. 'Excavations at the town of Enduring-are-the-Places-of-Khakaure-Maa-Kheru-in-Abydos: a preliminary report on the 1994 and 1997 seasons' in *JARCE* 35, 1–44.

Wenke, R. J., Buck, P. E., Hamroush, H. A., Kobusiewicz, M., Kroeper, K. and Redding, R. W. 1988. 'Kom el-Hisn: excavation of an Old Kingdom settlement in the Egyptian Delta' in *JARCE* 25, 5–34.

Werschkun, C. 2010. 'Resource procurement and management in Egyptian settlements of the Old Kingdom'. PhD Thesis, University of Liverpool.

White, D. 1999. 'Water, wood, dung and eggs: reciprocity in trade along the Late Bronze Age Marmarican coast' in P. Betancourt, V. Karageorghis, R. Laffineur, and W. Niemeier (eds) *Meletemata: Studies in Aegean Archaeology Presented to Malcolm H. Wiener as he Enters his 65th Year*, Vol. 3. University of Liège, Liège, 931–6.

Williams, B. B. 1993. *Excavations at Serra East: Parts 1–5: A-Group, C-Croup, Pan Grave, New Kingdom and X-Group Remains from Cemeteries A-G and Rock Shelters*. Oriental Institute of the University of Chicago, Chicago.

Winlock, H. E. 1955. *Models of Daily Life in Ancient Egypt from the Tomb of Meket-Me' at Thebes*. Harvard University Press, Cambridge, MA.

Xekalaki, G. 2021. 'On borders and expansion: Egyptian imperialism in the Levant during the Ramesside period' in *Heritage* 4, 3938–48.

Yellin, J. and Killebrew, A. E. 2010. 'The origin of Egyptian-style ceramics from Deir el-Balah: conclusions from neutron activation analysis' in T. Dothan and B. Brandl (eds) *Deir el-Balaḥ: Excavations in 1977–1982 in the Cemetery and Settlement: The Finds*. Institute of Archaeology, Hebrew University of Jerusalem, Jerusalem, 57–74.

Zahran, M. A. and Willis, A. J. 1992. *The Vegetation of Egypt*. Chapman & Hall, London.

Zorn, J. R. 1994. 'Estimating the population size of ancient settlements: methods, problems, solutions, and a case study' in *BASOR* 295, 31–48.

Index

Abadiya, 99
Abu Simbel, 53, 71, 109
Abydos, 27, 74
agricultural production, xii, 25–7, 31–3, 58, 104, 121, 132–3
   embanked fields, 36, 37–8, 41–3
   labour requirements, 41–5
Aksha, 4–5, 107, 119
Alexandria, 112, 116
allochem, 89
Amara West, 9, 24, 32, 35, 107, 119
   animal husbandry, 122–4
   architecture, 4–5, 19–20
   pottery production, 126
Amenhotep II, 77
Amenhotep III, 7, 77, 118
amphorae, 24, 70–1, 81, 125
Anath, 5, 114, 116
areas of excavation
   Area G, 83, 87–8, 90
   Area H, 12–13, 28, 93,
   Area N, 11, 35, 49, 101
   Area S, 11–12, 23
ash, 32, 47
Aswan/Philae Stela, 50
Atum, 128
awls, 99

Bahariya, 89
baking, 19, 25, 27, 28–32, 44
barley, 26, 36, 38–40, 122
basalt, 89, 128
Bate's Island, 2, 97
Beth Shean, 74
biosparite limestone, 85, 89, 92, 104
Bir el-Abd, 119, 124–5
birds, 57–8
blade blanks, 94, 97
bone pins, 58, 82–3, 97, 99–104
bowls, 12, 30, 71, 74, 79
brewing, 25, 28–9, 31–2, 45

calcium, 65–8
camp (military), 69, 71–2
Canaanite, 23, 92–3, 116
   pottery, 10–11, 67, 126
   shrine *see massebah*
caprines, 51–4, 56, 59, 104, 123–4, 130
cattle (*Bos taurus*), 48–52, 54, 123
ceramic coffins, 68
cereal processing, 25–7, 29–31, 122
chaff, 66
chapels, 7, 9, 10–11, 21, 35, 116
chert, 55, 95
chipped stone production, 93–9, 105, 129–30
chisels, 90, 92, 99, 127–8,
clay figurines, 68
clothing (Libyan), 84
company (military unit), 34
composite manufacture, 73–4
copper-alloy *see also* smelting, 56, 83, 99
cores, 93–5, 98, 129
crop yields, 26, 36, 38–41
Cyrenaica, 26, 37, 112, 118

Dahshur North, 77
dates, 36–7, 39
debitage, 93–5, 129
Deir el-Balah, 4, 76, 79, 93, 119, 122, 125–30
Deir el-Ballas, 85
Deir el-Medina, xiii, 13, 27–8, 55, 85
Denderra, 6
Dialogue of Ipuwer and the Lord of All, 7
dishes, 65, 70, 73, 75, 79
dogs, 46–8, 53
donkeys, 45, 53
door jambs, 16, 21, 90–2, 98, 114

Egyptian blue pigment, 3, 79
el-Ahaiwah, 74
el-Alamein, 1, 110–13, 115–17

el-Bordan, 112–13, 115
el-Gharbaniyat, 110–13, 115–17
emmer wheat, 26–7, 29, 38–9, 122
execration texts, 7
Ezbet Abu-Shawish, 113

fabrics *see* pottery (Egyptian)
figs, 36, 39–40
fish, 55–6, 124
fishing, xiii, 54–7
    cast-nets, 57
    fishing hooks, 56
    net sinkers, 57, 124, 163
flax plant (*linum usitatissimum*), 83–4
    cultivation, 84
    retting, 85
fortress terminology, 4–5
    dmiw, 4, 22–3, 109–11
    ḥtm, 4
    mktr, 4
    mnnw, 4–5, 22, 50, 109–10, 122
funnel-neck jars, 64, 69

gateway, 5, 133
Gebel Ahmar, 30
Gebelein, 6
glacis, 5–6
gnawing, 45, 47
goats *see also* sheep *and* caprines, 41, 51–3, 123
    kill age, 51
grain storage, 27
granary, 25, 27, 29, 123, 125
granite, 30, 90, 112–13, 115–16, 128
granodiorite, 128
grinder *see* handstone
ground salinity, 45, 55, 83, 86
Gurob, 9, 99

hairpins *see* bone pins
Hamada desert, 20, 115
hammerstones *see* pounders
hand spinning, 85
hand-made pottery, 73
handstone, 28–32
hares, 45
Harkuf, biography of, 6
Haruba A-289, 4, 71, 119, 124–5, 130
Hatshepsut, 7

Haua Fteah, 58
headrests, 92
Herodotus, 36
Hierakonpolis, 6
hoes, 27, 42–3
Horemheb, 53, 69, 71
horses, 45
Houron (Canaanite deity), 116
housing layout, 13–17, 21
    courtyards and streets, 17–19
hunting, xii, 54–6, 124
    arrow-heads, 54–5

Instrumental Neutron Activation Analysis (INAA), 125
iron, 65, 68
Israel Stela of Merenptah, 50, 109–10
ivory, 7, 100

Karnak, 7–8
Karnak Inscription of Merenptah, 109–11
kilns, 68, 81, 125–6, 130
Kom Abu-Girg, 113
Kom el-Ahmar, 110, 112
Kom el-Hisn, 27, 111–13, 115–16
Kom el-Nana, 35
Kom el-Nogous, 112, 115–17
Kom Firin, 4, 21, 50–2, 57, 86, 111–16, 118–24, 130
    excavation history, 114–15
    stone working, 128
    textile production, 127
Kom Rabi'a, 51, 86, 90, 100–1, 103
Kommos, 3, 11
Kurum el-Tuwal, 113
Kush *see also* Nubia, 50

Lahun, 27
Lake Mariotis, 112
lance points, 93, 97–8
Libya, 4, 7–8, 22–3, 36–7, 50, 118, 129
Libyan Palette, 6
Libyans, 3–4, 12, 97–8, 104
    Libyan Wars
        of Merenptah, 109–12, 118
        of Ramesses III, 111
        of Seti I, 7–8
    eighteenth Dynasty relationship with Egypt, 7

Middle Kingdom relationship with Egypt, 7
Old Kingdom relationship with Egypt, 6
resettlement of, 22–3
supporting farming at Zawiyet Umm el-Rakham, 37
as trading partners, 50–3
Libu *see also* Rebu, 8, 117
lintels, 11, 16, 90–2, 99
loom, 83, 86, 88
loom weights, 57, 83, 86–9, 126–7
Luxor, 71

magnetometry, 5, 116
manganese, 65, 68
Marea, 113, 115
marl, 9, 62–3, 66, 68–9, 71, 73, 77, 81, 124–5
Marmarica Formation, 25–6, 89
Marmarican coast, xii, 1, 8, 50, 59, 83, 90
    forts, 109–13
    in the textual record, 115–18
massebah, 11, 23
Medinet Habu, 22, 49, 111–12
Medjay, 22
Meketre, tomb of, 27
Mentuhotep II, 6
Merenptah *see* Libyan Wars of Merenptah
Mersa Matrouh, xi, 36, 38–9, 112
Meryre (Libyan chief), 118
Meshwesh, 7–8, 109, 117
migdols, 4
military supply chain, 4, 55, 59, 105
Minimum Number of Individuals (MNI), 47
Mirgissa, 97
mortars, 13–14, 19–20, 27, 29, 30–2, 87, 122
mudbrick architecture, 13–14, 17, 29, 90, 114–16, 122

Niau (*nꜣw*), 22
Nebre, 2, 4, 10–11, 50, 128
    biography of, 22–3, 37, 103, 109
needles, 99–100, 102
Ne-User-Re, 6
notched blades, 93–4, 96–8, 100–1

Nubia, xii, 23–4, 27
    forts in Nubia, 4–5, 107, 109, 117–21, 129–30
Number of Identified Specimens (NISP), 47

oil, 39
olives, 26, 36, 39
Optically Stimulated Luminescence (OSL), 36–7
ostrich eggs, 23, 39, 57–8
ovens, 13, 27–8, 31–2, 58, 122
    oven containing remains of dog, 46, 48, 53

panther-skins, 7
Pap. Vatican II, 36, 38–40
pestles, 29
petrographic analysis, 66–8, 125
pigs, 45, 48–9, 51, 53–4, 123–4, 130
pilgrim flasks, 73–4
pin-beaters, 99–100
plates, 64, 73, 75, 78–9
polishing stone, 97, 102
population composition
    age distribution (children), 21, 24, 35
    gender distribution, 23–4
    population size, 33–6
portable X-ray Fluorescence (pXRF), xii, 64, 68
pot-marks, 80–1
pot-stands, 70
pottery (Canaanite), 9, 11, 66, 125
pottery (Egyptian)
    analysis, 62–8, 126
    import, 3, 9, 61, 66, 69, 73–5, 79–81, 84–5
    incised decoration, 79
    local fabrics
        ZUR A, 62–8, 75, 81, 85
        ZUR B, 36, 62–7, 81
        ZUR C, 62–3, 65–7
    manufacture, 73–4
    polychrome decoration, 76–9
    slips, 64, 74–5, 79
pottery (Libyan), 3, 23, 37
pottery (Mycenaean), 3, 11
pounders, 90, 92, 99, 127–8
Prophecies of Neferty, 7

Ptah, 11
pulses, 38–40, 42–4

Qadesh, 53, 71–2
Qantir-Piramesses, ix, 79, 81, 107, 130
Quartzite, 29, 90, 127–8

Ramesses II, xii, 2, 11, 34, 77
    construction of Zawiyet Umm
        el-Rakham, 4, 8, 22–4, 37
    construction of other fortifications,
        107, 109–10, 112–19, 122, 124,
        126, 128
Ras Abu Laho, 56
Rebu *see also* Libu, 7, 109
Rhetorical Tanis Stela II, 23
rodents, 45, 53
rotation system, 72

saddle-querns, 28–30, 32, 87
Sa-Hu-Re, 7
Sai Island, 121
Sais, 51–2
sander *see* polishing stone
Saqqara, 69, 77–9
Scanning Electron Microscopy-Energy
    Dispersive X-Ray Spectrometry
    (SEM-EDX), 126
scrapers, 93–4, 98, 123
Sea People, 2, 8, 117
sedimentary silt
    for use in construction, 13–14, 16, 20,
        27, 92
    for use in the manufacture of pottery,
        62–3, 66–9, 71–2, 74–5, 77, 81
Sekhmet, 11
Senwosret I, 7
Sesebi, 121
Seti I, 4, 7–8, 117–19, 126
Shasu, 23, 109
sheep *see also* goats *and* caprines, 43, 45,
    51–3, 123
    kill age, 51
Sherden, 110, 117
sickle blades, 27–8, 43, 93–4, 96–8, 121–2,
    129
sickle sheen, 27, 93, 96, 121
sieve, 31, 55
Sinai, xii, 56

forts in Sinai *see also* Ways of Horus,
    4–5, 24, 112, 117–19, 122, 124–5,
    129–31
smelting, 4
socket-block, 87
soldiers, 8, 21–2, 71, 103, 115
Soleb, 7
spikelets, 27, 29
spindle whorls, 83, 85–7, 126
spinning, 85–9, 126–7
spinning bowls, 83, 85–9, 126–7
squatter activity, 3–4, 12–13, 86, 90, 104,
    109
stelae, 7–8, 23, 50, 109–10, 112, 115–17
    from the Temple, 9, 21, 34–5
    production of, 128
Suez, 22

tables (limestone), 92
Tale of Sinuhe, 7
Tel Gezer, 39–40
Tell Abqa'in, 4–5, 110–17, 119, 122, 127
Tell Edfu, 27
Tell el-Amarna, 7, 13, 19, 128, 130
    cereal processing, 27–32,
    faunal remains, 48, 51, 54
    polychrome pottery, 78
    linen manufacture, 86–7
    stone working, 91–2, 100–1
Tell el-Borg, 4, 14, 21, 119, 123–5
Tell el-Retaba, 4, 24, 35, 100, 122–4,
    127–8
    faunal remains, 51, 57
Tell Heboua I, 4, 21, 86, 117, 119
    cereal processing, 121–2
    textile and stone production, 126–9
Tell Heboua II, 119, 122, 125
Tell Ibrahim Awad, 27
Thebes, 30, 43, 130
Thutmosis II, 50
Timna, 56
titles (military), 21–2, 34–5
    standard-bearer, 21, 34–5
    general (military title), 21
    troop-commander, 21
    overseer of foreign lands, 21–2
Tjehenu *see also* Libyans, 6–8, 23,
    110–11
Tjukten [*tktn*], 22

Tjemeh *see also* Libya, 4, 7
trade circuit, Eastern Mediterranean, 2, 11

Userhat, tomb of, 77
Userkaf, tomb of, 103

vertebrae (fish), 55
vessels (stone), 89, 92–3
Vienna System, 61–2, 66

Wadi es-Sebua, 8, 34
Wadi Magid, 36, 41, 44
Wadi Natrun, 111
Wadi Qasaba, 36

Wadi Umm el-Ashtan, 36–7, 41–2, 44
water harvesting, 36, 58
   cisterns, 26, 43
   wells, 16, 22, 26, 31, 114
   rainfall, xii, 26, 41, 43, 132
Walls of the Ruler, 112
Ways of Horus, 5, 117, 125
weaving, xii, 86–9, 114, 126–8
Weni, biography of, 6
Western Desert, 6–7, 90, 112
   geology, 90, 93, 97–8
wheel-made pottery, 73
wine, 39, 71
Workman's Village (Tell el-Amarna), 13

Plate 1 Material related to the processing of grain excavated from Area K.

Plate 2 Material related to (a) fishing and hunting and (b) textile production excavated from Area K.

Plate 3 Material related to stone working and imported stone artefacts excavated from Area K.

Plate 4 Bone pins excavated from Area K.

www.ingramcontent.com/pod-product-compliance
Lightning Source LLC
Chambersburg PA
CBHW071832300426
44116CB00009B/1521